# Bread-winners

Also by Melissa Hogenboom

*The Motherhood Complex*

# Bread-winners

## and other power imbalances that influence your life

## Melissa Hogenboom

CANONGATE

First published in Great Britain in 2025
by Canongate Books Ltd, 14 High Street, Edinburgh EH1 1TE

canongate.co.uk

1

*British Library Cataloguing-in-Publication Data*
A catalogue record for this book is available on
request from the British Library

ISBN 978 1 83726 224 3
Export ISBN 978 1 83726 225 0

Typeset in Goudy by Palimpsest Book Production Ltd,
Falkirk, Stirlingshire

Printed and bound by CPI Group (UK) Ltd, Croydon CR0 4YY

The manufacturer's authorised representative in the EU for product safety is
Authorised Rep Compliance Ltd, 71 Lower Baggot Street, Dublin D02 P593
Ireland (arccompliance.com)

# CONTENTS

# INTRODUCTION

The closer we look, the easier it is to see the influence of power structures all around us.

Forget the stereotypes of power-hungry politicians or an overly dominant spouse – many influences are much more subtle, yet they are pervasive. The power of a slightly more senior person in the office; the perceived power afforded to a person with a higher disposable income; or power dynamics within the home when breadwinner expectations are outside the norm, which can have subtle as well as overt influences on personal relationships. These structures are so ingrained in how we operate in the world that we don't often stop to question them or realise how they affect us. You might think you are naturally more polite in the office, but it's our deference to those who have more power over us that can make us act more courteously or present less of our real selves at work, even if we are angry or upset. You might not realise that you instinctively judge someone with a high-earning job differently than before you knew their role. Much of western society values earning power and financial capital in a subtle but definable way: higher earners are often afforded more decision-making power at home, for instance, and are seen as aspirational, even though we tend to value 'worthy' professions such as charity workers and teachers more vocally. This contradiction shows the grip that money has over our lives – as financial power comes with an alluring promise of greater freedom.

This matters on a more personal front too. These structural forces then make their way into our domestic sphere, where paid work is often valued more highly than unpaid labour, both inside the home and by society at large. The same happens for 'higher status' jobs within relationships, with lasting repercussions on career progression as well as personal ambition. It might seem like a choice for one person in a couple to look for a more flexible career, but note who has the power and freedom to follow their ambition without being held back. Is it really a choice if your partner's inflexible work situation leaves you with no alternative but to work flexibly? And what are the implications when one partner is the significantly higher earner? Throughout the course of writing this book, it's become apparent that while some couples pool their money, many don't, and some even use their greater earnings to subtly 'bargain' their way out of household labour. It's also clear that if a couple goes against perceived norms and the woman is the higher earner and main breadwinner – which is becoming more common – it can have a negative impact on relationship satisfaction. It can also be positive and increase relationship quality, especially where men redefine their ideas of what being a caregiver means to them.

In the dawn of agriculture, farmers began to own land and property, which was passed down patriarchal line, whereas women moved away from their families when they married. And so began a very gendered divide of men as providers, with women as caregivers who had little economic ownership. This social norm, with its pressure to provide economic security, explains why out-of-work men experience relationship dissatisfaction. Not being able to provide is an instant signal to them that they are failing as husbands and fathers, as men. After centuries of these expectations, shifting the perception of breadwinner norms will take time. Fortunately, today we live in a society where change is happening in front of our eyes. Fathers are taking longer paternity leave, more women are primary or sole breadwinners than ever before and there is more awareness of how to bridge inequality gaps at home, from men and women alike.

All these changes are affecting relationships in myriad ways. Earnings at work can influence who holds the power at home, which can contribute to more equal partnerships and ease the 'male provider' norm. On the other hand it can also have negative consequences on male mental health and relationship dynamics. Earning potential translates directly to power at home too, especially in the division of labour, childcare and who is then more able to chase a more senior position at work.

As social psychologist Deborah Gruenfeld at Stanford University writes, power can also be used for good. She was surprised to find that 'power didn't turn everyone into a monster; in fact, sometimes it brought out people's most cooperative, most prosocial instincts'.[1] It's not just for self-enhancement; Gruenfeld told me that we can think of power 'as a tool we can use to take care of the people we care about'. In her view, power means having responsibility over others. What she's referring to is a subtler form of power, using our social skills. This view of power as a positive attribute benefits men and women alike – as both sexes are harmed by the pervasive idea that 'authority' is a prerequisite for power.

Thinking about it this way could instantly make you a better partner or parent, because every relationship has a social element to it, and every social relationship involves a form of power dynamic. By understanding the dynamics at play, our daily life will feel less of a challenge because understanding our social world is the first step to feeling more in control of it, and in turn, increasing relationship satisfaction.

*Breadwinners* will explore how norms can be challenged when gender roles are subtly altered, to both empower readers and highlight how – and why – society still needs to change. The book is grounded in evidence-based research and offers insights into inequality, relationship satisfaction, and the interplay of how power affects home and work life, in order to rethink traditional roles and push for a fairer, more equal society.

We will explore how to recognise and then shift the power imbalances in our lives, at work, at home and in our minds. I've spoken to dozens of scientists, many of whom have a slightly different interpretation of exactly what power is, but to me the commonalities are more revealing. Power, in its most basic form, can be understood as how we influence others. There are many ways to do this: we can control resources, impose rules, use words or actions; all of which allow us to change, manipulate or subtly influence someone else's behaviour. These resources could be material or emotional – food, money, affection and so on. For instance, in the case of a female breadwinner, she might hint that because she is so busy at work, she would value more support at home so she can focus on providing income for the family. It's the subtle assertion that her role takes her out of the domestic sphere that holds the influence here. Rather than explicitly stating that her role as primary earner means she deserves to do less at home, framing it as beneficial for both has the potential to create a fairer dynamic, one that shows both parties are contributing to the relationship, and both helping with the time available to them.

These are examples of softer power – subliminal messages, a compliment, a persuasive nudge, a persistent request from a child. All these interactions can affect our behaviour and often the person with the most power has the greatest influence. For better or worse, a higher earner has more licence to work late because their income is deemed more essential. Now consider how power affects social interactions. We don't realise it, but we are constantly part of subtle power battles. Crucially, the repercussions of power affect us all, whether we are in positions of power or not. As psychologist Dacher Keltner puts it: 'Power is not something limited to power-hungry individuals or organisations; it is part of every social interaction where people have the capacity to influence one another's states, which is really every moment of life . . . To be human is to be immersed in power dynamics.'[2] There's power at work, power over children (or being overpowered by them), power tussles with your romantic partners, or even your position in your social community. The influence of a group can also sway individual thoughts or actions and increase cooperation – a group dynamic has the power to elevate or advance individuals if it helps the group. In democracies, groups often vote for their leader – ideally one who will have their best interests in mind. Just as individuals can influence others, groups can also empower others. Research has shown time and again that power and status impact all aspects of how we socialise, and can alter human behaviour too. People in positions of power are less vigilant and feel more positive, but also show reduced empathy and are worse at seeing other perspectives.[3,4] In groups there's inevitably someone who takes the lead. Witness a group brainstorm or notice who takes on additional responsibilities: all these processes convey a certain level of power.

In large networks that need a lot of management, hierarchies even help group performance. They also mean we are incredibly aware of our status at work and at home. We understand what group we fall into, what seniority we have and what control (or lack thereof) this gives us. It's important to note that status is *related* to power and often goes hand in hand, but it is not the same. You can have high status but no power and vice versa. A bullying boss has a lot of power but little status, and a respected political prisoner has little power but high status, to give two extreme examples. Power can also change quickly, depending on who has access to what is deemed valuable. For instance, if the primary breadwinner tends to make more of the major financial decisions, but their partner comes into some inheritance or gains a big promotion at work, the dynamics shift for them to have more influence over household finances, work-life balance and domestic chores.

It's important to recognise that humans are a hierarchical species for better or worse. At some point in our lives, many of us want or *need* somebody else to lead us or tell us what to do. Junior at work? You need a manager to guide you. More senior? You need leadership to approve your strategic direction. A top-performing football team needs a commanding coach to call the shots. A parent? You seek advice from those who have gone through it before. It would benefit us enormously for those in positions of power to be socially intelligent, empathetic, and people we can depend on. It is reassuring when our boss empathises with us, understands us and motivates us to succeed.

Unfortunately, we need only look at any history book to see that power often lends itself to abuses and manipulation too, and so to understand power we also need to understand why the balance of it is crucial. This book will explore why it is necessary to understand how to shift this balance. We'll also learn how it is power itself that creates gender disparities. By that view the rise of female breadwinners should start to correct gender imbalances through the lens of power, a change we are starting to see in real time now, albeit slowly.

Knowing that power is pervasive is nothing new. In the twentieth century the philosopher Bertrand Russell wrote: 'The fundamental concept in social science is power, in the same sense in which energy is the fundamental concept in physics.'[5] Since then, many social scientists have been grappling to define how this fundamental force is so prevalent in everyday life. Modern research has uncovered numerous ways we can influence power, by understanding exactly how it works in the first place. Even recalling an instance where we have felt more powerful in the past makes us feel more confident, assertive and powerful. Being kind, having strong social networks and cultivating empathy and compassion can also help us get ahead.

In this book we'll explore how this influential form of power that involves empathy, perspective-taking and social intelligence can help all of us avoid the pitfalls of being 'overpowered'. We'll see how too little power creates more stress and reduces creativity; and how too much power decreases empathy and perspective-taking and even corrupts – as in cases of financial control and abuse.

A large part of how we perceive the world is heavily influenced by our brains' amazing predictive power, as well as the many subtle influences that shape how our brains respond to what is expected of us. The power of our thoughts can influence not only how we see the world, but how we absorb society's expectations into our homes. There are surprisingly simple techniques we can adopt that help alter how our brains respond to stressors such as power imbalances, which can help improve our well-being.

I'm going to delve into power dynamics in relationships, and look at how these affect every aspect of our society. First we'll look at our personal and social lives and hear how culture defines and creates imbalances. We'll then consider how power influences us, then we'll learn how our sense of self is intricately tied to the resulting social and cultural expectations. Finally, we'll learn how power dynamics change us at work, and how work itself is changing. We'll find out how power can be equally afforded to men and women to create a more balanced and happier society, and we'll learn how we all have the ability to influence this to benefit society at large.

Ultimately, this book will help readers to shift the power imbalances in their lives. To empower ourselves, we have to understand how the fabric of society and social relationships works. The chapters ahead will arm you with the knowledge and insights, backed by research and real-life examples, to help us all live a more fulfilled and equal life, one free from power imbalances.

# 1

## SUBVERTED POWER: THE RISE OF FEMALE BREADWINNERS AND STAY-AT-HOME DADS

'A trick has been played on you women; you work more and now you're still doing it *all*.'

—Alex

Felicity* is almost a textbook sole female breadwinner. She's 39, has one child and a second on the way, and works in a high-profile international development role. Her partner is a stay-at-home father and while this wasn't planned, he had not built up the work experience required to pursue a career, so it caused no tension when they decided that she would return to work after eight months' maternity leave, and he would stay home. 'That had always appealed to him . . . There wasn't a debate,' she tells me.

Felicity is one of the many female breadwinners I spoke to for this book, revealing an intriguing trend of subverting gender norms, with knock-on effects on relationships, good and bad. She revealed a pattern that many others shared too; while she does less childcare during the week, the household management is still largely left to her:

---

* Not her real name. The majority of women I spoke to wished to remain anonymous or use first names only.

[My partner] is [in] no way domestic at all. We often joke he was feral when we got together, and so the tensions that exist are not about the balance of childcare duties, he without question does the majority of caretaking. I get a chunk of time to myself at the weekends, but our real struggle between us is the other domestic and life administration responsibilities, which I still do the vast majority of, 99.9%. Everything from the mental load to the actual load.

Felicity's experience is far from unique; research shows that women tend to do most of the domestic work as well as carry the mental load in heterosexual relationships. One of the reasons that women don't hand over tasks is because patterns have become so entrenched, often due to societal norms. This means the inequality at home continues even in couples that aim to have an equitable relationship from the outset.[1]

I've spoken to dozens of female breadwinners and interviewed male stay-at-home fathers too, to understand how dynamics shift when a woman in a heterosexual relationship is the sole or primary earner. These stories are often backed up by published research – but also paint a very nuanced picture depending on circumstances. I'll feature some of them throughout this chapter to illuminate the more data-led insights and surveys. What's immediately apparent is that the increasing number of female breadwinners is changing the nature of how home and work life is divided.

First, some broad definitions. There are two types of breadwinners: sole and primary. The former is where only one person in a relationship is providing, the latter where both work, but with one earning more than the other. In the UK, it's rare for men to stay at home fully, but primary breadwinner women who earn more than their male partners are on the rise. In the UK this equates to about one in four couples (26%).[2] Interestingly, less than half of men asked in a 2018 YouGov poll felt a responsibility to earn more than a female partner – 43% felt this was their responsibility when asked: 'Do you feel a responsibility to be the main breadwinner in your relationship', while 16% of women said yes. The same survey found a generational difference too. One in four (24%) of the younger female participants aged between 25 and 29 were bothered when they earned less than their partner – whereas of the over-55s, only 5% were bothered to be out-earned.[3] When considering those aged 18 to 24 the pattern becomes even more interesting. Only a quarter of men (26%) in that age category answered yes to the question, showing an important generational change: younger men do not feel the breadwinning pressure as keenly. Among the over-55s this shot up to 46%. So the younger generation really does seem to be more likely to reject the notion that men have to be the main breadwinners. This kind of attitude change could see a new generation rejecting the outdated idea that it is predominantly a man's responsibility to provide for his family – paving the way for a more balanced home life and an increasing likelihood that women can pursue top careers.

This is in contrast to the 1960s, when as little as 3.5% of married women in the US identified as primary breadwinners of their household; that has now risen to 16% of women. Of that 16%, only 6% are sole breadwinners, although that is triple the figure in the 1970s, where it was 2%. Men still out-earn women in the majority of households, but the share of women in the US earning roughly equal to men has also tripled in the last half century. And even among that 16%, it's only when the wife is the sole earner that caregiving is found to be slightly more equal in terms of time spent on housework each week, though these breadwinner women still do significantly more housework. When the wife is the primary earner, she spends slightly more time in paid work but also on housework. Her leisure time takes a hit in all scenarios – when she is a primary breadwinner, a sole breadwinner or when she earns roughly equal to her partner, according to findings from a 2023 Pew Research Center survey.[4]

Another study suggests about 40% of children in the US are primarily supported by their mothers financially, though 25% of these children are supported by single mothers. This still means

15% are primary breadwinners in dual-income households.[5] In the UK about 15% of children are supported by single parents, and of those the majority are women – and in Europe the trends are similar.*[6] When it comes to female breadwinners, every income group is accounted for, but there are more female breadwinners in higher income roles than lower income brackets.[7] The lowest educated – who also tend to be the ones with lower earning potential – had least time being the main earner. The researchers of this 2021 study note that this increasing trend of female breadwinners is likely to continue, and that 'Overall, the final tallies indicate many more mothers, for longer durations, are primary family earners than is recognised by employer practices and government policies.' European data meanwhile found that in 27 European countries, almost 22% of households had female breadwinners, though this varied per country, with Slovenia being particularly high, at 33%.[8]

Frustratingly, policy has yet to catch up with this family set-up. Felicity, who we heard from at the start of this chapter, can't stay on maternity leave for as long as she would like, because her partner has no salary – it would put the family in debt. Company policies for parental leave often expect one earner to continue working, and while some mothers do go back extremely early, many need to recover physically, are sleep deprived and also *want* to breastfeed, while single-parent households have even less support.

In my household I started off as the higher earner, working an admin job at a GP-led urgent-care service in a busy A&E department. I then slowly increased BBC shift work in the national TV newsroom, taking each shift I could feasibly work in the time available outside my other job. At first I was running the autocue for the newsreaders, then, after some persistence, I worked on the production of the live TV news channel as a researcher. I would be assigned a story and oversee the end-to-end output of that story

---

\* 85% of the UK's 3.2 million lone-parent families are headed by women, and 15% (477,000) by single dads.

on each half hour that the news went out. It was terrifying. My partner worked in a pub while pursuing a career in music. Every penny he earned went to his rent and expensive rehearsal space. (Yes, very London, I know.) A year on from pub work he gained an entry-level role with a video production company on a minimal salary. A year or two later when our roles became slightly more senior and secure, our earnings roughly stayed equal – though I contributed more to the deposit for our first tiny London flat.

Fast forward 15 years, we are now married with two kids and he's the higher earner. Fortunately, divisions of our finances have never been something we've argued about, especially because I'm the one who deals with the related admin, such as our mortgage, our joint account, paying for childcare and sorting out what the children need, and he deals with household maintenance and the car. We both make sure we split childcare as evenly as we can, meaning there is no resentment from either of us. We both have autonomy but discuss any larger purchases together. I grew up in a household where my mother was the higher earner, and she was able to pursue her career despite stepping back for a few years when we were young, with my father working more flexibly. For many, the balance between home and work life is far from simple, especially when shopping habits or expensive hobbies are not given equal weight, as we'll explore. These imbalances often materialise more overtly once couples have children, but they can occur in child-free couples too.

Angie, for instance, feels 'awkward' because of the expectations her new job brings: 'I've been the default parent for three years and recently we had a baby. I have a new job and I feel he expects me to cover everything with my new big salary. Of course I plan to be more equal in our expenses but I also need to save money and pay for my debts. But I can see ££ in his eyes when he talks about my new job as he talks about what we will be able to afford now.'

Similarly, Eliza doesn't spend any money on herself and stepped back from her career to focus on her children:

He once again said, well what have you contributed anyway? I nearly choked and thought he was actually joking until he continued. He went on to say he can afford [a new house] with or without me, and wonders where all my money goes that I earn in my part-time role. I said groceries and family costs. I felt my face start burning with anger and I removed myself from the table and said it's not an appropriate discussion in front of the kids. I just don't understand how he can't see what I have contributed and feel very unappreciated.

## MONEY AND POWER

What we earn can fuel resentment and cause relationship stress. That's because with money comes power; some hold on to it in manipulative ways to control what it is spent on, whereas others use it as a subtle bargaining chip to do less housework at home, perhaps feeling that working outside the home excuses them from it, which can create a sense of injustice. In some instances, money becomes weaponised as a tool for control. For instance, animosity can quickly breed if one person in a relationship spends more money on hobbies while the other is carefully budgeting. Take Sarah, who never spends money on herself as she doesn't feel entitled to it, even though she does all the childcare: 'With my baby-daddy, he worked and I spent the money on our family; I would spend the rest on him, not myself, because I felt like it was his money and our benefits were for bills, so the rest was his to spend.' Or how about Amina, who is completely worn down by home-educating and caring for her children with additional needs, but can't spend any money on herself and feels infantilised by her lack of financial autonomy:

Before we had children, I worked full time and we had separate accounts, I didn't have to ask for money . . . My other half goes to the gym twice per week, he has motocross bikes and last summer was on them at a track all summer . . . I feel

so worn out and trodden down . . . I do so f***ing much . . .
Yet I get nothing, have nothing, no money . . . I want my
own money back. I don't want to ask for money, I don't want
to run things past him for approval. I'm not a child.

These examples show that a lack of money can be the barrier for
empowerment and liberation. When women earn more, their
economic power also translates into power at home. In many
relationships, money is intricately tied to who holds the power
– spending power, leisure power, and who makes the financial
decisions. As is now well understood, statistically, in most couples
the higher earner is the man in heterosexual partnerships – with
the woman spending more time on household chores.

Yang Hu, a sociologist at Lancaster University, studies how money
becomes gendered in families and how it affects housework. Many
people assume that money from income translates into power in
the household, but this is not always true. It's been found that
higher earners often 'hand over' money to their partner as an unsaid
exchange for doing less housework.

In a 2019 paper, Hu analysed data sets from the UK Household
Longitudinal Study, incorporating over 6,000 couples, to understand
how gender relates to who controls money at home.[9] His work
revealed that whoever managed the household finances (whether a
man or woman) also did more housework, as managing the household's money and paying bills is work in itself, and it's common for
the person who is in charge of the weekly food budget to also be
buying the food and cooking. However, if the woman had full control
of her earnings (rather than putting them into a shared pot) it
helped her reduce her housework. Women are therefore empowered
by their income coupled with autonomy in managing it.

The study also showed that men can exchange their way out of
household work simply by their earning power and by handing over
money to their partner, who then has to do the mental labour of
spending it or making it stretch. Managing the household spending
might include budgeting for food and clothes or paying for childcare.

'It's almost like they [men] created a mini marketplace in the home. They use that money, the money they have earned, to just buy their way out of housework,' explains Hu. This phenomenon is something researchers have called 'exchange-bargaining theory'.

Financial control clearly contributes to inequality at home but when there's a female breadwinner this exchange no longer holds true. As women's earnings go up, their household chores also go down – but only to a point. If her earnings rise above her partner's income, it starts to feel uncomfortable for most couples, and so women overcompensate by doing more at home because they 'deviate from the normative income standard (men make more money than women)'. Gender literally trumps money, as the authors of a report comment in their paper.[10] One unexpected reason women continue to do more at home is to protect a man's self-esteem, or to 'neutralise the deviance of a husband's economic dependence', as the authors put it. This 'gender deviance neutralisation' compensates for the fact that they are deviating from a long-established norm to 'regain a sense of femininity', something sociologists refer to as 'gender display', though most women won't likely realise they are doing so. In an analysis of data from over 6,000 couples in the US over the course of 18 years, it was shown that, on average, this deviance wasn't prevalent before children, but was found after higher-earning women become mothers.[11]

Thus in couples where the woman earns more, they tend to revert to traditional gender roles in their division of housework to compensate for the non-traditional set-up outside the home. This completely contradicts economic common sense, where, logically speaking – and indeed what we see where men earn more – the primary breadwinner should be doing less housework as their earnings create more opportunity for the family. But as is now abundantly clear, humans do not operate rationally much of the time. Tina, interviewed for a study on breadwinners by social scientist Noelle Chesley, said that she felt a lot of stress and pressure as her husband had lost his job, but the housework and childcare had not been fairly reallocated to him even though she was the one in paid work.[12] Felicity also experienced stress from 'doing it all'. Both she and her partner grew up in very traditional families, and despite being the sole breadwinner she does most of the domestic work.

Of course, this 'deviance' isn't universal and can change depending on a country's norms. It's more likely to be found in more traditional countries. For instance, 'West Germany' (i.e. the parts of Germany corresponding to the former FRG) shows very different patterns to 'East Germany' (the former GDR). In the latter, mothers have traditionally worked more than staying home. As one analysis put it, 'East Germany still differs from West Germany not only by a higher female contribution to household income, but also because East German women can earn more than their husbands without having to increase their number of housework hours.'[13]

Crucially, how tasks are divided can depend on individual couples' attitudes too. One recent Polish study found that women's beliefs about gender roles affect how much housework they do and therefore how much they show this 'deviance'. Couples with less traditional views were more likely to share chores equally, despite Poland being a country with fairly traditional views overall.[14] It follows that in countries where women rarely earn more than their partners (such as Egypt and India), men are even less likely to do housework, and in the rare cases where women do earn more, gender deviance is more likely.[15]

## THE HOUSEHOLD CHORE BARTER

Recent research on same-sex couples shows a slightly different story. There is a more equitable division at home across the board, but when one earns more than the other, the higher-earning partner also does less housework, though the disparity tends to be less compared to heterosexual couples, where, as we saw, women do more housework *even* if they are earning more. When partners contribute equally to household income, however, they are more likely to share household chores equally. One 2022 US study found that the higher earners spent 80 minutes more in paid work and 40 minutes less on household work per day, in both same- and different-sex couples.[16]

That men feel threatened by higher-earning women is due to how much our society runs on social norms – we want to fit in with others, and thrive on earning respect from our tribe. But it turns out that the more that this norm is challenged, the better outcome we see for personal relationships.

Chiara is the higher earner in her relationship and she and her partner both work full time. He is looking for work with the potential to double his pay, which would make him the higher earner. Her main concern revolves around him no longer thinking he needs to do his fair share of chores if he becomes the higher earner. Another woman, Linda, says she scaled back her paid work to go part-time, but her partner complains that he does too much child-care and that he would only help out more if she contributed more to the joint account. He earns significantly more and they each put the same percentage of their take-home pay into their joint account. In their case, her unpaid care-work at home is not considered as contributing, a pattern that affects many women: 'Is it me or should he be helping more? I'm always on the go and don't stop. Yes, he financially supports the house, but I work part-time and pretty much do everything else. I'm exhausted and tired of feeling selfish [for wanting more time to myself].'

Hannah stated that her self-employed partner was reluctant to do the school pick-up one day because he equated it to hours of lost earnings. He begrudgingly agreed but told her, in figures, what the financial loss would be, leaving her feeling guilty even though the event she was attending was important for her career:

I shared with him how it made me realise how much mental load I carry day-to-day and his response was, 'Well that's why you work part time' . . . I'm finding it hard not to feel resentful

... I really love the children and spending time with them, but it feels like I have had to do epic levels of organisation to come away, and this is with a husband in the house.

This example is a case of how our earnings can lead to a subtle level of control, and that paid work is seen as more important than care-work, a theme we will revisit. Financially, paid work time has to be protected for a family's financial security, but if there is some wiggle room, and the lower earner can spend time on career development, it will increase their earning potential too. The less time the lower earner has to devote to career-advancing activities, the less likely they are to advance, showing the importance of thinking longer term when it comes to the division of household and paid work.

Other intriguing patterns emerge when it comes to high-earning women. They have not been found to use their income to 'exchange' it for housework or use it to bargain or obtain power at home the way men do. Yang Hu found that high-earning women are more likely to become self-sufficient financially to bolster their own status, rather than controlling the household money. It's as if we are seeing a 'tale of two marriages', he says. On the one hand, we have men who are bargaining and exchanging, but on the other, we are seeing high-earning women with greater financial freedom. They find their power from their autonomy, whereas many men continue to expect there to be someone at home picking up the slack so that they can focus on earning. This often isn't deliberate but is part of a societal narrative many of us have grown up with where men are providers and women homemakers. We compare ourselves to those around us, with expectations formed by our parents' working patterns too. Most of my generation witnessed fathers who earned more and mothers who scaled back or did not work, especially as a generation ago it was financially easier to live on one income compared to today.

Lower-earning women are therefore even more susceptible to unequal households – and given the context of the gender pay gap, it's worth understanding the impact of women being forced to deprioritise their careers. This regularly happens globally, even in countries with high employment rates for women, and means they will be more likely to follow the path of doing more at home, when higher earnings could enable greater freedom. That is not to say that earnings alone will give women more power – but it specifically depends on keeping that money independent in some way, independence that can increase equality in their relationship. Given that one-third of marriages end in divorce, and women are more likely to be victims of domestic and financial abuse, it's important to be aware of these consequences. It's vitally important for women to maintain financial independence and a separate bank account, especially where women have even less power due to low female employment figures, such as in many highly patriarchal Middle Eastern countries, or in European countries with a low female workforce, including Greece, Italy and Spain.[17]

Though working patterns have changed, implicit attitudes can be slow to catch up, which is why a subversion of breadwinner norms provides us with such a powerful catalyst for progress. Tom, a stay-at-home dad also interviewed by Chesley, understood his partner's guilt and her sense that she was missing out on time at home. '[With respect to] the female side, my advice is that she has to be willing to go to work and then come home and not feel like she's guilty about, you know, having a career and not being home.'

When women in heterosexual relationships earn more it can reduce financial control by their higher-earning partner and increase independence. In a study looking at how couples managed their finances between 1920 and 1980, male power over finances reduced with time.[18] The more the woman earned, the more control she had over her finances. 'The trend of individualisation is particularly prominent among couples in which both partners have equally high earnings,' the study noted. Or put another way, among dual-earning couples both can put adequate focus on their careers, without one being unfairly held back to do more at home. This then also helps to create more independence and equality in a partnership, as well as greater relationship satisfaction.

To me that sounds like a happier way to live – it's not always easy, but recognising the self-fulfilling nature of how much caring is tied to earnings would help both partners in a heterosexual relationship realise that by both doing more at home, it helps reduce the load on women, and in turn, helps increase the household income because she has more focused time to develop her career.

As we heard, 'gender display' is deeply ingrained, so studying those who find themselves in this position sheds light on how rigid gender roles remain, whilst offering a glimpse into possible change.

Bethany is a health coach who works from home. Her partner now works in a coffee shop after leaving a bartending role which was paid more but was unsustainable for family life due to the late nights. During this transition he was out of work for four months, leaving Bethany as the sole earner. When he stopped paid work, Bethany was still doing most of the housework, which led to conflicts in the relationship: 'I told him he would have to leave if he couldn't contribute to the care of the home. We'd broken up and gotten back together recently, so he knew I was serious.' Only then did he take on more at home, and once he went back to work, they split tasks 50:50. Now she reckons they split it roughly 60:40 – with her doing less as she's doing a course alongside full-time paid work and remains the higher earner. 'Since I became the main breadwinner, things are much more equal and our relationship is much stronger than it's ever been.' Bethany's story shows what many couples have experienced: role expectations at home are hard to change. Even if the mother is out of the house more and earning more, expectations around housework still fall to her unless there is an active discussion or correction in how to approach it.

This pattern has intrigued researchers too, as it gives an interesting insight into gender dynamics and how work life affects them. For one research project, Noelle Chesley set out to interview stay-at-home fathers as she had heard anecdotally that they were increasing in number. She then recruited participants to do in-depth interviews to find out what processes were at play, but it wasn't as easy as she'd hoped. She thought that each participant would link her to another stay-at-home dad, but found she had to recruit the fathers via the mothers, as the fathers were not well connected socially. In fact, they were quite isolated. This isolation has been noticed elsewhere and is tied to the fact that it remains unusual for men to join mum groups. Another factor is that the majority of these fathers were out of work not because of choice, but circumstance, such as economic instability, job loss and so on.

Chesley's research involved interviews with 42 individuals in 21 couples, where the women earned either all or 80% of the household income – yet most of these women did not actually self-identify as the main provider, particularly due to the sense that this might undermine their husbands' masculinity.[19] As many of us know, being the main earner has long been core to a man's sense of identity.

Unemployment therefore affected their sense of self, largely due to social and workplace norms – men go out to work and women stay at home, so the story went in the 1950s 'ideal' family. This ideal was only relevant for those with the economic power to have this set-up – in many working-class families, women have always had to work; the same goes for single mothers. But the idea of the male as provider persists, despite the many different formations of a family, including same-sex couples and single-parent or single-income households.

One stay-at-home dad I spoke with told me how isolating it was to feel excluded from baby groups. He believed the mums just wanted to discuss 'womanly things' and saw him as a threat. Similarly, Felicity told me her partner really struggled in the early days, and even her family seemed somewhat judgemental of their set-up. At baby groups he'd end up only talking to the nannies 'because the mums were not interested'. Another, Steve Hull, who I met by chance through a local dad's network, had a more positive experience. He says he purposefully joined all the baby groups, without overthinking it. He was well aware he would be the only man in the group, but it didn't bother him as he'd always had female friends. 'The one thing I'd say is I wish there were more men there,' he added almost as an afterthought. This spurred him on to find other local dads and he subsequently set up a text group called 'Overworked and underpaid', recognising how hard their roles were at home. They would meet up regularly, which made it less isolating. 'We had cheeky lunches at each other's houses, we'd cook nice meals for each other, then send photos to our wives. That was fun, though most of the time it was bloody hard work.'

While Steve and his overworked dad friends may be an anomaly, it certainly shows that with a bit of effort, it's possible to find a group of like-minded dads to meet up with. Unfortunately, a lack of a network for stay-at-home dads was echoed by others. Belinda, a medical professional and higher earner, found that her partner's lack of connection with other parents was a key reason she organised social events, even if her partner was the one taking them to an activity or playdate. Both work a three-day week but most of the dads in their area work full time and cannot meet up during the day:

Before we had children, 10 years ago, we both worked full time but I made much more money so paid almost all the bills. For holidays and trips away, I would pay for flights and hotels, and he would pay most of the spending money while there. That is still our arrangement now we have children. Since having children we both work full-time hours over three days a week, splitting childcare almost equally. He makes hardly any money so I pay all the bills, mortgage, most of the children's activities. We are a loving, happy family and work hard to make our household and childcare equal but I still do most of the work.

## THE RISE OF THE STAY-AT-HOME DADS

With the rise in sole female earners there is also a corresponding rise in stay-at-home dads. In the US it's about 5%, but the true figure is difficult to establish because men often find another way to define themselves.[20] Another study found that 18% of stay-at-home parents are dads,[21] while a UK analysis has found that fathers are spending 18% more time with children at home compared to before the pandemic. Unpaid domestic work for men increased too.[22]

It does a great disservice to men when we stereotype them as being lower empaths and deficient in 'softer' skills like nurturing. It's clear that when men stay at home, they can become just as competent as women in all the skills needed for family life to function, as long as expectations are set out from the start and women don't continue to take on most of the organising around the house. Evidence shows that primary-caregiving fathers are just as equipped for child-rearing as mothers.[23] Several emerging studies now also show that dads experience similar brain changes to mums, and that the changes are greater if they are the primary caregiver. This shouldn't be surprising, because when we become skilled at a new task our brains change accordingly, or, put more simply, we learn by doing and corresponding brain networks specialise as we learn. Fathers also show more hormonal changes than non-fathers.[24] When we look at hunter-gatherer groups like the Agta people of the Philippines, who are egalitarian and share everything, the brain changes are even less surprising, because egalitarian life has been part of numerous human societies since the dawn of our existence.

Unfortunately, stay-at-home dads aren't just ostracised socially, they can feel it emotionally too. The isolation is problematic because childcare, playgroups and the school run are part of their everyday routine. To feel excluded daily can take its toll. In one research study, interviewees described being upset because they felt their children were excluded from playdates because they didn't feel welcome there as dads. They would attend playgroups but be excluded at coffee meetings after, for instance.[25]

Alex, a father of three, stays home with his kids three days a week and is a freelance writer outside his childcare commitments. He suggests that men who take on more childcare responsibilities will feel less alone if they meet other men doing the same. Nevertheless, he has noticed he gets certain looks, where people seem surprised to see him so often at the school gate, but it doesn't bother him. Other men, he says, don't seem to understand. He explains how he and his wife both cook and do the laundry. She keeps track of appointments, but he sorts the bills. When I ask him if he thinks housework should be shared more equally he instantly replies, 'Absolutely', and says that it's like 'a trick has been played on you women; you work more and now you're still doing it *all*.' Alex says he and his wife didn't talk about the divisions initially, but by their second child they had learnt by doing – and it worked for them. And although he says they fell into the routines he describes, he also talks about how he made a conscious effort to be present, especially as his dad was rarely around when he grew up. It's a clichéd saying, he says, but time goes quickly. 'When they're 15 they won't want to be with you. So maybe spend as much time as you can now.'

Clearly it takes time, communication and trial and error, but home dynamics for fathers like Alex and Steve really do change family life. They are more present in every aspect of their child's life, and research shows this kind of involvement is more likely to increase relationship satisfaction, reduce maternal gatekeeping and create stronger bonds between fathers and their children. The children in turn will grow up not expecting the same norms their fathers experienced, showing that these family set-ups provide real hope for generational change. US data shows that stay-at-home dads with breadwinner wives are the only family dynamic where men do more caregiving than women. Fathers in these households do 14 hours per week of childcare, while mothers do an average of 8.4 hours. On the other hand, these dads also have the most leisure time, about 47 hours per week compared to 24 hours for women.[26]

Role reversals of household chores are seen more often in female breadwinner families. Steve told me he doesn't let his wife near the laundry, and Mary said her husband took over all the cooking and doesn't trust her to do the food shopping as he likes to budget. He'll buy cost-conscious food from the local supermarket while she'll order more expensive organic vegetable boxes, without always communicating. He once ordered an online delivery the day after she had ordered a vegetable box: 'We won't have communicated, and we'll both have got loads of tangerines, for example. So we'll end up with 100 tangerines to eat. That genuinely happened over Christmas.' Despite food being his domain, they are both, as she puts it, 'controlling in the kitchen'. Now that she's working again after her third maternity leave, it's easier for her to let go because the kitchen is out of sight and out of mind. Subverting the norms once again has been useful for her as the primary earner. Precisely because she felt the kitchen *should* be her domain, even though she rationally knew that was nonsense, it was hard for Mary to let go of organising the food.

There's a good reason why women like Mary feel this responsibility acutely. Women are judged on how they run a house in a way that men aren't. One striking study showed participants a clean or messy room and were told it either belonged to 'John' or 'Jennifer'. If they believed it belonged to 'Jennifer' they judged the clean room as messier than if they were told it was 'John's room'. This showed that they were more disapproving when the space belonged to a woman even when the photo was identical. Participants also held women more responsible for cleaning up the messy room. The best thing about the study was that men and women noticed the mess equally, showing that it's a myth that men don't see mess. Same-sex couples by the nature of their set-up fall outside these expectations – there's nobody who can hide from the mess or be expected to tidy it up more.

\*     \*     \*

For most of the breadwinner women I spoke with, there was no deliberate decision for their partners to stop working or be the lower earner; it tended to be circumstantial. It was when it was a clear decision to prioritise a woman's career that couples sounded most satisfied. That said, many fathers prefer to cite reasons such as illness or being retired rather than out of work due to childcare. A 2023 Pew Research poll found that in the US only 23% of all stay-at-home fathers noted that they *chose* to stay home for child-care reasons and reported they were not working because they were 'taking care of home/family', though this is up from 4% in 1989. Other factors stated were unemployment, being ill or disabled (which was the highest figure at 34%), studying or retired.[27] The figure for women who said they chose to stay home was a lot higher, but it has decreased from 86% in 1989 to 79%.

Chesley's research found that men had concerns about defining themselves as a stay-at-home parent. A key reason is due to their self-esteem, or social judgement; as one stay-at-home dad said: 'It stings your pride a little bit that your wife's the one out making all the money', while another stated: 'A big thing is you can't let your ego [say] that you're the man, you're the breadwinner – you got to let go of the ego . . . you got to be humble sometimes.' Another, Brendon, had good reason to feel judged: family members labelled him 'the house bitch'.

A gradual drift into a particular set-up was the case for Beth and her husband. 'We didn't choose who was the breadwinner; I was able to pursue a higher-paid career after I graduated university. My partner dropped out of university and has been working in retail ever since.' In another case, Dawn's partner was out of work for 11 years, leaving her as the primary breadwinner:

This started when he was made redundant. At that point my youngest was about six months away from starting school. He didn't know what he wanted to do so we said he would have a little bit of time off and look after my son until he started school.

At this time, I was working two days a week in a government job, term time only, and growing my self-employed business. It was supposed to be temporary, but he then didn't get a job, just talked about it a lot!

Again, this shows that without direction, patterns can become ingrained. When couples discuss the impact of being unemployed and help each other with their careers, it can prevent resentment. Otherwise, unemployment of either person in a relationship can increase the chance of divorce, an effect that seems to be universal, as it's been found in the UK and Germany, and many other countries, including Denmark, Finland, Norway, Sweden and the US.[28]

Women are more able to give tangible reasons for unemployment, such as caregiving, whereas there is a greater social stigma when men are out of work.[29] Couples tend to be judged more negatively when a man is unemployed compared to when a woman in the relationship is unemployed. It's harder for men to find other identities too. If a woman with children is unemployed, she can often reconfigure herself to being a stay-at-home mum who is taking a few years out for the kids, or she can immerse herself in various voluntary positions, school PTAs, charities and so forth. It is harder for men to become involved in similar activities, because, as the academic Helen Kowalewska told me, men are thought of as agentic, 'going out to work and not necessarily as emotional or nurturing as women can be. Men are more likely to be left isolated and lonely because they don't have the same groups to fall back on in times of job loss as women might.'

The differences in household labour for female breadwinners is most notable at weekends, with women taking on more overall, although much of this is because women tend to do more than their male partners to begin with. It's only on weekdays that female breadwinners spend less time with children and on housework than their stay-at-home partner. At the same time, a heartening pattern emerges among stay-at-home fathers. Compared to breadwinner fathers, at weekends they show more involvement in parenting and other household tasks, likely a result of their increased familiarity with their children's daily routines during the week. One female participant observed, 'It's more of a team environment . . . it's become what it is supposed to be.'

Despite that, the tasks the female breadwinners did at home were still those that tend to be stereotypically considered 'women's work' – laundry, cleaning and cooking, and, of course, the mental load, the 'thinking about doing', a hidden workload that can be ever-present. Even though these women were in full-time paid employment, once back at home it was difficult for them to let go of these gender-defined roles, which are conditioned from a young age.[30] Then there's the urge to overcompensate at home that we heard about earlier. Women are expected to be primary caregivers, and can be judged for not seeming motherly if they are the ones working most, meaning they feel pressured to put in extra hours at home. This was true for Scarlett, especially around housework: 'Childcare is very equal but I feel like I'm more attentive/likely to notice kids' bids for attention. He is much better at keeping track of them and preventing dangerous situations. He also cooks most of the meals and does most of the shopping for the household, so that is helpful to balance. Cleaning and mental labour is almost entirely mine, unfortunately.'

Scarlett's experience tallies with that well-established tendency to judge women more than men on childcare and how tidy their house is. In Dawn's relationship the split was not as equal:

I always did way more stuff at home, especially cooking, child-care responsibilities, anything that needed organising for the house – this includes all finance, all holidays, birthdays, Christmas, sorting cars etc. During this time [of unemployment] he did a bit more – he would usually do the weekly shop and did take on more of the dropping off and picking up from school – but only really if I wasn't there. I was still the default parent. Not even at this time did our labour get anywhere near 50:50.

These examples do not mean that progress has stalled – bread-winning mothers have at least been found to reduce housework on their working days. 'To me the overall point is that we are fighting an entrenched system,' Chesley told me. The system impacts men too. Another interesting finding was that men who had experienced being stay-at-home parents found they had stronger attachments to their children. They knew the bedtime routine, knew where the right size socks were – though they helped out more with childcare rather than housework, perhaps because childcare is an immediate need as the demands are visible and constant: meals, clothing, attention . . . Housework can wait. As Chesley explains: 'There are things that are happening that are pushing people towards greater gender equality. But there's some resistance in some of these more entrenched patterns. That resistance is both in our heads, the embedded culture, and the idealised versions of what family life and parenting is supposed to look like. And it's also in our institutions in terms of what supports different work and family behaviours.'

This certainly matches Belinda's experience. She and her partner home-educate the children on their non-workdays. Their conundrum is that they are paying for an expensive renovation. If Belinda worked one extra day and her partner worked one less, the family would earn more overall. She explains that her partner is resistant to the idea as he would otherwise feel 'like a kept man' – something she attributes to toxic masculinity, embedded at a young age. 'I am finding it frustrating as my earning potential is so much higher than his, it feels like an obvious solution. I think if my partner was a woman, this would not be an issue, this is definitely a gender thing. We work as a team to run a household and family, and money is just part of it.'

## WHEN BREADWINNING LEADS TO RELATIONSHIP DISSATISFACTION

A study published in 2023 looking at female breadwinners exposed just how strongly the norms of who should provide can affect and even harm a relationship. The study found that relationship satisfaction was lower when the woman was the main earner.[31] Well-being increased if both worked or only the man worked. Well-being for the man was lower when the woman was in employment – compared to if she was also out of work. The study exposes the powerful ways gender roles, expectations and norms link to well-being, as well as the stigma and emasculation men often feel. Once again it shows just how important positive role models and a supportive male network can be.

This study analysed 42,000 responses from the annual European Social Survey. The data set involved responses from nine European countries between 2004 and 2018. Participants in the survey ranked their life satisfaction between 1 and 10, with 10 being highest, and were asked about employment, income, values, age, education and so on.

The team found that life satisfaction was higher when a man and his partner were out of work compared to if a man was jobless and his female partner wasn't. If a woman was sole earner, men rated their satisfaction as 5.86 on average, compared to 7.16 if the man was sole earner. Women were not as bothered; they rated their satisfaction as 6.33.

Take that in for a moment. This is staggering: unemployed men were happier if their partner was also out of work than if she was getting paid. The reason for this can be linked to the fact that breadwinning is closely tied to masculinity. If they were out of work their very identity as a male provider and therefore 'good husband' was at stake. This was especially negative for them because most hadn't chosen to stop working but had lost their jobs. The visible reminder that they weren't working but their partner was could be one of the catalysts for this dissatisfaction.

As it was all based on survey data which measured well-being, we don't have the insights from this study to know the exact details. It can be true that whilst these men prefer to have more household income, they still experience lower well-being if they are not the ones providing it, compared to when nobody is providing any income at all.

There are a few reasons for this. I spoke with Helen Kowalewska, the sociologist responsible for the study, who told me that if nobody in a relationship works, it becomes a norm, but if one goes to work and the other doesn't then it can accentuate a man's unemployed status and adds to his feelings of inadequacy. If a man is out of work but sees his partner going to work each day, it serves as a constant reminder of his own status as unemployed. That sense of a man needing to be the provider is so strong that his female partner working when he is not lowers his happiness.

This follows many other studies that show male unemployment is more psychologically damaging for men than female unemployment is for women. 'There's a real difference between men and women and how they perceive their own unemployment and also their partner's unemployment,' Kowalewska explains. If either partner was out of work, women's feelings of well-being remained the same. The study therefore revealed a stark difference between how men and women perceive their own unemployment compared to their partner's. Kowalewska was not surprised at the findings, but a bit 'sad because it feels like we should be further along than that'. It's especially disappointing because solo female breadwinners on average had lower salaries than solo male breadwinners, as would be expected with the gender pay gap. In fact, highly educated female breadwinners had comparable salaries to men who had reached only low to medium levels of education, a phenomenon the researchers have dubbed 'the female breadwinner penalty', which 'reflects women's secondary labour market position'.

Similar patterns are revealed elsewhere. A study looking at Australian couples found that relationship satisfaction reduces when there's a female breadwinner compared to when both are in work or when only the man is earning. Again, this was exacerbated if it was due to male unemployment,[32] because 'the loss of the bread-winner role could diminish men's self-worth and simultaneously reduce women's regard for their partner, thereby reducing both men and women's satisfaction with the relationship'. This was in part attributed to the fact that housework and childcare is not equal even when a woman is the higher earner. You can imagine why this would fuel resentment over time. Reassuringly, the authors urged a note of optimism – that the negative impacts on female breadwinners should reduce or disappear once cultures and wider society place greater value on gender equality.

This work reveals that relationship satisfaction decreases when expectations are abruptly altered. If a female breadwinner is in place because of a deliberate choice, as is the case for a few stay-at-home dads I spoke to, relationships can benefit hugely.

Tela Mathias, for instance, is a high-powered tech professional living in the United States. She is the sole breadwinner, and her husband does everything at home, all the housework and all the childcare. Without his support, she says, she wouldn't be able to function. 'My husband absolutely enables me to have the life that I have. I love my job, I love my work, I travel all the time.' It doesn't come without guilt, she has some concerns about her career causing her to be less present with her children because she's not fulfilling 'the myth of the American working mum'. However, this set-up has been hugely positive for him too as he is fulfilled by providing everything she needs for her career. 'He would never want to stop me from achieving the dreams and hopes that I have.' Her husband has shown that for women to be able to lean in, men need to feel comfortable with leaning out. If this set-up works, relationship satis-faction can be extremely high.

Happiness can also increase if there are no expectations at all. A high-powered media professional I spoke with, Ada, is a single mother by choice. She told me how she found dating extremely challenging because men seemed to feel threatened if she was deemed more successful than them, but when she dated people better off financially they acted as though her career was less important. She's now a sole breadwinner single mother and says the decision to go it alone has felt extremely liberating. While it's hard work, there's zero resentment about dividing tasks.

Couples without children are more likely to divide tasks according to time available.[33] One cross-cultural study found that among northern European couples without children, 76% shared responsibilities for both paid work and domestic chores, a figure that drops significantly once children arrive (though this differs per country, as Chapter 6 will explain).[34] As one mother, Gabrielle, said, before children it was broadly equal in her household: 'My husband used to sometimes do a lot more than me, but the house responsibilities shifted disproportionately towards me once we had our baby, and now I still work full time, go to school and have the house and baby to take care of, while my husband added an extra 30 minutes of new responsibilities to his day . . . It's been a hard fight.'

In other cases, it's also far from equal. A 26-year-old academic, Emily, told me that her situation had become more imbalanced over time. 'It wasn't always this way, but properly moving in together has just made it worse and worse. I can't remember the last time he did anything except laundry without me asking in over a year.'

## FAUX POWER

The rise of female breadwinners highlights just how complicated gender expectations are. Belinda's set-up at first appears quite equal, but there are less visible inequalities:

We both cook on the days we are not working and take the children to their various activities. We work together to fold and put away laundry, load and unload the dishwasher, tidy, vacuum, do bedtimes. I end up cleaning the kitchen most often, I don't remember when he last cleaned the bathroom or did any laundry that wasn't just for himself. He would if I asked him to, but the mental load is still mine.

Belinda also experienced what the 2023 Pew survey noted, that 'society values men's contributions at work more than their contributions at home'. Only 7% believed the opposite, that 'society values men's contributions at home more than those at work'. Men feel appreciated and are rewarded by colleagues and bosses for a paid job well done more than the much less visible and unpaid labour at home.

Women have historically been seen as power-holders at home, but sociologists see this as 'faux power' as it doesn't translate into wider society. Power over domestic tasks is judged as less important. This reveals an interesting merger of two worlds, where generally, the clash of personal power at home does not complement the power of the higher earner. It shows what psychologists have called 'positional power' and 'subjective power'. Subjective power, also sometimes called 'sense of power', is the capacity to influence or control your partner by changing their thoughts, feelings and even behaviour to align with your own, while positional power relates to income, social class or occupational prestige. An individual with high positional power can have a lower 'sense of power' at home in terms of the domestic decisions and social engagements, but at the same time, overseeing the running of the home is a power that is a consequence of inequality outside it. This means that someone with more subjective power at home is likely to have less relative power overall.

This is not surprising because unpaid work isn't valued as highly as paid labour,[35] even though society depends on the former to function. The pressure to provide is one Belinda's partner feels keenly, resulting in financial worry for her. However, from the same survey, some more positive findings have also emerged. About half (49%) responded that they valued women's work at home and in the workplace equally, with 31% saying that 'women's contributions at home are valued more than what they do at work.'

For some female higher earners like Felicity, it made financial sense for her partner to stay home as he had not built up a career, meaning both were happy with the arrangement. However, there are class differences too. If a man from a lower-earning profession stays at home due to precarious labour conditions there is a very different outcome. One study looked at lower-income couples where women had become sole breadwinners very rapidly due to men losing their jobs; the team found that women increasingly entered the labour market to compensate for lost earnings. Núria Sánchez-Mira conducted numerous interviews with couples in Spain to see the impact this had on their household.[36] She found that men talked a lot about how they would like to 'be the man of the household and bring in income' – it was a real tension in their identities. However, for the most part they were not as closely tied to being the breadwinner compared to 20 years ago, and the couples had 'flexible attitudes'. They understood it was not polit-ically correct to be concerned about the man being the higher earner but would later contradict themselves. Pedro was out of work for four years while his wife was the breadwinner and said: 'I would like to be the man . . . Yes, I'm not going to lie . . . You always like to be, but it's not a macho thing . . .'

In another couple, Lorenzo overestimated how much he earned and mentioned several times that he earned more than his partner had, showing that he was 'undervaluing the woman's economic contribution or overvaluing that of the man'. Despite this, the study found that women saw great value in their work 'as a source of economic independence and female autonomy, as opposed to an eventual dependence on their partners'. Judith, who was a bread-winner for over three years, said:

If you are a woman and a man supports you, you are always tied to that. This is one of the reasons why I never want to stop working, because you always have the freedom to say: 'Look, I'm sick of you and I am leaving.' I don't have to . . . be with this person . . . I don't want to because they support me economically . . . I think everybody should be able to support themselves.

Overall, working more did trigger these women to demand extra help at home, but while their partners increased how much they cooked, overwhelmingly the women still did all the laundry, cleaning and general household management, something that resulted in conflict. A lot of these patterns happened because there was no communication over who did what. In one case, however, Julia, who was working out of the home for long hours, explicitly expected her partner to do more – which he then did. 'I wouldn't have stood being away [working] and coming home with him having done nothing [. . .] It didn't happen.' In turn, Jorge acknowledges that 'When I forgot to do certain things and I wasn't working she would remind me, "Hey, mate, you aren't working . . . okay?"' While no couple achieved 'an equitable division of the overall workload', female breadwinners noticed increases in men doing more housework and childcare. This reveals that power dynamics at home can change when expectations are clearly communicated.

## THE FATHERHOOD FORFEIT

It's clear that a man's self-esteem is negatively affected when unemployed,[37] and men are twice as likely to be depressed when out of work compared to women, which can contribute to poor physical health, making it harder to get back into work.[38]

A confounding factor here is that, as we've heard, out-of-work men don't tend to have as wide a social network as women who don't work for pay and who are more likely to be involved with community, volunteering and school groups. I certainly met many other mums when on maternity leave and was quickly welcomed to numerous meet-ups.

It's worth understanding these experiences because a rapidly changing job market means many of us may experience bouts of unemployment. It's therefore increasingly likely that many more women will be the sole earner at some point. One US study found that 70% of mothers could be the primary earner before their first child turns 18.[39] In order to help the next generation, the focus of policy therefore needs to be on how to best help women get ahead, especially as it is women who are more likely to be single caregivers. Women are also reaching higher levels of education, with potential to earn more, and more women than men are obtaining university degrees.[40] These higher-educated and higher-earning women tend to make more of the household financial decisions too.[41]

Another reason that stepping back from work is especially challenging for men is because of a phenomenon dubbed the 'fatherhood forfeit', a term originated by Jasmine Kelland, who conducted numerous surveys with parents and managers. In one study, a fictional father who applied for a part-time job was viewed as less competent and committed than mothers were. Kelland then asked managers to rate either mums or dads for part-time jobs. She found that managers judged men negatively and even viewed them with suspicion when they requested a part-time role, while mothers who applied for part-time work were viewed more positively.[42] The fathers were less likely to get a part-time role in the first place and tended to be considered a 'secondary parent' regardless of their working hours. Men who wanted to work part-time experienced other forms of mistreatment, such as being teased or considered idle and uncommitted, as one participant noted: 'There would be a lot of piss-taking . . . "You are a bit of a wuss" . . . "She rules the roost . . . wears the trousers" . . . that sort of thing, there would be a lot of "You are not a real man" . . . "What is wrong with your wife" . . . It would be gentle but it would definitely occur.' Several men were also asked: 'Where's mum?' when they requested flexibility.

These judgements occur because we still don't accept men in the domestic sphere as much as we accept women at work. When we question or judge dads as caregivers it creates an extra burden on women to continue doing the bulk of it. There are so many structural forces that make women do more and men do less, and, as is clear from Kelland's work, constant microaggressions too.

Because of this, many couples stick to patterns that are more socially acceptable. That 'gender deviance neutralisation' we heard about earlier is at play. Most people who make these comments are not intending offence, but are simply voicing societal norms. However, it's crucial to challenge such assumptions because they can perpetuate and reinforce stereotypes in an unhealthy societal feedback loop.

While some fathers hid their caregiving responsibilities in fear they may be judged for it, Kelland noticed another group that she has dubbed the 'f**k-it fathers' – though in her paper she used the term 'disregarding discourse'. These were the dads who successfully combined working flexibly with childcare, and did not worry about how it affected their masculinity or how they were judged. Their desire to be there for their children overruled outside perceptions of what they *should* be doing. They had a 'sort of maverick, ground-breaking type of personality', Kelland laughs. One said, 'Have any of these troubled fellows tried Not Giving a F**k? It worked for me', while another stated: 'There has never been a shortage of a***holes in the world and they tend not to bother me.'

Unfortunately, most dads who needed it tended to work flexibly without asking formally, because of the reasons explored. Kelland's analysis came from hundreds of comments on an article in the *Guardian* newspaper titled 'The Masculine Mystique', exploring why we haven't yet decoupled professional power from gender.[43] It wasn't only work-related. Men expressed concern that a desire to stay home with children wouldn't be viewed as an attractive quality by potential partners. One stated: 'If, on our first date 25 years ago, I had said my ambition was to be a stay-at-home dad, I doubt there would have been a second date, let alone marriage and kids', while another wrote: 'If you act like feminists tell you to then you won't get laid.'

These sentiments may have some truth to them in certain circles due to the assumption that care-work is not masculine, but this doesn't tell the whole story. Women like Felicity, and an investment banker I spoke with, Tatjana, show it's quite common for educated women to marry men with lower or minimal career prospects, which is linked to the fact that today more women are educated to a higher level than men. Due to this education gender gap, in heterosexual marriages at least, wives are commonly more highly educated than their husbands.[44] 'We find that highly educated women tend to partner more often "downwards" with less educated men, rather than remaining single more often,' notes one 2017 paper on the topic.[45] As this trend continues, we can expect more female breadwinners too.

We live in a world where more people are apparently striving towards equality, yet persistent gender norms around work and family life remain. But as research in this area also shows, norms are slowly changing. The biggest predictor of how we view gendered roles is what we see in our own homes.

Today there is an interesting attitude shift taking place. Millennial and younger men are more inclined to *want* to take on equal parenting duties compared to generations before them, but there is still more understanding needed from employers to enable flexibility for all, for men as well as women to take parental leave, and for society to let go of the expectation of overwork, which harms caregivers – who of course are most likely to be women.

The persistent rise of female breadwinners reveals that they are here to stay and policies to help them progress will benefit future generations. Generational shifts often take time, but we are witnessing change happening before our eyes – so notice and support male caregivers, have conversations early on in your own relationship so that you both expect fathers to be more involved, and most important of all, keep an eye on your female-breadwinner friends – they have an extra taxing job, emotionally and physically, if they are combining paid work with the majority of housework too.

## KEY POINTS:

- A female breadwinner disrupts typical gender expectations and can affect her male partner's self-esteem. Such women may be increasing in number but attitudes towards breadwinning and caring are slower to change.
- Female breadwinners have greater financial control at home but still do more housework and childcare to compensate for disrupting gender norms.
- More men want to be actively involved at home but workplace pressures and societal expectations can make this difficult.
- Men are subject to a bias called the 'fatherhood forfeit' if they openly show they need to work flexibly for childcare.

## ACTION POINTS:

- Set out expectations early in a relationship for a more balanced home life, and don't let outside expectations affect what is working for you or your family.
- Consider whether you are doing more housework as a penalty for your breadwinner status and divide free time outside of work to overcome that.
- Challenge expectations and judgements of dads as caregivers and encourage couples as well as your colleagues to expect men to take on flexible working as much as women do.

## 2

## MONEY TALKS: HOW MONEY AND POWER CAN DOMINATE

'I do not wish women to have power over men; but over themselves.'

—Mary Wollstonecraft

Like with many aspects of social life, how couples view and divide money often starts with expectations. Many of us expect men to earn more because most still do, and these societal norms then reinforce this expectation. This was drilled home to me especially dramatically one beautiful summer evening in 2015. I found myself on top of a mountain overlooking Florence, in a stunning and no doubt expensive restaurant with my then boyfriend. I'd been told to dress nicely but had no idea where I was going. As soon as we arrived, I knew we were expected, as two chairs were adorned with rose petals, and ice-cool champagne was waiting. Yes, it was romantic, and, yes, this was the night my now husband proposed to me as the sun was setting over the city, but I'm not writing about this to be sentimental. I mention it because there was also an extremely amusing moment – in retrospect steeped in old-fashioned chauvinism – that came to mind when I started researching the topic of financial expectations and disparities.

It was the type of restaurant that didn't even have prices on the menu (or so I thought). When the bill arrived, it was given to my partner, who paid it without showing me. I commented that it was amusing that the menu had no prices next to it and he was confused, as his did. While the bill more often gets given to a man when a couple is dining, this restaurant had gone one step further and removed prices on the menus given to women. Not only were men expected to pay, they were also expected to be the only ones aware of the cost, reminiscent of a time in not-so-distant history when women rarely had incomes of their own.

## MANNING UP AND WOMANING DOWN

While many expectations around money are much more subtle, this example exposes an attitude still prevalent in everyday life – we not only assume men make more money and are therefore more likely to pick up a bill, it also actively harms a man's self-esteem when he is *not* assumed to be the one with financial power. The BBC presenter and author Katty Kay, who is a primary breadwinner, laughs when she recalls how, when out to dinner with another couple, both she and another high-earning woman let their husbands pay because it felt so uncomfortable to disrupt this norm, and the lingering idea that, as Kay says, men still feel the need to pay 'because society expects it'. This has shown itself in a remarkable real-world example. In the US census, couples have been found to twist the truth when they report their earnings. When women earned more than their husbands, they under-reported their earnings on census data, while men over-reported theirs. The authors who discovered this aptly titled their report: 'Manning Up and Womaning Down', stating that couples who 'violate the norms that husbands out-earn their wives' lied to maintain the status quo.[1] This small lie may seem innocuous, but it exposes a problematic viewpoint that could even persuade women not to reach for their full earning potential. We've long known that individuals are prone to over-reporting socially desirable behaviours and under-reporting negative ones on survey data, which is exactly what seems to be going on here. It reveals just how powerful our assumptions are of the links between money and status and how intricately money is tied to power. In same-sex couples there is less likely to be an assumption of who will pay based on gender, as one gay friend told me, he sometimes pays when he knows he's the one who earns more, but more often splits the bill. Another said he always splits unless it's clear there will be a second date, when one might pay this time with the promise that the other will the next.

Having money or lacking it can affect our sense of self, as well as how we view success. Individuals who come from privileged backgrounds tend to act more confidently, show higher levels of extraversion and expect to earn more, compared to those from less privileged backgrounds. A contributing reason is that those in the more privileged group don't have the numerous stresses that poverty exacerbates. Economic insecurity contributes to a feeling of scarcity and a lower sense of self-worth, whereas those with means can focus on self-improvement and education, and have numerous choices available that can enhance their lives.

The divide between the rich and poor is perhaps the starkest reminder of inequity and is linked with how powerful we feel. Take a study showing that students from poor backgrounds had increased levels of stress when confronted with class inequality. The participants took part in an implicit association test looking at class divides. It measured their responses to class by noting reaction times between positive words versus negative ones about wealth and class. The results showed that most of these participants had an implicit bias that favoured the higher classes, as most of us are conditioned to want to achieve wealth and status and are applauded when we do so. Poorer students with a higher social-class bias showed the most physical stress as measured by inflammatory cytokine, a protein important for regulating our immune system.

This is evidence that those in poverty are more likely to face adverse health issues and feel chronically stressed simply by operating in a world that favours wealth. The feelings of rejection for these participants contributed to worse academic performance too.[2] The opposite happens for high-status individuals, who tend to believe they have more control over their lives and face less stress as a result.[3] It follows that relationship satisfaction is affected when couples come from different financial backgrounds. Just as power inequality affects relationships, research has shown that relationship satisfaction declines when there is a large socioeconomic divide between a couple.[4]

## LOW STATUS SELF-BIAS

These insights are important to understand when considering power dynamics, because they show just how much we are influenced by others, and how that affects our confidence and mental health. And while we may have become used to the hierarchies that favour wealth, power and class, our brains know these categorisations are deeply unfair. If these hierarchies didn't exist, we would all feel more comfortable interacting with individuals across social divides.

Those from lower socioeconomic status (SES) backgrounds, for instance, believe people view them more negatively than they really do. An analysis of over 6,000 participants showed that those from poorer backgrounds believed that others saw them as less competent and emotionally colder than they really did. This resulted in more self-blame, and being less able to accurately predict how others viewed them.[5] When it came to seeking 'higher power' positions (which could increase earnings), this research also found that because of this low self-regard, these individuals went into self-preservation mode. Rather than trying to compensate for the misguided negative judgement they felt others made, they dropped out of competitions for power altogether. This was because of the disconnect between how they perceived themselves and how they felt they needed to act to get ahead, namely more 'warmly and competently', which itself can become a self-fulfilling cycle that further deters their motivation for success.

Meanwhile, a person from a higher SES background is more likely to believe that they're going to be perceived positively. When judged negatively or rejected following a job application the low

SES participants blamed themselves, while the higher SES participants blamed aspects outside their control. If you blame outside
events, you are less likely to be put off pursuing similar goals – if
you don't expect to fail, it can't possibly be your fault, after all.
Whereas if this is an inbuilt expectation because of how you grew
up, that rejection feels inevitable; you might be more likely to give
up altogether than put yourself through an experience you believe
will be negative. This happens because many people have negative
stereotypes about those living in poverty. These studies show that
people revert to blaming themselves when they feel uncomfortable
or out of place, which can have lasting consequences when it comes
to experiencing a power imbalance.

Interestingly, in follow-up work when researchers asked participants to define their socioeconomic status, they had very different
interpretations of what it meant. In some cases, people had an
external, comparative view, where they considered their history of
family wealth or compared themselves to the elite, whereas other
people looked at their own life in the present moment, and whether
they had an 'easy comfortable life' with enough income.[6] This
suggests that there's more than one way to interpret socioeconomic
hierarchy. When it comes to relationship dynamics this is revealing,
because it shows your background does not necessarily determine
your later sense of self, and you can adopt the status of a higher-
earning partner. This also shows that in an established relationship
where resources are fairly distributed, a higher-earning partner's
wealth can change the perceived social status of their spouse. Your
idea of status can change simply by being in a relationship where
assets are shared. This is exactly how the Agta of the Philippines
operate, as material 'wealth' is shared in the group, meaning nobody
suffers from a lower status if the group has adequate resources. This
creates a more balanced dynamic, according to the scientists who
have studied them.

We can all look at our own backgrounds and re-rationalise any
rejections as having been outside of our control rather than thinking
we didn't fit the part, which can help motivate us to continue

chasing certain goals. And if we truly don't fit the part, use that insight to motivate ourselves to get more experience, which will increase our confidence next time around. I've certainly attributed job rejections to the simple fact that another candidate may have been more experienced, rather than judging myself – though self-doubt inevitably crept in too. Without a more positive mindset, getting into journalism would have been impossible. I felt outside my comfort zone and experienced imposter bias until I realised just how common this was, and that it wasn't due to my own inability. I also purposely surrounded myself with aspirational role models, meaning I could use their feedback to improve. This isn't always easy, but seeking a mentor outside an immediate team or even company can help – and most people feel honoured to be asked. It just takes a few extra steps to reach out for advice and prepare yourself for honest feedback. Indeed, studies have shown that seeing other successful women can help women feel empowered, more confident and therefore perform better in leadership roles.[7]

## THE LEADERS OF TOMORROW ARE ALREADY BEING SHAPED NOW

Evidently, having money can elevate status and help perpetuate success. This financial security often fosters aspirational attitudes which are then passed on to future generations.

A friend who went to one of the UK's most prestigious boarding schools told me that the benefits he felt from attending had little to do with the teaching, which was at times mediocre. Instead, he said his schooling instilled in him the confidence to talk to anyone in any room, whatever their background. This type of cultivated confidence really can help get you ahead. His classmates are now all top-earning professionals in fields like law, politics and finance, showing how easily privilege perpetuates privilege, and why the traits that many power-holders have are honed at an early age. Many of us, knowingly or not, tend to surround ourselves with people from similar backgrounds, status and even ethnicity. If we surround ourselves with successful people, we are more likely to chase it ourselves.

All this goes to show that if we feel an imbalance at work or home we would all do well to look back to our childhoods to see what traits we honed, or what we missed out on, as it could address some incongruences of how we view money or scarcity. If those differences in views create regular conflict, that's where problems can persist and where we can address them.

## LIFE'S NOT FAIR AND WE HATE IT

Social comparisons can drive us to succeed or at times can be demotivating, especially if we feel we can never match up. Comparing ourselves financially to others reveals why a discrepancy of earnings can create a feeling of imbalance. We instinctively know that those in power have influence over us, diminishing our control.

A lack of equality feels so uncomfortable precisely because we don't like knowing others have more than us, especially those we see day to day. As stated previously, the Agta group divides resources, which protects group members from 'the detrimental effect of wealth inequality'. If one member of the group finds honey, there is an expectation it will be shared. This also means it would be unusual for any household to go without because resources like food are not accumulated privately. Mark Dyble at Cambridge University, who studies the Agta, tells me that true change can't come about unless we stop our obsession with materialistic goods, where wealth separates the haves and the have-nots.

In our society, this would translate as fairer pay and more affordable access to childcare. Agta women are free to provide and contribute as much as men, as there is so much support available to help them with childcare. For those with children it's only when we can pay for childcare or have access to family support that both in a relationship can start to contribute equally financially, and power will feel more balanced. On a societal level this could equalise the gender pay gap and normalise breadwinning for men or women, decreasing the likelihood of resentment due to one career being prioritised. Dyble pinpointed that the ownership of 'stuff' is also a key driver towards inequality. Just as he'd noted with the Agta, cooperation and sharing resources results in a fairer distribution of goods.

This also explains why we are wired to seek parity and fairness and why it physically and mentally affects us when it doesn't happen. It can be about small and large disparities; my children will regularly compare the amount of milk in their cups to check it is exactly equal. They do this for toys too. When playing with wooden blocks, there was visible outrage when one had one more block. My youngest, aged four, happily gave me the spare block to ensure they both had the same. It turns out this behaviour is embedded deep in our evolution.

There's a famous social experiment with monkeys that went viral, much to the late primatologist Frans de Waal's surprise. He was testing fairness in a group of capuchin monkeys and revealed that a sense of fairness was clearly present in the troop. As a reward for completing a task he first gave the monkeys pieces of cucumber, and they were perfectly happy with their lot. Then he gave one a cucumber but gave another a grape. They were side by side so each could see what the other received. The one who got the cucumber was outraged, throwing a monkey tantrum.[8] Just like monkeys, we all instinctively know that it's unfair when someone else gets something better. It stings.

When I spoke to de Waal several years ago, he explained that when traits are universal across the animal kingdom, it signals that they are ancient. Morality and a sense of fairness are crucial for our survival. Even young toddlers will share rewards when given the opportunity to do so. In experiments that have been rigged so that one participant gets more than another, they notice and share with the child who got less.[9] Three-year-olds will share stickers if they perceive their toy (puppet) partner has worked hard to receive the reward.[10] This same trait has some more amusing side-effects. Children will throw away a reward instead of having to share it unequally, a process called 'inequity aversion'.[11] The behaviour clarifies once more how our obsession with 'status' as a society runs deep, because having something someone else does not gives us a feeling of superiority and the other a sense of injustice, especially when we are comparing ourselves against those from our own group.

Meanwhile adults, just like children, can also show annoyance if someone else has more material goods, be it money or a bigger house. Participants in an experiment called 'the ultimatum game' sacrifice their own reward so that a fellow participant won't get more than them – which goes some way to explaining why female breadwinners annoy unemployed partners so much. In this game, one participant can choose to share money with another (the responder). However, the responder has a subtle form of power: they can choose to reject the offer, at which point both get nothing. If a responder is offered what they deem an unfair sum, they prefer to reject it, even though it means they get nothing. In one version of the game, a participant was given $20 to divide with their invisible partner and were told they could either give some away fairly or unfairly, but if the responder rejected the offer neither got any money. Most often they chose to give about half, meaning they each went away with $10. But some cunning participants realised that giving $7 and keeping $13 gave the responder enough of an incentive to accept. Even though it was unfair, it was found to be a large enough amount to not risk losing. If, however, they only offered $3, the responder tended to reject it, showing that they gave up a financial incentive to punish the unfair partner.[12] This study reveals just what lengths we will go to when we see a disparity in rewards, and that we actively dislike it when we have no control over someone else getting more.

A team of neuroscientists have gone one step further, and analysed the brains of those playing the ultimatum game to show just how deeply our sense of fairness is embedded. They found that when given an unfair offer, the participant's anterior insula, associated with negative emotions like anger, was more active. Even more interesting is that our decision-making seems to take a cue from our brains. Before participants rejected an offer, this same area would light up – meaning neuroscientists could predict from brain scans alone whether or not a participant would reject an offer.[13] This work again shows that the brain has evolved to react to unfairness, and our emotional response to it then influences how we act.

The crucial thing when it comes to money and how we navigate relationships often comes down to control. Most of us cannot immediately control the financial rewards available to us, which explains why a superior financial status has the ability to elevate our social standing and therefore power. As power has the potential to corrupt and warp our sense of fairness, it can further exacerbate the cycle of inequality between those at the top and bottom. This highlights why an income disparity within a couple can cause a power imbalance, as well as relationship dissatisfaction if it is not adequately addressed.

## MONEY SECRETS

It's unfortunate that a lack of parity conflicts with our generally altruistic and cooperative nature. We want to cooperate, but when our relationships are imbalanced and others have power over us, it affects our ability to do so. It's a great flaw in our nature that we are primed to want to achieve more than others, but we do so because we get rewarded for it by society, and garner greater status from financial success.

It doesn't help that in many western countries we are extremely secretive about money. In the US and the UK, it's taboo to ask others what they earn.* But we are clever creatures; there are numerous signals we give out to indicate wealth, from the obvious

---

\* This is not the case in Scandinavian countries and some East Asian countries. In Norway and Sweden income tax data is publicly available.

cliché of flashy cars and designer handbags, to the more hidden signs of wealth, like so-called 'stealth-luxe', the understated dressing of the uber rich. We are most satisfied when we achieve more relative to those around us, an effect even visible in the brain.[14] Decisions around money can be such a sensitive topic that the majority of the breadwinning women I interviewed asked me not to reveal their identities. The reason for this is revealing. These breadwinners weren't only talking about chores or earnings, but revealing intimate insights into how being the higher earner affects who holds the power, as well as how happy or dissatisfied this made them feel in their relationships.

Money therefore represents more than a basic need; it's intricately tied to how successful we feel as a provider and as a member of society. Felicity, who we heard from in the last chapter, is fine with her breadwinner status, but she's aware that others judge her partner for having no income. Another stay-at-home dad I spoke with told me that whilst being there for his kids feels like his most important role, he has lost a sense of purpose as he is no longer working in a vocation that once gave him a professional identity.

This feeling is further exacerbated because in our capitalist, individualistic society we are often fed the idea that more is better, that working hard will give us financial rewards, and that if you are poor, you must somehow therefore be to blame. However irrational it may be, what we earn is often closely tied to our self-worth, especially for men, because of the entrenched expectation of being the breadwinner, despite societal changes occurring in front of our eyes.

## DIVIDE AND CONQUER

What we earn affects relationship dynamics in some unexpected ways. In dual-income families with children, it's simply not feasible for both in the relationship to work the type of demanding job that involves a 60-hour week. Someone has to either put a brake on a certain career path, or, if they earn enough, outsource the labour for childcare and domestic work – and often feel guilty for that too.* That's exactly what the academic and author Anne-Marie Slaughter did. She worked long hours away from home, until her teenage son was having a difficult time and she felt she had to choose work or family. She chose the latter and felt guilty for it in a way that women, not men, are often conditioned to feel. She wrote in her book, *Unfinished Business*, that she had 'suddenly become categorised and subtly devalued as just another one of many talented and well-educated women who showed great promise at the start of their careers . . . but then made a choice to take a less demanding job'.[15] The double bind of having to pick one or the other limits future earning potential. This can be financially damaging, with lifelong consequences for our pension, financial freedom, and career prospects, and shows why female breadwinners have this additional mental burden of feeling like they have to sacrifice one or the other.

It's largely women who make this choice, in part because a flexibility bias exists for men too. Even if they want to take more time off for their children, men are judged as being less committed for doing so. Men can be thought of as less masculine when they request flexibility, despite both sexes often wanting it equally. One recent report found that 75% of men wanted the option to work more flexibly,[16] though flexible-working requests tend to be declined for men more often than for women. This leads to fewer men requesting it. It's these kinds of structural forces that make it hard to shift power imbalances at home too. If a higher earner is subtly conditioned to work longer hours and less flexibly, their earning potential will continue to increase, and their career will continue to be prioritised.

Meanwhile, women who become mothers are judged as less committed and ambitious at work simply by being mothers. The

---

* The great irony of this is that they are outsourcing domestic labour to someone less fortunate than them, usually a woman, who needs the money but is perhaps facing similar work-life balance issues at home.

difference is that women, as Slaughter herself felt, expect to *have to* prioritise family over work in a way that men don't. This contributes to the motherhood penalty,[17] the now well-established finding that women's earnings reduce after each child, while men continue to earn more and work many more hours because they are expected to, further exacerbating inequality at home.

If we can create more parity by both partners in a couple having the opportunity to devote an equal amount of time to work, then nobody has to 'lean out'. Even better would be to create a culture that does not value overtime, as putting in extra 'facetime' at work is impossible for those with caring responsibilities. At an internal employee awards session in my office a few years ago, several winners were congratulated for going 'over and above' by working in evenings and at weekends. It's exactly these kinds of comments from senior management that send a signal to others that this behaviour garners status, rather than being an anomaly. If companies want to create earning parity rather than simply talking the talk, they need to be extra mindful of the language they use and the company culture they want to exemplify. One new mother I spoke to felt she had no choice but to quit after her request to work more flexibly was denied. She felt as though the company valued that final half hour of facetime more than the loyalty she had shown for the previous five years.

We've heard how breadwinning women can negatively affect their male partners as they feel emasculated and judged. Unfortunately, it remains the case that when men earn less, women respect them less – which is perhaps a reason why lower-earning men are slightly more likely to cheat. The percentages are tiny, but the reasons why are revealing.[18] Their status as lower earners threatens their masculinity, and spreading their seed elsewhere helps reassert it, punishing their higher-earning partner in the process.

A higher-earning woman creates a dissonance between her expected identity as a lower earner, versus her reality. This makes divorce more likely in couples with higher-earning women, or when men are working part-time or not at all, because it can feel so uncomfortable for men to earn less. Some of these patterns are influenced by whether a man opted out of work voluntarily or involuntarily – with the latter the most damaging for a marriage.[19] As Esther Perel said in her popular TED talk, we expect our spouse to 'fulfil an endless list of needs', to be our lover, friend, parent, confidant, emotional companion and intellectual equal.[20] So when something disrupts our romantic ideal, it's no wonder that the relationship can suffer in the process.

The increase in higher-earning women globally is causing a change in attitude. In the 1995 World Values Survey, participants were asked to respond to the statement: 'If a woman earns more money than her husband, it's almost certain to cause problems.' Of US respondents, 36% agreed or strongly agreed, with similar responses from Europe. The same statement from the 2017–2021 survey was an entirely different story, with only 10% agreeing in the US and 8% in the UK. Similarly, in response to the statement 'When jobs are scarce men should have more right to a job than women', only 5% agreed in the US, with similar results in the UK. Unfortunately, many countries show far less progressive views – in Nigeria, Egypt, Bangladesh, Pakistan and Myanmar, well over half agreed.[21]

Here's where it's a double bind. Earning less affects a man's identity, but so does doing so-called 'feminine work' such as caregiving, which again goes some way to explaining why higher-earning women still do more housework than their lower-earning male partners. Plus, as we've heard, men use their status as higher earners to 'bargain' their way out of housework. This is exactly what Nisha found:

Whenever I talk about equality at home, him helping out with housework more, he always brings up that he earns more, and that it's 'not equal' in that way either. I just don't know what to say. He works five days, I work four and look after our daughter the other day. In my mind that's an equal amount

of 'work', and going part-time to spend a day doing childcare
was not something he ever wanted to do because he didn't
want to sacrifice his career progression and because 'it's not
the done thing' where he works . . . In every conversation we
have about money I end up feeling like a failure for not making
much. I'm so sick of it.

Meanwhile, Georgia, who works for the US government in the UK,
found herself prioritising her partner's career when she had a child,
although she had already built up a substantial nest egg to ensure
that she was not a 'financial burden' for her partner. 'I hate that I
have to think about it this way . . . so in that sense I feel like I pay
for myself.' While they divide housework, the mental work of raising
their child falls to her. 'It was almost like parenting was my project,
also because it was my only child and he had other children.'

Georgia is an interesting case as she continues to maintain
financial power due to her income, but in a less fulfilling role.
Despite this, the power shift occurred because she wanted a child
more than he did, meaning she felt she had no choice but to step
back from her career, something she still feels regret over. 'It's not
terrible but it's not fulfilling; I've plateaued in my ability to advance.'
Her example shows that stepping back may be what is thought
necessary in the moment, but it could have lasting career as well
as earning repercussions for the future.

## WHEN MONEY OVERPOWERS

Given that money and providing for the family is stubbornly tied
to masculinity, when one person in the relationship seeks to hold
on to this power it can create financial insecurity, a pension gap
and, in the worst cases, extremely toxic situations involving financial abuse. I've now read and heard of countless examples where
higher-earning men hold on to their money without any discussions
about a joint bank account or pooling it together. This often starts
before children, when bills are more manageable, but as women

are more likely to work part-time after having children and there-fore have a reduced income, it can become a challenge. Zahrah, for instance, had no reserves to fall back on when her husband went away on a work trip, but she knew from experience that asking for more wouldn't get her anywhere:

I work part-time around the school hours. He [earns] three times more than I do. He does pay the bills and I pay for the food shopping . . . I don't think this is fair as I barely have anything left after buying for the family! He has always said his money is his and I've never actually known how much he has. We have been together for 12 years . . . He hasn't asked me once if I'm OK with money while he has been away, he's not offered to help me with anything. BUT if I ask him he absolutely hates it. So I've gone 14 days struggling, just so I don't have to have him say 'I knew you were going to ask me . . . you're a leech sometimes.'

That financial abuse like this exists is often due to the abuser wanting full control and power over another. It might be because they have less power or status outside the home, and can exert it inside, it might be that power at home has warped their empathy, or it could be a generational pattern where they witnessed similar abuse growing up. Each situation is different, but certainly the loss of power in one domain has been shown to push individuals to seek power in another. Think of bullies who come from troubled backgrounds, when they exert power in other places due to a lack of it at home.

Once a couple has children it can feel more challenging to leave a relationship. Most couples don't talk about expectations when they are first in love, and abuse can gradually build. It can then be harder to disrupt these patterns to enact meaningful change. Worse, if one in a couple holds or controls the finances, the other has nothing if they leave, often keeping the less powerful one tied to the relationship.

Fortunately, there are steps non-breadwinners and lower earners can take to overcome this type of control in the first place, but expectations have to start early. Kristin Laurin, a psychologist who studies people's beliefs and motivations, set up a relationship contract before her latest partner moved in. Her previous relationship had not ended well and she wanted to ensure similar patterns didn't occur. At the beginning of a relationship there is not yet a status quo to overcome, Laurin reasoned, so she laid out her expectations and had her partner agree to them. She also recognises that because she is older than her partner and is the higher earner, she felt comfortable with enacting this type of expectation early on. Other tactics include regular communication, lists to divide chores, and sharing finances 50:50 or in equal shares proportionate to earnings. Especially if children come into the mix, considering finances as shared for the family can be helpful too, as it affords each person in the relationship an equal role in the household finances, without one feeling disempowered.

## MORE HOUSEWORK = MORE SEX

The complicated relationship we have with money and how that translates at home shows that it's important for us all to understand these impacts. Only then can we learn to recognise and undo the more unhelpful financial pressures. For instance, if men do more housework, it is better for the marriage all round – and studies have shown that in couples where this happens they have more sex; presumably because it's easier to get in the mood when nobody feels resentful about having to pick up the slack. Couples with egalitarian views on housework and paid work have been shown to communicate better, leading to increased sexual confidence and frequency,[22] while couples with an unequal distribution of childcare do the deed less often.[23] If the dishes are done, the meals are planned, the kids camp is booked, then there's more breathing room for fun. If there's a shared physical load, the mental load may decrease for women too, creating more time to enjoy each other's company.

There's even a link between how much housework and childcare men do and the country's fertility rate. South Korea scores lowest for men doing chores, and lowest for average number of children too. In countries where men contribute to housework and childcare the most, they have the highest fertility rate, while in countries where men don't do as much, women are resistant to having more children.[24] This fascinating pattern links a few of the research areas we've been exploring. Throughout history, men with higher status and more power have tended to have more children, but because power contributes to gender inequality, declining power leads to fewer children for men, and in parallel increases the number of women who consciously forgo having children altogether, as it allows them to gain greater power. These patterns show that a domestic issue can quickly become an issue for the global economy as a whole, considering the decreasing birth rates in many countries.

All the examples we've explored show that the complicated interplay of earnings, work, status and home life have wider consequences than we might expect. Women might opt out of work, thinking they can't manage to balance home and work life, without realising this sets them up for domestic and financial imbalances that are hard to claw their way out of. Female breadwinners may not realise that their status means they can still end up doing more domestic work at home. Men might want to spend more time with their children without realising they will be judged for it by friends and employers as less committed workers or as less masculine overall. It is only by changing these patterns that our assumptions and expectations will begin to be shaped differently. We are living through a time of rapid change, and if we address these imbalances as soon as they occur, then when our own children grow up, they may not be having similar discussions. We no longer live in a world where we should teach our sons to be providers, as our daughters are increasingly likely to be so too. In fact, we could all learn from the Agta people and operate on the assumption of equality from the outset.

## KEY POINTS:

- In couples where men earn less, women have been found to under-report their earnings while men over-report theirs, exposing the discomfort couples feel when it comes to this imbalance.
- Lacking control over income creates an uneven playing field, empowering some while marginalising others. This power imbalance can breed resentment and amplify inequality.
- People from privilege tend to act more confidently and extraverted, and are seen as more powerful, while visible inequity causes stress.

## ACTION POINTS:

- Sharing finances ensures both partners have an equal say in managing the household spending, preventing a sense of powerlessness for the lower earner and future-proofing finances in case a relationship breaks down.
- Having more open and honest conversations from the outset models positive change and helps destigmatise how our financial status at work affects power at home.
- Don't let the higher earner exchange their way out of housework. Sharing housework might even lead to more sex!

## 3

## HETERO NORMS: THE LINGERING HARM OF STEREOTYPES

'When everybody is equal, we are all more free.'

—Barack Obama

The psychologist Susan Fiske never expected to set foot in the Supreme Court, but that's exactly where she found herself in 1989, in a landmark case about gender discrimination brought by a senior manager at Price Waterhouse called Ann Hopkins. Fiske had the right credentials, having extensively documented the effects of stereotyping individuals in race, class and sex divides, and was developing interesting theories about power and its many influences. Little did she know at the time, but Price Waterhouse v. Hopkins would leave lasting ripples years later in how companies consider gender stereotypes.

As Fiske and the court heard, Hopkins had been passed over for a promotion because she wasn't deemed feminine enough, but Hopkins had never pandered to such suggestions. Instead, she rode a motorbike to work and acted as she always had, in a direct – some would even say abrasive – manner. It wasn't Fiske's job to analyse Hopkins's character but to take account of whether she was unfairly stereotyped. Hopkins was even referred to as a 'lady partner candidate' rather than simply a candidate. 'She was held to a standard of womanliness that was not relevant to her job,' Fiske tells me. She was also a single-mother breadwinner (whose daughter would go on to closely follow in her footsteps).

Hopkins, a maths graduate with a background in aerospace, was a skilled employee. When it came time for potential promotion to partner in 1982, she was the perfect fit – she was said to have brought in more business than the other candidates she was up against. Out of 88 potentials, she was the only woman. She wasn't given partnership that year and so applied the next year too, and was again denied. When asking for feedback, she got an unexpectedly honest response. She was told she needed a 'course in charm school', that she acted too aggressively, was impatient, spoke improperly and was abrasive. She was acting too much like a 'man', in other words, and not how women at the company were expected to act. She had even been told by a well-meaning colleague that she should 'walk more femininely, talk more femininely, dress more femininely, wear make-up, have her hair styled, and wear jewellery'.[1] Aware that this was nonsense, and that she was being treated this way not because of her work but due to her sex, she resigned and sued her employers, citing the 1964 Civil Rights Act.

The findings Fiske was uncovering about gender stereotypes were new to social science at the time, but apparent to anyone in a male-dominated workspace. She found evidence for stereotypes we have long known existed, which is why lawyers had started to take note. Fiske was glad she could play a role in revealing why particular assumptions gave employers the power to discriminate, further perpetuating certain power dynamics.

As for Hopkins, she went back to work after a seven-year legal fight during which she was an unemployed single mother with three young children to support. The district judge filed in her favour: she returned to the same company that had not promoted her, was given $400,000 in back-dated pay, and was finally made partner. Asked about the impact of the case, she seemed to shrug it off and said that raising her three children was a 'much more preoccupying concern'. She would continue to work at Price Waterhouse until her retirement in 2002. Hopkins died in 2018 aged 74. Her case has had lasting repercussions on the legal landscape of how we define what it means to be a woman as well as how an individual chooses to identify. It was the first case law available that subsequently made it illegal to discriminate on the basis of gender stereotyping, and has since been cited numerous times in other lawsuits – most commonly involving LGBTQ cases where individuals are discriminated against based on how they present.

Hopkins's story is bigger than gender discrimination alone, but shows that your personal identity can affect you in the workplace too, even where it shouldn't. After she won her case, Hopkins was visited by dozens of individuals from the LGBTQ community seeking advice after they had been subjected to both subtle and overt prejudice. While attitudes today have become more progressive, assumptions around what it means to be a family are still closely tied to a heterosexual norm. Intriguingly, it is those who defy expected conventions who can show the rest of us that breadwinner norms don't have to dictate who holds the power.

## SAME-SEX COUPLES ARE MORE EQUAL

Take Cara, 42, and Alice, 30, a UK couple who have been together for 11 years and have a three-year-old together. When they were visiting schools, they had additional concerns to the usual questions parents ask, about results or enriching extra-curriculars. On each school visit they asked how a child with their family set-up would be received: would teachers be supportive, be aware, use inclusive language and so forth, instead of assuming a typical mum-and-dad set-up? It intensified the already stressful experience of choosing a school. They experience London as a tolerant and inclusive place, but despite the increasing number of same-sex parents, they don't meet any others at the school gate, and they regularly come across subtle assumptions of what a family should be.

There is something more reassuring we can learn from couples like Cara and Alice. We heard earlier how in heterosexual relationships female breadwinners still do more at home, which made me wonder what happens in same-sex couple households. Are they better at sharing housework more equally? You probably won't be surprised that the answer is yes. There is now research on this very topic that finds that same-sex couples share childcare and housework much more equally. They cannot divide tasks according to gender norms, which means they don't fall into some of the common patterns different-sex couples find themselves in.

## 'IF IT'S EVEN HALF A PERCENTAGE DIFFERENT THE OTHER WILL COMPLAIN'

Cara carried their child and took the majority of her maternity leave, whilst Alice took two months. As they had their child during lockdown, Alice was able to be regularly present throughout the first 10 months too. There were no long commutes or late nights in the office, and she could help when she had breaks from work. When I asked about the division of care in their relationship, Alice replied instantly that 'it's 50:50 and if it's even half a percentage different the other will complain'. They share the workload based on what each is better at. Neither likes to cook so they aim to do it together to make it more enjoyable. Now with a toddler around this is more difficult, but they divide and conquer where they can, meaning they share the pleasant and the more mundane. Speaking with them both I realised that they attribute this balance to several simple but important behaviours and habits:

- Communication of each other's needs, especially when things are not working, so that there's time to enact change before it leads to negativity.
- Prioritising their family: both say they could work more overtime with the hope of higher earning potential, but they don't want the added stress.
- Flexible work: they regularly work from home and are able to fit in household tasks in the time that they save from having no commute.

The first, communication, is the one aspect they think has been most vital – and the one everyone can work on. It sounds simple but when we are stressed it's harder to communicate – and if our partner is more powerful, they may lack the empathy to understand how we are truly feeling. We are also prone to overestimating how much others, even close family, understand what we think.[2] Without us explicitly stating it, our partners may have no idea that resentment is building.

Before becoming parents, Cara and Alice discussed in depth how they would raise their daughter and what it would mean for their careers. Couples who assume tasks will be divided 50:50 often don't talk about how that will work in practice, and so without a concerted effort to subvert norms, life quickly becomes unfair. Once children enter the family, tasks become even more entrenched, and in the majority of cases, women tend to take most or all of the parental leave available. They are the ones who then become the experts at home. When they go back to work, if there is no handover period, they continue to do many of the tasks they did when on leave. From a mental tab of which clothes and shoes are the right size, to vaccine appointments and school research, women tend to do the bulk of the anticipating and planning, as well as doing the work involved in these tasks. Cara and Alice didn't find themselves in this situation. Both formed strong emotional bonds with their child, unlike many heterosexual couples where children tend to bond more closely with their primary caregiver, typically the mother.

Still, despite *both* being equal primary caregivers, Cara and Alice find that others categorise them. Alice says she has firmly been put in the 'dad' box because she is not the biological mother and looks least like their child (Cara and their daughter are of mixed heritage, while Alice is white). They say that people find it hard to know who to contact about playdates – something mothers tend to organise most often. Whilst they don't have gendered divides at home, they are still subject to outside preconceptions because of the idea that when two women are raising a child, one might take on a typically masculine role and the other a feminine role, when that is not necessarily the case.

A large body of studies confirms what they experience – that same-sex couples tend to divide tasks more equally at home. A 2023 report using American data shows that same-sex partnerships tend to allocate time for paid work more equally from the outset, meaning there is also less likely to be an income disparity, though still, when one earns more, the lower earner does more housework.[3] One review looking at 15 years of data found that lesbian couples engage in a more equal distribution of household labour than heterosexual couples, and that lesbian women often opt to eschew traditional gendered divisions of chores in favour of other factors such as quality of the task or ability.[4] Another in-depth study revealed recurring assumptions. Nandi, aged 37, said: 'It's maybe the people outside the house that will see me as the more masculine one but inside the home there are no roles.' Her partner Jasmine commented that these preconceptions occur because Nandi presents as more masculine, so she gets put in the 'man' box.[5] Our constant need to categorise others fuels these misconceptions. Even when a couple doesn't fit the heterosexual narrative, we might still subconsciously assign stereotypical traits to each partner.

It's certainly easier for Cara and Alice to fall outside expected divisions, but they work hard to maintain the status quo. Cara is more senior, and paid more, and they could just as easily have fallen into a situation where she, as the higher earner with more positional power, could have used this status to do less at home. As we've seen, it's often a power imbalance that contributes to gender inequality, but for same-sex couples power outside the home doesn't have quite the same effect inside the home. Precisely because Cara and Alice fall outside the 'heteronormative standard', it led them to make conscious choices about parenting and dividing tasks. It took work, but it means their household feels truly balanced.

Speaking to child-free gay men I heard similar patterns, that tasks are divided more according to who is better at them. George, for instance, tells me he is more disorganised but enjoys cooking, while his partner sorts the house and keeps it tidy. When I was researching the mental load for my previous book, I started by asking everyone about divisions in their relationship. An acquaintance, Brandon, told me that he definitely carries the least mental load, with his partner, Jeremy, doing much more of the thinking and organising. They each excel at different tasks, but the key is, neither of them fall into particularly gendered roles. Both help clean and cook, and both can dedicate equal time to their careers. All the same-sex couples I spoke to did not assume the other would do more, though it's worth stating that those I spoke to do not represent every relationship.

## THE BIRTH PARENT

Maaike van der Vleuten, a researcher who studies gender dynamics among same-sex couples, found that financially, they seem to be more equal too. When analysing earnings between couples, she found that there were much larger financial gaps for different-sex couples than for same-sex couples. Her data spanned four Nordic countries known for high levels of equality, Sweden, Denmark, Finland and Norway, showing this gap was not specific to one place. Interestingly, combined household income didn't differ, meaning there were no financial repercussions (nor benefit) for a smaller earnings gap. Simply put, in heterosexual couples it was much more common for one partner to earn more and the other less, but for same-sex couples it was more common for both to earn more equally – though on average the household earnings *overall* didn't differ. Financially, then, it doesn't penalise the household for there to be an earnings gap, but it *does* penalise the lower earner, and, conversely, a smaller earnings gap translates into more balanced power at home.[6]

Meanwhile, mothers in same-sex relationships experience a significantly smaller motherhood penalty after childbirth compared to mothers in opposite-sex partnerships. This is reassuring as it shows that being a mother isn't in itself deterministic of this penalty; instead, the problem seems to be linked to deeply ingrained gender norms at home and the lack of support that comes with mother-hood. It once again shows why breadwinner women are bucking against so many expectations.[7]

There are also differences between male and female same-sex couples. Van der Vleuten noticed a double standard affecting women when she herself was subject to comments when her partner was pregnant: 'My career was very important, and now I'm a young mum I get comments of "How can you be a good mum and still work full time?" – I think you would never say that to a man.'

Female same-sex couples have been found to divide tasks even more equally than do two men, perhaps because they are the gender more likely to have expected inequality, so they enter into a rela-tionship with more awareness of this divide and make a conscious effort to overcome it.[8] Of course, same-sex couples are not exempt from gender norms either. One study found that male couples usually work full time, but female couples are more likely to both work part-time. Female same-sex couples often both have a desire to be pregnant at some point, which gives them a shared experience of pregnancy and birth, as well as an opportunity to discuss which role each will take. Interviews with Swedish lesbian couples revealed that both partners spent a lot of time discussing who would first carry a child, anticipating in advance the impact this would have on their career and home-life balance. This is not something male–female couples routinely do, but tend to only notice greater inequity after a child arrives – at which point it becomes harder to correct it. Veronica, one of the interviewees, decided to carry her child precisely because it would help her 'switch focus from work'. If her partner carries their next child, she will have experienced what it is like and it will allow her to relate more easily: 'Veronica indicates that Viveca had a stronger desire to carry, but choosing Viveca as the (first) birth mother was mutually seen as a potential risk to their relationship, a risk of inequality in the division of care (and work) since it would enable Veronica to "just keep going" [at work]. Hence, the risk of future inequalities – due to their current differences – made Veronica and Viveca adjust their decision.'

More importantly, because motherhood can create such a drastic imbalance, both women having an awareness of how motherhood affects their sense of self means that 'both mothers escape – or enact – the less recognised identity of a non-birth mother', creating a 'lesbian maternal equality'. The individuals the researchers interviewed therefore all wanted to carry a child at some point.[9] It's hard to pinpoint exact figures, but one US source suggests that about 16% of same-sex couples are raising at least one child, and, unsurprisingly, more same-sex female couples have children than do male couples, and they are more likely to adopt and foster than heterosexual couples.[10]

## ADOPTION

Ben Fergusson and his partner, Tom, have been together for 18 years, and in 2018 were among the first same-sex married couples in Germany to adopt a baby. Due to the generous parental leave available, both Ben and Tom were able to take seven months off at 70% of their salary – the first two months of which they took together to help them ease into shared parenthood. Among UK heterosexual couples, the father is usually back at work after two weeks, leaving the mother alone. Ben tells me how the lack of social expectation about who would stay home made the decision easy – they'd both share it. This is still how they approach parenting six years later. The idea of one person having to do most of the shared tasks seems completely absurd to him. They both found early parenting hard, and he remembers wondering how mums do it with the added difficulty of breastfeeding and perhaps a lengthy physical recovery too.

Ben has written at length about how he and his husband noticed the double standards of expectations, and how it remains so normalised for women to take on the bulk of childcare with little support: 'When there's no social expectation about which parent stays at home and looks after the baby, the idea that either of you would do it single-handedly seems crazy. If my husband had suggested going back to work after two weeks, I'd have thrown the television out of the window,' he wrote in 2020.[11] He explains that it's straight-forward for them to share the home and parenting load when there aren't any obvious external pressures. Neither career is devalued, and neither faces an earning penalty because there's no positional power imbalance forcing one of them to step back.

The power inside their home is unaffected by their caregiving roles. Because their home life is balanced, both can pursue chal-lenges at work equally. They largely split tasks based on what each of them likes doing and have found a balance that works. Just like Cara and Alice, they communicate about every aspect of care and workload to keep it that way.

Naturally, unless you are the rare exception, relationships are seldom perfect, and power imbalances can be found among same-sex couples too, where there is often still one main bread-winner and one who does more domestic work – it's just less likely to occur than in heterosexual couples because there's less societal pressure to follow a gendered script. In heterosexual couples, if childcare costs more than a salary, women often give up work entirely, even though it harms their career prospects should they want to go back, and affects pension contributions and financial security. They become more financially dependent on their part-ners, further upsetting the power balance, and making them vulnerable should anything happen to the marriage. Ben recalls that although he was the lower earner, it didn't even cross his mind to scale back more than his partner. Instead, they worked out their finances around childcare, both opting to reduce hours to watch their son as there was no power tussle of who had the more important job. Ben is aware that their relationship is much more equal compared to his heterosexual friends, who, he says, don't seem to be aiming for equality, but to take on a greater share compared to the generation before:

I've got lots of lovely, straight male friends who from their point of view, in comparison to their dad who was absent, they are heroically covering childcare. They're doing an amazing job. They do it in a way that's better [than before] but it's still the case that while men are more involved it's a degree of difference rather than a complete revolution. What I notice is, often, the mum has been looking after the kid all week and then she gets an hour lie-in at the weekend, and I'm like 'How about the weekend off?' If I look after T for a week because Tom's away, I'll be like, I'll do a week's writer's retreat. It's not tit-for-tat, but my expectation would be, if you wanted to go and do something for a week, then I get to do something . . .

What Ben touches upon lies at the heart of the issue many heterosexual couples with children face. Even if the will is there, society hasn't caught up to enable couples to share the load without friction. There's unaffordable childcare, the expectation of long hours, meaning both can't equally pursue the types of careers that require overtime, especially as women are conditioned to feel more guilty for being away from their children for long days. To make things more equal at home, Ben says men should feel comfortable with scaling back or going part-time if finances allow – which is exactly what some men now do if their partner is the main breadwinner. Men can also ensure they are more involved at home, because inequality at home means less time available to do paid work, as well as the hidden mental preparation required for advancing in careers, networking or CV updates. When I'm knee-deep in school or homework admin, it's hard to think about that next career step, but because we both prioritise my work goals too, I've been able to get ahead and not fall victim to the motherhood penalty. And when both in a couple are able to take account of what the other needs, it naturally has a positive impact on relationship satisfaction.

## CONGRATULATED FOR THE BARE MINIMUM

Ben and his husband share tasks as much as they can. What surprised Ben is that he isn't subject to the comments, criticisms and subtle judgements many mothers face, but is instead congratulated for doing the bare minimum. Ben and his partner have found that, with the support that comes from an equal partnership, the hard days are somehow a little less hard. There are difficult moments too, subtle assumptions, questions about where their son's mother is and quick, polite corrections. They have to pay more attention around Mother's Day and check with the school that their son won't be asked to draw a card for mum. It's not 'pure harmony' at home, he says. They have the usual disagreements most couples have, but to avoid anything escalating, tasks are discussed and divided. They also have full confidence in the ability of the other to do everything needed for the household to function – which is not always the case in heterosexual couples, where women in particular become more proficient in domestic tasks. This specialisation can lead to women losing trust in their partners to get it right and end up 'gatekeeping', leaving them detailed lists or constantly checking in – something I've certainly done in the kitchen. It's demotivating at best, demoralising at worst for the partner trying to help out if someone else is hovering about telling them they would do it differently. Even if you eat later than planned, as long as it's nourishing and everyone is fed, that's the most important thing. Even if you're more proficient in the kitchen, without leaving your partner to it they'd never learn to improve.

## LAUNDRY AND DIRTY PANTS

Clearly those of us in heterosexual relationships can improve upon how we counter gender expectations and the stereotypes that Ann Hopkins fought so hard to avoid. Given that there is a clear link between unequal housework and unhappier relationships, we would all do well to remember that dividing tasks at home is better for the entire family's well-being, leads to closer bonds and allows both in the relationship equal time to focus on work. If this sounds a bit simplistic, take that as a positive, and know that we can all start by communicating how much time each of us spends on tasks and then dividing them according to either skill set or time available.

If one in the couple is the higher earner by a large margin, be aware that continuing to prioritise their career and working hours will push this gap even higher. If one of you works part-time, then divide leisure time away from children – for those who have them – equally, so that each person can hold on to their own identity and follow their own passions. Carving out equal leisure time will allow each partner to pursue their own hobbies and foster more gratitude in the relationship, hopefully making them feel more fulfilled and present in family life.

For those reading this without children and considering having them later, noting these patterns early on and discussing who will take on which areas of housework and childcare will help prevent future resentment building up. Often it's only once children are in the mix that couples confront expectations of divisions of care, because until then nobody has the responsibility to be home at a particular time. The earlier conversations can be had, the greater chance you'll have of tackling these responsibilities more equally from the outset. If you need another reason to do this, discrepancies in how couples perceive their division of housework can be a major source of relationship dissatisfaction and can even lead to divorce. When couples disagree on their division of housework, even if men believe they contribute equally, women often feel they shoulder a heavier burden. This perception gap leads to lower relationship satisfaction for both partners, with women more likely to consider separation. Resentment and hostility can also fester.[12] Remember that one person in a relationship tends to do more invisible work, which often isn't realised by the other because it's so hard to measure. If couples take stock and recognise these contributions, and divide what can be divided, it is bound to lead to greater relationship satisfaction too. The first step is the awareness of what needs doing, followed by making a conscious effort to divide and conquer.

So, take note: if you're the one who persistently anticipates needing to do laundry, but your partner will only do it when they have run out of underwear, then talk about it. It may be that they don't see the need to do it as often, or simply don't think about it as much because you've always anticipated it, leading to greater resentment over time.

Precisely because many of the patterns discussed so far are specific to male versus female roles, it's worth us all learning why this can hold us back professionally and personally, taking action before resentment builds – and before we pass on these norms to our children. This is important because children's preconceptions about gender are heavily influenced by what they see their parents doing. Ann Hopkins's case beautifully illustrates this. I tracked down her daughter, who is now herself a business leader in the tech industry and is a sole breadwinner with a stay-at-home male partner.

Tela Mathias, aged 46 when I interviewed her, speaks of her mother fondly and is brought to tears twice during our conversation. She recalls hearing Ruth Bader Ginsberg say her mother's name in court on 8 October 2019, in another landmark case that would make it illegal to discriminate against sexual orientation or gender identity in the workplace, a case won in 2020. 'The only case law was my mum's case law,' she explains. 'So not only was her case a landmark, these new cases are landmarks on the back of my mum's.'

Her mother, she says, described herself as a 'reluctant civil rights landmark, gardener and pie maker' – but only if asked. Otherwise, she went about her work as normal. Back at Price Waterhouse, Hopkins found herself reporting to someone who'd received the promotion she might have got. Mathias tells me she once asked her mother if this bothered her, to which Hopkins replied: 'No, because I did it my way.' Still, growing up during the lengthy legal battle had an immediate impact on the entire family. Mathias felt she grew up under the shadow of a larger-than-life woman, but it made her determined to speak out in favour of anyone who faces discrimination, even subtly. As her mother had, she works in an extremely male-dominated industry, and while overt sexism is rare, she once called out a senior client for using the word 'girls' about women who worked in his office. Generally, she feels well respected at work because of the air of competence she knows she exudes, a self-assurance that her mum helped encourage.

She once asked her mother how she could ever hope to have a similar impact, to which Hopkins simply said: 'There's nothing special about me, I was the right person at the right moment in time.' The case understandably caused considerable stress; both she and one of her brothers later experienced alcohol addiction, as did Hopkins, who also outlived her youngest son, who died in a car accident aged only 21.

Her mother's fight and case certainly left a mark. If you remember Mathias it's because we heard from her earlier, as she's a sole bread-winner with four children and a stay-at-home husband. When speaking with her it was apparent that their set-up was heavily influenced by her mother. Her to-the-point communication style echoed her mother's too, and it's clear her business success owes much to that early encouragement.

Hopkins is an extreme example of one lone woman overcoming an individualistic society's approach to equality and gender. What is revealing is that when gendered expectations are not subject to heterosexual norms, interesting patterns begin to emerge that we can all learn from. It's why Hopkins became a powerful advocate for defying stereotypes – she had realised early on that we need not act in gender stereotypical ways, lessons her daughter now continues to act out.

## KEY POINTS:

- We are all influenced by gender stereotypes, and we transmit these to our children.
- Women tend to become the experts at home, holding 'faux power' because they have less power outside it.
- Same-sex relationships tend to be more equal as they cannot divide tasks according to gender norms.

## ACTION POINTS:

- Communicate what can help make home life more equal. It's harder to communicate when stressed, but without discussing our needs tasks will continue to be unfairly balanced.
- Don't see the household as the woman's domain. This will help avoid internalised pressure on women to do more at home.
- Couples can work at anticipating the invisible labour that needs doing.

# 4

## CARING CAN BE MASCULINE: THE CHANGING FACE OF MASCULINITY

'I think daughters can change the perception of their fathers.'
—Ruth Bader Ginsburg

Today, despite the rise in female breadwinners and equality measures targeted to retain female leadership at work, men still hold much of the power. These differences have long been attributed to a range of essentialist viewpoints, arguing that men and women are different when it comes to many personality traits, leadership styles and so forth. While there is some truth to that, it largely reflects how we are socialised.

Everyone no doubt has an anecdote about the different expectations of boys versus girls. As a child I was shrewdly aware of this as I was a tomboy, and always had male friends. This gave me a subtle form of status among the boys, especially because I was good at sports. I was only considered a tomboy because the activities I liked were seen as more typically boyish, reflecting ingrained expectations rather than the more logical approach that many children are interested in a range of activities. If gendered toys didn't exist, I wouldn't have been given the label 'tomboy', and likewise there would be no reason why boys who act 'girly' should be teased. Even today my son won't touch anything pink, and when my daughter was only three, she would already list *girls toys'* versus *boys toys'*, despite me telling her that all toys are for everyone. If we need reminding of how much these categorisations are social constructs, pink used to be considered masculine – and young children don't show any preference for pink until about two years old, the preference getting stronger with age when socialisation fully kicks in.[1] Since becoming a parent, I've noticed even more how gendered the world is. It's the first question often asked during pregnancy: do you know what you're having? A real human baby doesn't quite seem to suffice. Some would comment that I was lucky to have a girl first, because they're apparently easier than 'wild little boys'. Again, this is a misconception – both my children are extremely rambunctious.

Societal obsession with gender is unhealthy, not least because anyone who steps outside of gender norms is often instantly judged, questioned or, at worst, discriminated against. It would therefore help to understand how and why our gendered assumptions begin, because this has a big impact on how we view power throughout our lives, and on who is expected to achieve it.

We all know the more obvious gender expectations of loud boys and quiet girls, or bossy women and authoritative men, but it's the more subtle ones that creep under our skin. Pregnant women report more movement if they know they are having a boy, compared to if they don't know the sex, and have been shown to overestimate their sons' motor skills, and under-estimate their daughters'.[2] Mothers and fathers have been observed acting differently towards their daughters and sons, with mothers talking more to daughters,[3] and fathers taking part in more rough play with sons.

Fathers also talk more about emotions to their daughters, but more about physical achievements with their sons. One striking study found that fathers' brains even respond differently to the happy faces of their daughters compared to their sons. This reveals that dads are much more attuned to their daughters' positive emotional expressions, as their brain was active in areas important for emotional regulation and feelings of reward.[4] Language differs too, fathers being more likely to use achievement-based words such as 'top', 'win' and 'proud' for sons, while using more analytical language for daughters. They have been shown to sing more and speak more about sadness to their daughters than to their sons. Even the researchers of the study were surprised at how early this gendered behaviour begins, as fathers hadn't noticed they were behaving differently. With all this in mind, you can easily see how boys are socialised to be more aggressive and girls as more talkative and emotional.

How we are socialised plays a major role in our outlook on life later, and most of our archetypes are of the father earning more than the mother, with mothers picking up the domestic work at home. But when this is reversed, it can help us rethink our idea of masculinity, as well as how couples make financial, caregiving and career decisions.

James, a Canadian professional working in London for a software company, was raised in a household where his mother was the higher earner, though both his parents had good jobs. They were out of the door early, meaning his mother was never the default parent at home doing more household chores. Just like Tela Mathias, James grew up with an expectation that women can have high-powered careers too. Fast forward a generation and today his partner works in the financial industry and out-earns him. He supports her career and values her passion and ambition. Unlike the research we heard about earlier, where a man's self-esteem can be affected by having a higher-earning partner, he feels the opposite. 'I came from a household where this was normalised. My mother was very career-focused, I think that probably helped [inform] the way I interact with my family and my son,' he tells me.

They have one young child with another on the way, and because James works from home, he does more childcare during the week; more of the pick-ups, drop-offs and organising at home. But he and his wife split things fairly evenly at weekends. He consciously ensures he's there for his son, not only caregiving but spending quality time together. For him, fatherhood means being present. 'That's probably the biggest thing for me. I want to make sure that [my son] knows that I'm there for him both mentally and physically.'

For him masculinity isn't tied to what he is bringing in from outside the home, but to time spent ensuring he can be a good role model.

James is an example of how expectations can shift based on our upbringing, something referred to as 'intergenerational norm transfer'. Numerous studies show that this is a potent force in shaping our understanding of who holds the power. It's how we first recognise that power imbalances cause gender imbalances, due to how patriarchal society is structured. Worst of all, this is drilled into us from an extremely young age and goes on to inform many of the more subtle forms of power play we see at home. If these power plays don't manifest, we grow up expecting a more balanced home ourselves. I grew up in a household where my mother, as a GP, was earning more than my father, who worked for a charity. His role was more flexible as my mother had patients to see, but she rarely finished late, so it meant both were readily present and around for caregiving. It was my dad who spent two hours every week driving me to basketball practice, finishing work early to do so. He was the one who kept our kitchen organised and tidy too, though my mum did the majority of the cooking. This upbringing certainly helped inform my expectation of future success and roles at home, and that a caregiving role would never solely define my identity.

Early behaviours and attitudes have lasting consequences. Assumptions about how men and women should act can affect emotional availability and how we form close connections. One manifestation of such an upbringing is that the suicide rate among young men compared to women is staggeringly high. In recently published UK statistics, three-quarters of suicides were male.[5] This is often attributed to men having to act in unrealistic, stereotypically masculine ways, and the fact that they are less likely to get support when struggling. The longer society perpetuates unattainable ideals, the worse it will be for the next generation.

How we raise our children is not just important for equality, but also for the well-being of families as a whole. Traditional masculinity is often 'evidenced by the dominance of men over women and other, less powerful men',[6] depicting men as dominant, strong, stoic, independent and powerful – which, as we'll hear, are concepts that are changing. Even when we recognise this, our social conditioning is so deeply ingrained that it requires conscious effort to challenge our implicit assumptions. Every time I hear 'boys will be boys' it further cements just how entrenched our conditioning is. It matters because it affects how children view femininity and masculinity, with lasting repercussions. Assumptions about masculinity harm men and women alike, but we are at a crucial moment where we can change the narrative.

## CARING CAN ALSO BE MASCULINE

How we are socialised explains why the male-breadwinner norm is so embedded, and why stay-at-home fathers can feel alienated. If capitalist society reinforces the idea that our value as an individual is based on our output, our success at work and our earning potential rather than raising and caring for others, we have a problem. It means that if you aren't achieving at work or earning as much as your peers, it will continue to affect your self-worth as an individual.

Women are *expected* to be caregivers, meaning they already have to change their identity if they become mothers. This still creates a motherhood penalty for them, but men haven't had to think about changing their identity to caregivers for much of recent history. Changing breadwinner patterns as well as increased paternity benefits are now confronting men with care-work in a way that previous generations did not experience, which is bound to feel uncomfortable for some, but hopefully rewarding for many in years to come.

One eye-opening study in 2013 showed that men felt threatened if their romantic partner experienced success in several tasks. This was found among both US and Dutch participants, showing it was not only specific to one country. Men experienced a lower self-worth when their partner succeeded in a task than when their partner failed. This, the authors reported, was because 'Men are more likely than women to interpret a partner's success as indicating that they are not as good as their partner.'[7]

Fortunately, in 2021 another team aimed to replicate the study and didn't find these differences in self-esteem.[8] The authors wrote that 'Heterosexual men may find the success of their romantic partner less threatening today than they did in the past.' When a replication of a study fails it's never entirely clear why, but as their study was done almost a decade afterwards, the authors propose that it could simply reflect that cultural change is happening, something that has also been reflected in survey data showing that many men no longer perceive women earning more as problematic.

## RISKY PIONEERS ENCOURAGE CHANGE

Patterns are visibly changing, especially when children come into the mix. We've heard a lot about how mothers still do more child-care, but it's worth recognising that fathers are spending more time with children than in recently recorded history. For many families this is now a basic expectation. More men in the UK and elsewhere are taking parental leave, and some employers, clearly keen to retain talent, are increasing paid parental leave for all. At the same time, society is slowly welcoming other forms of masculinity, or, as one study puts it, 'the new male'.[9] This includes the following: decreased homophobia, acceptance of gender diversity, emotional bonding and closeness, compassion, vulnerability and even bromances, among many other traits once considered 'softer' and not masculine. Other studies have found that more men are rejecting misogyny,[10] are showing willingness to be more equal in relationships, and taking on more laundry, cooking and childcare during paternity leave.[11]

In 2015 the UK government instituted shared parental leave but take up has barely hovered above 2% because, in most cases, companies have maternity pay policies, whilst men only get two weeks' statutory pay. It's not financially possible for many men to take more unpaid leave. For breadwinning women, it makes more financial sense to share parental leave, but this is logistically problematic when you factor in breastfeeding and physical recovery after birth. Breadwinning women therefore face extra financial challenges when they take maternity leave, especially if the family relies on her income. My own employer recently changed its policy, such that 'maternity leave' became 'parental leave'. Now both male and female caregivers have access to 18 weeks' leave on full pay – take up, as you would expect, is increasing.

Finances can be a barrier, but so can the judgement men experience when they step back from careers or ask for reduced hours for caregiving. Fathers are more likely to face stigma when taking parental leave compared to mothers, because it's so far from the norm. Mothers expect their careers to stall when having children in a way that fathers don't. They even get what's dubbed a 'fatherhood bonus'. Fathers tend to be perceived as more competent, promotion-worthy, and focused on their work than non-fathers and even earn more.[12] The opposite pattern is true for mothers versus non-mothers.[13] The stakes are high, professionally, for prioritising your kids over work, especially if male partners aren't willing or able to support equally with care.

Perceptual change is one thing, but to enact change at home, someone in any social circle or company has to lead the way and be a 'risky pioneer' (taking inspiration from the 'f**k it fathers'). Often they have to be confident enough in their role to request it, or to ask early on to have flexibility written into their contract. When men who take parental leave are more visible and there is less stigma associated with it, uptake has been shown to increase.[14] Knowing your worth and managing upward expectations all come into play here, as long as policy supports it too.

## REBALANCING REQUIRES REGULAR COMMUNICATION

Greg, a software engineer, was the first at his company to request paternity pay. I spoke with him and his wife, Ruth, who were keen to share how they maintain an equal work-life balance. It's hard, but they each recognise the importance of balancing work and caregiving equally. His company offered 13 weeks' fully paid parental leave for men. As Ruth had recently started an important new role shortly before their second child was born, he knew that he needed to support her by increasing time at home. While he was slightly worried about how others would perceive him, his family needed him more and by this point he was confident and experienced enough to feel comfortable with reducing his hours.

This enabled Ruth to continue progressing with her communications company, meaning her salary remains slightly above Greg's. It was the shift in mindset of them both being available and both being clear that they needed flexibility to progress that enabled them to share things equitably at home. Now, each time their work patterns change they discuss how to rebalance life at home too. Greg will soon reduce his hours to work four days, spending one day with his son, which Ruth has also been doing. Each takes ownership of the activities for one child, including organising and paying for them. They make meal plans and pass the baton if one is fed up with cooking. They know they are bucking the trend but attribute their balanced home life to regular communication, as Ruth explains:

Having that shared parental leave did set the precedent. A friend said to me when I had [my daughter], 'I have great optimism for you because my husband and I have tried to be equal but it's really hard.' I think the advice I would give to anyone who's trying to do it equally is that you just have to look at it every few months and say, is this equal or have we slipped into gendered roles?

Of course, some aspects remain gendered. 'Or perhaps I'm socialised to pick up on things more than he is, such as I'm the one combing every three days for head lice for weeks on end. How did I pick that one up?' As they reveal, putting in the hours tangibly makes both parents feel equally responsible and invested in their children. It's been shown that if fathers share childcare early on, they are more likely to continue to be more involved later too, which is critical for the family's well-being. Children with more emotionally invested and sensitive fathers at three months show improved cognitive development at 24 months,[15] a benefit that continues as children age. This effect lasts, as children with emotionally supportive fathers show greater well-being and positive relationships with others aged 10.[16] Quality time with dads has even been linked to educational attainment later on, while time with mothers has been found to be important for emotional behaviours, likely because dads behave differently to mums when it comes to caregiving.[17]

It's clear that numerous overlapping factors are important for a child's development – sensitive caregiving being a primary one, whether it comes from the mother, father, same-sex parents, a single parent or a blended family. The idea that a mother's time is best is a fallacy that continues to fuel motherhood guilt, and as this assumption subtly influences women to downplay their careers too, it has repercussions for family earnings and happiness.

For decades, most western parenting research was really research centred on mothers, with dads and other family set-ups ignored. Now research on fathers' involvement is highlighting that being emotionally sensitive to a child's needs is key. It just so happens that it's women who are conditioned to be more emotionally sensitive than men, and men are less likely to show their emotional selves. My daughter, then aged six, once said to me: 'I'm emotional because life is getting harder. Daddy doesn't have emotions,' perhaps because she has never seen him cry, but she has seen me cry. Children pick up on emotional differences early on at home and these expectations continue to be reinforced outside the home. Knowing the studies, I'm now concerned I speak more about emotions to my daughter than to my son, which I can still correct.

As men in caregiving roles increase, how we divide care really matters. Traditionally, fathers have been more playful with children, with mothers doing more of the mundane aspects of care. The difference in how parents care is therefore related to who is the primary versus secondary carer, rather than innate differences between mum versus dad. One influential 2014 study found that primary-caregiver men from same-sex couples show brain changes after becoming parents in similar areas we see for women, showing that a father's brain is also 'sensitive to childcare experiences'. The study found that the more time fathers spent caring for their babies, the more their brains changed in areas important for parenting.[18]

This resonates with single dad Victor, the primary carer to his daughter. While he organises every aspect of his daughter's life, he has found the role difficult to navigate, especially because dads in popular media and day-to-day conversations are often still stereo-typed as being useless or disengaged. He felt left out at the school gate too and was at first rarely included in conversations around childcare. He noticed that the assumption was that he wouldn't know how to respond to routine questions about sickness, school events or social development. At the other end of the spectrum, he also experienced an overly positive reaction where he was congratulated for simply being out with his daughter. He was once asked if it was a 'special daddy–daughter day', which was confusing for his daughter to hear too, since this was routine. 'We're asked to be gender neutral in every conceivable place apart from parenting,' he told me. Over the years he has noticed a shift. A seemingly small but emotional turning point for him was when the other mums at the school gate took a group photo of 'the mums' and included him. 'It kind of brought a tear to my eye. I was like, finally I'm being recognised for what I do.' This shows that a change in our perceptions clearly can and does occur – it simply takes longer when it revolves around men caring (as it does around women breadwinning). It took years of simply being a routine primary-caregiving dad for the other school mums to see him in this way, as being just like them. Just as we all learn from doing, societally, a change in perception clearly happens from seeing too.

## PESKY ASSUMPTIONS OF MASCULINITY

It was once believed that for women to gain positions of power, they had to act more dominant and abrasive, like men. Now there are subtle indicators that men should do more of what women do, from laundry adverts targeting men, to self-help advice gurus on social media teaching men how to maintain the balance and tune in to their emotional side. More importantly, for lasting change we first need to dismantle the stereotypes of what masculinity means today. Academics are aiming to do just that, but as with much of what we've explored, awareness still lags behind reality. Generational change takes time, which is all the more reason to talk about these issues now.

Alex, who we heard from in Chapter 1, talked about how his father's lack of presence growing up contributed to him wanting to be around his children more. On the opposite end, Felicity feels that her partner's upbringing influenced his expectations around the home, as his own father did not contribute to any household chores either. As she takes on so much of the mental load, it cements this pattern.

Imbalances like this have led researchers to propose that men are like 'care commanders' and women like 'care footsoldiers'. The idea is that the commanders get involved in decisions around the more visible aspects of the household, commanding what needs done, whereas women are the ones doing the day-to-day menial tasks.[19] These differences can be seen as a direct consequence of unfair power dynamics, where the more powerful person in the relationship has a strong influence on how labour is shared. The reason this kind of imbalance originates in the first place is because women are disproportionately represented in caregiving roles. Women are then, in turn, seen as more suited to caring. It's a classic case of perceptions perpetuating reality and vice versa.

This also explains one of the great misconceptions I often hear when people are describing 'female' or 'male' traits. Many people believe that women naturally have more empathy, but as power distorts empathy, couldn't that very empathy be a direct result of *having* to be so perceptive to what those in power want, as well as having less power to begin with? Women, after all, have been socialised from a very early age to put others' interests first. That's exactly what a team found in 2018, in what was the largest genetic study on empathy to date. Empathy, they noted, is in part hereditary, but of the genes involved, there were no sex differences. Any sex differences found were instead largely attributed to socialisation.*[20]

How we are socialised to think about gender has a long-lasting impact, especially in situations where men or women don't conform to certain norms. Take the fact that conversations are more likely to be interrupted by men; as this is a social norm it also goes more unnoticed.[21] Men tend to speak for longer and interrupt more than women.[22] This starts early. Boys as young as three have been shown to interrupt girls three times as much as the other way around.[23] What we can learn from this is to shift some of these forces which start so early by understanding, and encouraging more junior people to feel empowered to speak up more. At the same time, dominant leaders should give more space for other voices in the room to have their say, while individuals in senior positions can call out interruptions.

## THE 'ALL SCIENTISTS ARE MALE' FALLACY

A fascinating body of work has revealed that stereotypes among children are also changing. In one landmark study between 1966 and 1977 almost 5,000 school-age children were asked to draw a picture of a scientist and about 99% of them drew a man. The few who did draw women were all girls. This experiment gives us a very quick insight into the stereotypes school-aged children had of scientists at the time, which, due to lack of female representation, wasn't wildly inaccurate.

---

* Prenatal hormonal influences are also believed to play a role.

This experiment has now been replicated numerous times. An analysis looking at a combination of 78 experiments over the years involving 20,000 children has shown that the number drawing female scientists is on the rise – hurrah. It's now 28%, though it was mostly girls who did so. The older the children were, the greater the likelihood of drawing a male scientist was, revealing that gender assumptions become more embedded with age.[24] This experiment is especially revealing because scientists are generally viewed as more 'agentic' and less 'communal', i.e., competitive and independent versus the more stereotypically female traits of 'sociable' and 'help-ful'.[25] As the authors of the analysis say, girls 'may now develop these interests more freely because these stereotypes of scientists have become more androgynous over time'. As scientists strongly influence the direction of future research, we would all benefit from encouraging more girls to follow STEM careers.

This shows that as society changes, attitudes clearly do too. In the 1960s scientists were overwhelmingly men, and depictions of them even more so. Women scientists are now more visible in books and in the media – in my workplace, colleagues pioneered the BBC's 50:50 project, where we report the gender balance of experts and contributors to our content and aim to reach parity. I've experienced the effect this has; sometimes it takes a few minutes longer to reach out to someone new rather than an oft-quoted source, but it is reasonably easy to find equally qualified female commentators, and we expect colleagues and freelancers to do the same. The more we do so the more unacceptable an imbalanced programme, article or film is. Until we tracked the data, we didn't realise just how often producers would reach out to the same tried and tested, authoritative voices in certain fields, without seeking greater diversity.

## GEN Z AND TOXIC MASCULINITY

While attitudes are changing, it's important to note that the results are mixed. In 2024 a report from King's College London found stark divides in young people's attitudes. Younger men feel that they are harder done by compared to women, with 17% thinking that feminism has done more harm than good. Other findings include:

- About one in five men (22%) reported that it was harder being a man than a woman today.
- About half the respondents think it's harder to be a woman than a man, compared to 69% 20 years ago.
- One in six men say women have better lives today than men.
- More men than women think doing housework 'applies equally' to men and women, but at the same time the majority recognise it applies to women more than men.
- More young men (aged 16–29) think the term 'toxic masculinity' is an unhelpful term compared to young women, while almost half of young women (47%) find it a helpful term, compared to 29% of young men.
- On a more positive front, 46% overall said equal opportunities for women have not gone far enough, though 13% said equal opportunities for women have gone too far.

These findings reveal that while both sexes still believe women have it harder, younger men are slightly more likely to think men have it harder – perhaps due to a greater focus on the recognition of men historically having more power, which they feel they are losing. Given what we've explored, it shows those who traditionally hold more power feel threatened when a previously marginalised group becomes more influential. It could also be due to the mistaken belief that when others gain power, you lose it. This shows that while changes are taking place, there are fractured views emerging in different age groups. Parents should take note of how they talk about gendered behaviour to their children. We all have the potential to influence their views by modelling equal lives at home, which extends to prioritising careers and leisure time as equally as is realistically possible.

## CARING, EMOTIONAL FATHERS

Despite some of these fractured views, it's encouraging to know that the simple act of caring can challenge traditional notions of masculinity.[26] It's not only care that's important but also 'about men disavowing domination or inequality', explains Karla Elliott, a gender scholar. 'It's not just about men doing that fun stuff that's really rewarded. It's about them getting into those kinds of messy, gritty parts of care-work.'

She found three interesting consequences when men take on more of the care at home. First, they start to let go of the idea of the man as being the more dominant one in a couple. Second, they express more emotions, and third, they reject the male-breadwinner norm and instead see their role as being responsible for the family, rather than only providing financially. This shows that masculinity can be reframed to include caring, which would be a key step for care-work to become less gendered. Fortunately, although stay-at-home dads still have strongly embedded views around gender norms, they begin to slip away from these attitudes simply by doing more childcare. In one eye-opening study featuring in-depth interviews with 25 stay-at-home dads, they experienced overwhelmingly positive changes in their relationships. It also forced them to construct what Elliott calls 'alternative masculinities'. Take Henry, who said: 'I've never had to feel that I had to prove myself to anyone to be, you know, like a manly man or anything like that. I have no problem with my wife being the "head of the family". That doesn't bother me at all. If she wants to be the boss, that's fine . . . If this is what I need to do to . . . have a good family, then I have no problem with that.'

They spoke about having more emotional recognition of others, that they felt more in touch with their nurturing side and were able to relate to others better. Crucially, they showed greater appreciation of care-work, and the ideas of male and female roles became more fluid. By being more involved caregivers, the men started to define masculinity differently and they indicated that they wanted to be respected for doing care-work. One said of being a father: 'I want to prove to everybody that I am good enough, that I can do this, and I'm going to be a damn good man.' Another noted that he can do just as much housework as women, but that he finds it challenging when friends discuss his wife's career, making him 'feel ignored'.

The rise of stay-at-home dads could even pave the way for a new type of masculine identity that does not rely on any existing assumptions but combines both typically male and female traits. Kevin, for instance, refutes the idea that staying home makes him more like 'mum' in the relationship: 'There are still plenty of people that say "Oh, you're Mr Mum." No, I'm not Mr Mum. I am a dad who stays at home and does everything . . . A dad that's doing this is being a dad . . . I'm Mr Dad.'

Clearly, caregiving can shift attitudes, but among the interviewees that felt devalued, it was tied to the fact that unpaid labour is still less respected than paid work. Adding to this complexity, ambitious women can face additional judgements, which is why some women downplay their career aspirations or even avoid careers with long hours altogether. This reminds me of the 'manning up and womaning down' phenomenon, where women lied and reported lower earnings. The concept of a 'patriarchal bargain' helps explain these trends, where women have been known to downplay their own achievements or even criticise other women, precisely because they know that is what patriarchal pressures demand – helping them fit in with rigid gender norms and avoid rejection or judgement when challenging the status quo. As many families depend on two salaries to get by, judging mothers for working or for pursuing careers that have the potential to elevate them into positions of power, risks stalling the progress we so desperately need.

Ruth – who we heard from earlier – finds it stressful to combine family life with a full-on career, leaving her tempted to work fewer hours. 'We can both feel the strain, but I'm the one that wants to make the sacrifice to do something about it. I feel like it's usually the women that are feeling that, and who will step back from work.' She realised she was falling into a typical pattern and so instead of her sacrificing work time, Greg shares the caring load. Both of them now purposely work more flexibly to help share childcare.

## WHEN BALANCE BECOMES SACRIFICE

Sacrifice seems to be the common theme when talking about work-life dynamics. This reveals something many writers are increasingly voicing out loud. Nobody truly 'has it all', because you can't give everything to work or home life in equal measure. Prioritising one area means less time for the other. What we can do is support each other for a happier family life. It's support and a shared load at home that gives everyone more breathing space to pursue other interests. A more balanced dynamic can only occur when men are just as likely to take time off to look after their kids as women currently do. While the will is often there, the practice has not become the norm, aside from the maverick 'f**k-it fathers' – a group which Greg, Steve and Alex clearly fall into.

Care is such a fundamental part of human existence, but we largely gloss over its significance lest we be seen as unreliable or less dedicated to work. It's ironic that we don't place more value on it considering we're all only alive because someone cared for us too – and as we age, we will need the same ourselves. Our ancestors got us to where we are today by shared caregiving, yet individualistic and capitalist needs are surpassing human caregiving ones. We have the power, knowledge and insights to redress this. You can start now too.

## KEY POINTS:

- Fathers spend more time with children than in the past, which creates stronger bonds. For many families this is now a basic expectation.
- However, fathers talk about emotions more with daughters than sons. Brain scans even show they're more responsive to daughters' happiness, suggesting a stronger emotional connection to daughters.
- As fathers spend more time with their children, their idea of what masculinity means is changing and is redefined to include caring as well as being more in touch with their emotional and nurturing side.

## ACTION POINTS:

- As we are exposed to norms and expectations from an early age, we can correct this by acknowledging how our upbringing shaped us and being mindful of the norms we pass on to the next generation.
- For a happier family dynamic, we should stop valuing ourselves primarily based on our economic output or breadwinner status, and instead value how we help care equally for our loved ones.
- Men should take the parental leave they are due. If your company hasn't updated its policies, politely suggest that they look into it.
- Learn from the f**k-it fathers and prioritise your family's needs rather than how others may judge you if you work flexibly.

# 5

# UNDERSTANDING POWER: HOW POWER DYNAMICS AFFECT US ALL

'Power tends to corrupt and absolute power corrupts absolutely.'
—Lord Acton

We are a species full of contradictions. On the one hand we are incredibly cooperative and kind: we'll help save strangers or donate to charities and help out in our communities; and yet we are also self-serving, prone to aggression and anger, and capable of premeditated violence and murder.

Then there is a phenomenon that's been dubbed the 'power paradox', which exposes this great contradiction in spades. To become powerful, we need to use empathy, kindness and compassion, but once in a position of power, those very traits we used to get there start to diminish and a more stereotypical type of power emerges. We have evolved socially intelligent minds that help us understand the desires of others and use this insight for good. However, once an individual gains power, many of the traits needed to get there in the first place become dampened. Clearly, power can corrupt.

We can all wield extraordinary amounts of power, whilst at the same time being subject to power dynamics that shape us. Psychologists continue to study various forms of power because it exposes interesting nuances about how society and individual relationships function, and what aspects of that we can control. It turns out we can control more than we might expect. And to understand how all this plays out, we need to look at some intriguing recent experiments from the field.

One of the leading researchers who has studied power in everyday life is psychologist Dacher Keltner. He wasn't entirely sure how to define power twenty years ago, but as a young psychologist at an eminent university, he had the tools to study it for himself. He wasn't satisfied with the idea of power as being Machiavellian in nature, where ruthlessness gets you ahead, as we all have varying degrees of power, and the traits we use to wield it can be positive.

It started in college dorm-rooms. Fresh-faced students arrived at the University of Wisconsin–Madison, where Keltner had been allowed to observe the status of those living in group dormitories and see how dynamics changed.[1] First, he asked what type of influence others had over them with a questionnaire, and gave them personality tests. He was looking at how highly they scored on the following: enthusiasm, kindness, focus, calmness and openness. If they scored on the lower ends that would mean they were more likely to be unsociable, exploitative, neglectful of rules or shared objectives, likely to complain and to ignore the ideas of others – in other words, they were more likely to be selfish and rude.

He returned several months later to understand who had the most perceived power in this relatively small group. The results? Enthusiasm was one of the key traits that the high-power dorm students had shown, followed by kindness, calmness, openness and focus. The students who scored low on those traits did not rise to power. His findings, that 'the nice guys' did not finish last, have been replicated in other universities and in a basketball camp. Other studies have come to similar conclusions in real-world settings such as hospitals, management or schools, showing the finding is not confined to a subset of middle-class college students. In fact, leaders had aspects of the same five traits Keltner first identified in the dorm group. A large review of leadership traits concluded that extraversion, openness to experience, conscientiousness and agreeableness were significant predictors of leadership.[2] Even hunter-gatherer groups have shown that power tends to be bestowed upon those who consider the benefits of the entire group. The anthropologist Christopher Boehm argued that it was key for our success as a species to cooperate rather than compete. Humans, he wrote, 'were egalitarian for thousands of generations before hierarchical societies began to appear'.[3]

## NICE PEOPLE FINISH FIRST

When it comes to social relationships, the individuals who are more controlling or abusive are often so because they are losing power. Bullies are rarely respected and seek to maintain their power by controlling others. One study found that individuals with low power gave the most electric shocks to others because 'the relatively powerless individual may attempt to restore equity by using the highest levels of noxious stimulation he or she has available'.[4] This experiment reminded me of the times when, if my brother felt hard done by, he'd always retaliate with something much worse than I had done. Similarly, parents often shout when they are losing control, not when their children are being compliant, and so on. This is referred to as retaliative aggression and explains why it occurs when those in a conflict don't have equal power. The imbalance can lead the person with less power to have a stronger retaliatory response if given the chance because they feel disempowered. If you've ever plotted revenge in your mind against a bully who has wronged you, you'll know the feeling.

Power comes in many guises. It's often closely associated with status, social class, financial capital, seniority at work, being the higher earner in a relationship, or a combination of these. Power tends to involve the ability to influence or control others. It differs from status, which is the ability to garner respect and admiration from others, though often the two are linked. Recent research has found myriad ways that power can influence others, giving us access to subtle forms of hidden power. A smile to a stranger makes them more likely to smile; an insult can cause hurt or even instigate conflict; telling a customer a smaller portion will reduce their calorie intake influences the portion size they order.[5] Those are three very different examples of subtle influence with varying degrees of agency, but all three show that we have the ability to influence others constantly, whether we are aware of it or not. It's how we do so that matters. For instance, we can influence our partner at home to achieve greater equality, commitment and help, while in the workplace we can influence colleagues to create a better working environment.

We all intuitively know what 'soft power' means. When I started researching power dynamics, I began to wonder if 'soft power' is the true power that helps us understand not only society today, but how we evolved the way we did in the first place. Soft power is the magic glue we use to resolve a conflict by communicating, taking each other's perspectives into account and presenting other points of view, rather than shouting or blaming each other. We use it when we compromise with our friends or partner and we use it when we show empathy, compassion and active listening, all of which make others feel understood and validated, meaning we can offer solutions. At home we can use positive reinforcement to encourage more of the behaviours that are beneficial. Conveniently, research has shown time and again that kindness elevates.

History books would have you believe that power mainly relates to how an individual or group can manipulate or gain advantage over others both overtly and subtly. However, soft power can be even more influential, especially in today's connected world. Soft power is a technique I unwittingly use all the time both at work and at home. I've already mentioned how at times I hover around my husband when he cooks, but it's demotivating for him when I make comments that may come across as criticism rather than help. It's more beneficial for us both if I let him get on with it, and he admittedly finds it more satisfying to try a new recipe without me meddling. If I don't 'gatekeep', or worse, criticise, he's likely to cook more often. Research backs that up: expectations of women often lead them to become more proficient at certain tasks, leading to gatekeeping or micromanaging at home. However, the more encouragement mothers give, the more involved fathers have been found to be,[6] whilst gatekeeping can lead to less involvement.[7] As more men engage in family life, the entire family benefits. It 'may help produce a more gender egalitarian division of labour and more progressive gender roles in children later in their adult lives', as one 2021 review put it.[8] The soft power then comes with knowing when to let go of tasks that we can easily hand over to our partners, and accepting that they may well do things differently to us. The more a person in a relationship gatekeeps, the less their partner will do. It's more rewarding for both parties to contribute, as an equal partnership makes both more invested in family life.

Steve – who we met back in Chapter 1 – is a clear example of finding satisfaction in his role as a stay-at-home dad. He told me he couldn't imagine not being there for his kids – and found a way to make it work by leaving his job, and later embarking on a new self-employed venture where he can choose to work around school drop-off and pick-up times. He explains he could earn more by sending them to clubs but wants to be there for them. 'If a husband doesn't pull their weight, it's because of ingrained gender expectations, or because they're not approaching their relationship in a unified way,' he says.

Similarly, Mary M firmly states that if women lean into their careers, men also need to lean out, which many don't feel able to, in part because they are not expected to. She works hard at dividing labour but has to do this actively to avoid falling into old patterns. She also talks about her frustrations at going against the norms, and for her, part of it is letting go of control:

There's a huge opportunity for men to be more active caregivers. Society pushes men to be primary breadwinners but a lot of time they would prefer to spend more time with their children and don't want to miss out on everything their children are doing. And by being a dual-income couple and sharing childcare, you can end up with both people happier and more fulfilled and able to choose the roles they play in society. One of the interesting things we noticed is that the odds were stacked against [Mary's partner], because all the playgroups and networks were all women-based.

## THE POWER PARADOX

Soft power is also hugely beneficial at work: the traits needed can create more cohesive workforces with better communication. Interestingly, female leaders tend to display soft power more than men.[9] Companies are now increasingly training leaders to focus on empathy and compassion, showing that we can all benefit from leaning into a softer form of power, and for good reason. One recent study found that employees with empathetic leaders were more likely to successfully balance their work and personal lives, as well as experience more positivity, productivity and innovation.[10] Power is therefore defined by psychologists like Keltner and Gruenfeld as how we can alter the emotional, economical or even physical state of another person. And it can happen all the time. But there's something counterintuitive that happens once an individual reaches power. As we saw above, the very traits they employed to get there – understanding, empathy, listening calmly to others – diminish once they gain power.

So what's going on? Power can distort our thinking – the power paradox in action. Keltner also noticed something curious: some individuals in positions of power show the exact profile of someone with damage to the brain's frontal lobe, causing a form of sociopathy. It can make people ruder, overconfident and egocentric. They are then more likely to cheat and act immorally.

It's no surprise then that 12% of business leaders have been found to show psychopathic traits – compared to about 1% of the general population.[11] Some amusing and clever experiments illustrate this perfectly. In one, a team asked three individuals to work on a task and randomly assigned one as the leader, the 'power' position. This participant was asked to award the others points for effort. An experimenter then carefully placed five cookies in front of them, meaning only two of the participants could take a second cookie. Social politeness means most people don't take the last one to avoid seeming rude. The results from the experiment were revealing: the person who had been designated the leader invariably took a second cookie. They ate more messily and didn't worry about crumbs falling all over the place, 'with lips smacking . . . apparently unconcerned about what others might be inclined to think'.

This sounds like an innocent example, but there are many other indications that power corrupts from real-life observations. One particularly illuminating experiment monitored how drivers of expensive or cheaper cars behaved. While car ownership is not necessarily a direct indicator of wealth, it is certainly linked. Researchers noticed an intriguing pattern: the drivers in the cheaper models followed the rules, they stopped at pedestrian crossings and did not cut in front of other cars at a busy four-way stop, where the earlier car to arrive has priority. You probably already guessed what happened when they observed the luxury cars. The more expensive the car model was, the more impulsive the driving that was observed. Drivers of expensive cars were more likely to cut in front of others and were less likely to stop at a zebra crossing. The study authors noted that 'privilege prompts self-serving impulsivity'. Having a perceived higher 'status' because of your wealth noticeably increases self-entitlement.

In fact, simply having power warps what is called 'perspec- tive-taking'. This was shown in a simple study where participants were primed to experience power and then asked to draw a letter E on their forehead.* Sounds simple, right? Funnily enough, the

---

* A quick note about priming, as it's a method many of the studies here feature. Participants who take part are asked to recall a situation where they felt powerful or powerless. In some cases, they are asked to write it down too as this helps activate memory. It's a quick and easy way for the memory of an event to activate the associated feeling.

people who felt more powerful were less likely to draw the E back to front, as you would do if you were drawing it with someone else's visual perspective in mind.[12] This implied that they were thinking about themselves, not others. This experiment captured the public attention and has been touted as a 'five second test' in order to understand if you are a leader or follower. Perhaps try it on your friends or even colleagues. Dinner and power dynamics would make for an interesting evening.

Studies have also found that power decreases perspective-taking both at work and at home. These 'flaws' clearly occur for a variety of reasons. In theory, those in power don't have to spend much time worrying about what others think of them in the first place, and they no longer need to take others' perspectives into consideration for their everyday actions. They can ignore advice, delegate tasks and set deadlines with competing priorities. They are the ones who invariably control tasks or resources and are also therefore less reliant on others' views. If you make the rules, you simply can't second-guess everyone else's view before implementing them. It's a paradox, because these same perspectives are exactly what they needed to interpret to gain power.

Likewise, in personal relationships, if one individual has more power, they are more likely to act in a controlling manner, influence decisions or fail to consider a partner's viewpoint. An individual with low power in a personal relationship is more likely to help their partner pursue their goals over their own, as well as adopt their partner's goals as their own, which researchers aptly call 'goal contagion'.[13] Think of a family moving because the higher earner gets a new job. They would have more say over such a decision, but this person also has more sway in prioritising their own hobbies.

If you don't have to worry about others, the 'powerful can plunge headfirst into action and pursue goals without restraint', Adam Galinsky and Deborah Gruenfeld wrote of their letter E study, adding: 'Failing to take others' perspectives, objectifying others in a self-interested way, and stereotyping others may all be part of the cognitive toolbox that power holders use to stay in control.' Or look at it more positively: those in power simply have too much going on to think too deeply about others. Our brains have a limited ability to process information, which anyone who has tried to listen in on a meeting while attempting to write an email will easily understand. Those with greater power have the authority to pick and choose which task to prioritise, with little consequence.

A key tip if you are feeling the tugs of power and apathy is to remind yourself to take stock of how others feel, so as not to fall victim to the power paradox. By considering other perspectives, you should be able to maintain your position while fostering a more positive and inclusive environment. If you need a little nudge, reminding yourself of the responsibility you have over others can help. That's why engaging in an open dialogue with others rather than making assumptions can foster greater compassion and therefore connection.

## ECONOMIC EMPOWERMENT

You might wonder why modern life is littered with power structures in the first place. It's in large part due to our extremely social nature: we literally had to cooperate and be social to survive – and these skills have been co-opted by the powerful. Evolutionary psychologists say that some of the changes our species faced when we began farming – moving away from communal living to small family units – are causing lower fertility rates today, as it's much more stressful raising a family without the support of a village. Today, those who have children are having fewer on average than our ancestors did. Population levels in many countries are no longer at 'replacement rate' – which is the average number of children we need to replace ourselves. This trend shows no sign of reversing either, meaning there could soon be many more older people in care and not enough people to care for them.

There are several obvious reasons why. As anyone who has
looked at nursery fees will know, two kids in full-time childcare
easily costs more than an average UK salary. This economic conflict
can translate into pressure for a dual-income family to prioritise
one career over the other, with the lower earner picking up the
childcare slack and often reducing their hours or stopping work
altogether. Societal pressures then affect relationship dynamics at
home, meaning one starts to have greater economic power than
the other, with lasting influences on the domestic front too.

There's another quite compelling underlying reason that could
be at play here too. Evolutionary psychologist Mark van Vugt and
colleagues recently published a paper that attributes the lack of
population growth directly to a desire for greater social status. 'We
show that activating a desire for status can lead people to prefer
reproductive trade-offs that favour having fewer children, thereby
predicting preferences for delaying both marriage and having a first
child.'[14]

On the face of it, this is somewhat depressing: that we need to
be unencumbered in order to achieve status. But look at it another
way and it starts to sound slightly more empowering. Many of us
now have the *choice* to delay having children, or else forego it
altogether. In the not-so-distant past, men and women alike were
fully expected to have children and judged negatively if they didn't.
Today, while some expectations remain, it's becoming more of a
norm to choose to be child free.* On the other hand, if it's a choice
between work or children then it's not a true choice, especially
when this is a compromise due to economic barriers, so it remains
a complicated conundrum. Many couples stop at one or two children because of the sheer financial cost at home and to their careers.
This is felt due to lingering effects of the motherhood penalty.
Child-free couples meanwhile aren't beholden to the career sacrifices many parents have to make, minimising conflict with regards

---

* There's even an acronym for working couples in this scenario – DINKs
  – which stands for 'dual income no kids'.

to who has to leave the office earlier and potentially sacrifice their career advancement to do so.

## THE BRAIN'S PREDICTIVE POWER

Our society is carefully organised in many hierarchies, with certain groups dominating others. This can be subtle or more overt in politics or leadership. Social hierarchies can also overlap, meaning wealth often begets wealth and marginalised groups stay oppressed, especially in the case of race and gender. Today more of us can attempt to climb corporate or social ladders to gain more power, but this is often only achievable with a certain amount of privilege in the first place. We have the knowledge to change some stubborn hierarchical structures. While hard power got us into these hierarchies, soft power may well help us undo some of the more toxic dynamics. In terms of how, the brain is a good place to peer into for solutions.

As with so much of what we think and feel, how we influence and are influenced by others starts with the brain. Before we are even consciously aware of it, our brains make implicit assumptions – their 'predictive power' – that affect us in both surprising and at times alarming ways. Understanding how these processes work helps us to figure out the dynamics that sometimes control our lives.

What if I told you that you have the power to change your own brain, and that doing so would have many benefits, including boosting cognition, mood and well-being? Sounds rather dramatic, doesn't it, but you really do. Our mood and outlook in life are crucial tools we have that can influence how we perceive others and how we are seen. Our mindset can transform our lives. We could all do with learning how we can use the power of our brains to protect us from the very forces and individuals who try to control us, especially because powerlessness causes chronic stress, and feeling devalued results in increased levels of the stress hormone cortisol.[15] The evolutionary response that helped our ancestors escape dangerous predators is activated today when we feel disempowered.

At the start of 2023 I embarked on a daily guided meditation course led by a cognitive psychologist. Twice a day for 15 minutes, I practised focusing my mind on the present moment, making me aware of just how busy the mind tends to be. I had my brain scanned before and after the course, and the results were remarkable. After only six weeks I had managed to change the structure of my brain, by a small yet measurable amount. If I had continued for longer the results would likely have shown a bigger change – but I had a deadline, time really was of the essence. Meditation is known to be effective because it alleviates stress, and stress is toxic for the brain, limiting its natural capacity for change.[16] Although I set out to 'hack my brain' for a TV documentary, the results were backed up by the scientific literature. It was empowering because I could do the intervention without many major life changes. The more I read about how our cognitive processes are affected by those around us, the more I realised that it's fundamental to learn how to combat certain stresses and pressures.

Learning how to train our minds so that we are not negatively influenced by others is an important skill we can all hone. By living in a society which values status, attainment and success in ways that are not necessarily healthy or attainable for many, we can become victims of this constant pressure even if we are not overtly seeking to gain power, but simply want to avoid being manipulated by it. The impacts are far reaching: if we better understand the power our minds have on our well-being, it can improve our empathy, help us overcome conflicts and minimise stress. Having delved into the science of neuroplasticity, it's clear that we all have it within us to change our outlook on numerous forces that influence our daily lives, in work and at home. It's in part thanks to the effect our brains' amazing predictive power has on our state of mind.

## WIRED TO BE SOCIAL

As soon as we're born, we demand social connections with others. In our formative years our brains depend on constant interactions with caregivers and loved ones to form healthy relationships. If we are deprived of these it has lasting effects on our development, including a detrimental impact on school performance as well as cognitive and emotional difficulties.[17] In other words, we are wired to be social; we physically need close connections to thrive.

Let's look at the impacts in more detail. Friendships are a crucial glue that binds society together. To be sociable is a superpower. In fact, people in positions of power also tend to have more friends. One recent study found that children who come from poor backgrounds are likely to earn more if they have friends from across class divides. The study had a staggering conclusion: our social ties as children can increase success later in life.[18] Other research has come to similar conclusions – our social networks are important for educational achievement too. If a friend is studious, we might seek to act the same, but if your friendship group mocks those who aim to do well at school, it might prevent you from trying as hard. As one study put it, friends 'provide support and resources and can both encourage and discourage academic achievement'.[19]

The clichéd saying 'It's who you know' is more powerful than you might think. Why? Because friendship increases social capital, which can be defined as 'the strength of an individual's social network and community'. Friendships are so powerful because unlike other connections, friends have a tendency to help each other without even being asked. Habits, fashion and aspirations are contagious. We know, for instance, that if friends in a social circle stop smoking, it will spur others in their network to do the same.[20] Friends help us define expected norms. If those around us aspire to become artists, musicians or lawyers, it might sway you along those lines too. You get the idea. This shows that just as we can influence others, others can influence us. As Keltner says, true power is our ability to do greater good by influencing the state of others.

How we interact with friends is often effortless. When we get on with someone, we rarely have to think about what to say next or worry about whether we are saying the right thing. If you're a little bit socially anxious, remember this: research has shown that we tend to come across as better than we think we do, a phenomenon termed 'the liking gap' which is where people assume they are less likable than they are perceived,[21] as outlined in David Robson's fascinating book *The Laws of Connection*.[22] If we understand this bias, we'll learn to expect that others find our conversation rewarding in return. It's a subtle form of power to know – and therefore expect – others to find you interesting; just don't let it go to your head and begin to dominate every conversation going forwards, which, as we'll see, is a common pitfall of those in power.

Similarly, we can all affect our mindset both during and after uncomfortable interactions. Instead of feeling crippled by the discomfort, lead, ask questions and show kindness. The result might surprise you. Our brains are attuned to social connections with others, even if they are strangers. Research has shown that an individual's happiness improves even during a simple positive social contact with a barista in a coffee shop, compared to if they went in and didn't interact.[23] It's not a fix for loneliness, but for anyone who lives alone, there's great comfort in knowing that everyday interactions can improve our well-being.

## PRIMED TO BE HAPPY

Of course, it's human nature to get sucked into others' moods, which can be detrimental if we absorb someone's negativity. If your partner comes home after a bad day in the office, you may find yourself starting to take on their negative emotions. Knowing the science behind it can give us more control over how our brains respond in such a situation, which will help keep our minds more positive and could even strengthen social bonds and therefore improve relationships.

Here's why. Our brains are built to not only react, but predict certain behaviours based on past experiences, and our own moods play a role too. This has interesting repercussions for social interactions, dominance hierarchies, and how we can learn to make friends without the anxiety of wondering whether we have said the wrong thing.

Our own emotional state also influences relationship dynamics. One study found that individuals perceived neutral faces as either happy or sad depending what stimuli was first presented to them. If they had been primed with a positive face, they found a neutral face to look happy, and vice versa.[24] This reveals that even subtle outside events easily manipulate our day-to-day interactions. The researchers call this 'affective realism', which simply means that our inner emotional state affects how we experience the world. Our emotions can warp our reality, meaning it's probably best not to judge someone as rude if you were in a bad mood when you met them. They may have thought *you* were the hostile one.

It works the other way too – our inner state can affect how others perceive us. Our emotions are contagious; people have been shown to synchronise their emotional expressions while in conversation with each other.[25] We have the power to influence the positive or negative emotions of others, but most of us don't think about this too deeply. It's only once we start to become finely attuned to the influence we have over others that we can use it to our advantage. The reason this happens is because our emotions impact the way our brains process sensory information, which has consequences for our decisions.[26] An awareness of this could be a powerful tool when it comes to relationships. You might have a certain sense of power over one aspect of your life but feel powerless in others, for instance if someone leads a team at work but is out-earned by their partner at home.

What's interesting is that the very idea of being 'in power' has an impact on our cognitive processes. Those in positions of power have been shown to be more decisive, take more risks and handle stress better. As we discovered, people in power can start to behave not only as if they are superior, but as if they are above the law – remember the expensive car experiment we heard about? Here the power paradox shows its true face. Another revealing experiment showed that those in power have a different profile in the brain's mirroring system, which is when neurons fire when we see someone perform an action as well as when we perform that action ourselves. The brain is doing what the rest of the body also does in many social situations where we often tend to mirror facial expressions, body posture and even accents, all to create cohesion, affinity and connection.

The experiment was surprisingly simple. To elicit a feeling of power, participants were instructed to recall a time when they experienced control over another person, and asked how it made them feel. Other participants were asked to recall a time they felt they had no power at all, while a third group were simply asked to think about what they did the day before. Next, participants were asked to watch someone grip a rubber ball, while their brain waves were observed. Those in the 'higher power' states showed less excitability in the parts of the brain that corresponded to the movement than did the 'low power' participants.[27] The neuroscientist behind the work, Sukhvinder Obhi, told me that it was astonishing that he was able to see the effect of social mimicry in the brain with such a simple experiment. The less powerful are more likely to mimic others but the effect diminishes the more powerful an individual is. 'When you feel very independent you see yourself as very disconnected from society and other people, but when you feel interdependent you feel connected,' he said.

To understand whether mirroring could be induced, in a follow-up study participants were told how the mirror system works and asked to try to use it. Unfortunately, it didn't work; they could neither increase or decrease mirroring when asked to do so.[28] Naturally, squeezing a ball is very different to mirroring a pain response, but the fact that it is automatic gives us some indication of how little control we sometimes have over how our brains react to external events. This work is so revealing because it shows the impact of power by observing the brain's neural processes, which will in turn help us understand why we behave the way we do.

Perhaps more importantly, interesting effects also occur when people feel powerless, which most of us can relate to. Maybe you've had an unfair speeding ticket, or have experienced bullying or unrequited love. Those who feel powerless show increased stress and, as a result, lower cognitive function. The impact of stress is well understood – it can affect the areas of the brain important for regulating our emotions. We already heard how important friendships are, but if we're chronically stressed, the help we most need from friends could be harder to access because the parts of our brains fundamental for forming social connections in the first place are impaired.[29] When we feel stressed from a relationship conflict, it can therefore cause us to feel disempowered. To begin the journey to feeling more empowered, it's important to tackle stress levels first, or the vicious cycle of stress and feeling powerless will continue, further affecting our relationships in the process.

## ADDICTED TO POWER

Social hierarchies are difficult to navigate objectively, because feeling superior can be addictive. It releases chemical messengers that affect our mood, notably the neurotransmitter serotonin. Recall a time when you won an argument. You knew that you were right, and it was infuriating to be told otherwise. When they finally conceded, you felt justified, superior even. It feels good to be right, and that others know it. This feeling then tells the brain to seek more of it as it acts on the dopamine-fuelled reward network of the brain.

That's exactly what can occur with those who have a higher status and higher levels of social support. They have been shown to have higher levels of dopamine receptors, meaning they literally feel more rewarded. They experience a greater sense of pleasure and satisfaction from everyday life, which can create a positive feedback loop. These individuals would then be more motivated to continue feeling this way, which could further enhance their status.[30] You might remember a time you were recognised by your peers, socially or at work. Recognition feels good – that's a dopamine hit right there. As your day-to-day life becomes more social and successful, these dopamine hits become more frequent, and greater power will lead to more people telling you what you want to hear. Would you tell your boss their new idea or strategy is terrible? Probably not . . . You can see how easy it then becomes for power-holders to have a distorted reality, and for those who are disempowered to tell their superiors what they think they want to hear rather than what they really think.

A reason why we are sometimes oblivious to the effects of power is because power may not be understood very well even by those who hold it, in personal relationships, friendship groups and even among colleagues. Social psychologist Pamela Smith found that 'power' is a loaded term, and that many participants in her research didn't think of themselves as having or wanting it. Indeed, other research has found that it's not a 'fundamental human motive' to desire power, or to want to ascend more once in a position of power, whereas desiring status is. As one review paper put it: 'Status is more stable than power and thus provides a more reliable and enduring basis of social rewards.' We crave status because it's intricately tied to how others respect us, while having a low status creates a psychologically negative response.

On the other hand, some people even actively avoid power.[31] In some experiments, Smith would therefore not mention the word at all. Instead, she'd ask the participant to take a role as 'manager', to which they reacted more positively than if she said they would have power over someone. This reveals that many of us don't always understand how much power we have over others – including, as we saw, how female breadwinners affect perceptions at home. This hopefully unlocks something for you. It explains why managers don't necessarily realise the stress they cause when they ask someone more junior to complete a task, if they haven't first checked workloads or helped them prioritise. It explains the stress of an unequal relationship at home – if someone feels powerless to make financial decisions, they may not realise how much this affects them, whilst the higher earner may not be aware of this power imbalance at all. It could even affect how we later feel about how our parents treated us, when we had very little power at all. If children feel they have no agency they quickly lose self-confidence. We would do well to remember that many of these imbalances occur because our social standing can change our fundamental cognitive processes, which affects how we treat others.

It's hard to let go of power if you are a beneficiary of its effects. As Henry Kissinger famously said, power is the ultimate aphrodisiac. One thing related to power is when we feel as though we are winning. This also explains why those in power want to hold on to it. The feeling that comes from winning is also literally addictive. Recall the last time you dominated in some way over another, say in sports, or you won an award. You might have felt that rush that winning gives you. This is the brain releasing a feel-good hormone, which is a useful signal to our brains to seek that feeling again.

Winning was crucial for survival when we were competing with other species over resources, and so the brain developed clever ways to signal to our minds that we should do more of it. Competition has literally helped us evolve and survive in social groups, has helped increase brain size,[32] and contributed to humans developing social hierarchies and status.[33] Today this very same trait has been co-opted in social relationships where we constantly compare ourselves to others. If we have lower power, social comparisons to those who have more can feel uncomfortable, whereas those with more power can feel dominant over others.

Interestingly, our brains have a bit of a flaw. The more we win the less satisfying it can become, so, like a drug, we keep chasing for a stronger hit. When we chase success and become used to achieving it, it can become less rewarding over time, something referred to as the 'hedonic treadmill'. The initial burst of endorphins we get from external recognition may feel good at the start, but the more normal this feeling becomes, the more we adapt and chase another rush.

The hedonic treadmill seems to have ancient origins that prevented us feeling too satisfied. Add in a bit of social competition and comparison, and every achievement can feel outdone by another, and the dopamine hit our brains receive quickly fades. You'll find that many ambitious people experience this contradiction. When is enough 'enough'? It's important to understand, because it explains why those who get external validation from power continue to chase it, and why many millionaires want more money, thanks to the brain's expectation of reward.

A process like this can be benign, especially as it has beneficial origins, but sometimes social comparisons cause us to feel jealous and can start to hinder our progress. The dopamine hits we are seeking can instead turn into cortisol if we start to feel overwhelmed by competition, feel inadequate, or set ourselves up for unrealistic goals. The more upward comparisons we make to individuals we perceive to be much better off, the more stressed and demotivated we can become. We see this play out increasingly in the home too; when women out-earn male partners, men often feel emasculated because they are comparing themselves to the expectation of the male-breadwinner norm. The more we change this narrative, the more comfortable men will be when they are not expected to be primary providers.

## HOW SOCIETY CHANGES THE BRAIN

We heard earlier that we have the power to change our own brain. The opposite happens too, whether we want it to or not: social pressures from outside impact our brains for good and for bad.

Neuroscientist Nicolas Crossley told me that inequality has a detrimental effect on the brain. Inequality, he says, leaves a visible scar, we just can't see the brain to notice it, even if it has tangible psychological consequences and continues to perpetuate power imbalances in society. In 2023 he, along with dozens of colleagues, published a ground-breaking study that showed that a power imbalance physically changes the brain. The team analysed over 7,800 brain scans from individuals living in 29 countries and found that women in countries with more inequality had thinner cortical thickness.

The changes were located in brain regions involved in emotional control and resilience to adversity, and in areas affected by stress-related disorders such as depression and post-traumatic stress disorder – the anterior cingulate gyrus and the orbitofrontal gyrus.[34] The women had thinner parts of these brain regions as a consequence of daily inequality, precisely because they faced a harsher environment compared to men. It's a bit like how gardening gloves become weathered after years of use, and the more weathered they are, the less effective they are at protecting your hands.

The reason for these brain changes is because stress affects how neurons connect to each other, and crucially, stress inhibits brain plasticity, which is the brain's natural ability to adapt and change over time. The effects could also be related to the lack of opportunities that women in some countries have compared to men, especially in education. We know that in countries with greater gender inequality, girls perform worse at school. Women from countries that score high in inequality also have more mental health issues. This reduces opportunities to develop crucial brain connections. Each time we learn something new, neuronal connections in our brains increase – neuroplasticity in action.

In more equal countries, these brain differences were diminished, and similar cortical thinning was not found in the male brains either. Intriguingly, in countries with high inequality, men have slight brain changes too. The results are a damning confirmation that everyone benefits when society is more equal, including men, who benefit when their wives are not exposed to a world that affects their mental health, especially as mental ill health also perpetuates poverty. It's a vicious cycle.

## POWERFUL PEOPLE TAKE RISKS

What can we take from all this so we don't fall victim to the brain's self-fulling process – where feeling powerless begets reduced cognitive ability as well as increased stress?

Conveniently, there are cognitive tricks we can use both on a personal level and to help others. Pamela Smith found that those with power are better at thinking 'bigger picture', which in turn increases abstract thought. In her research, she often primes individuals to feel powerful, which is a trick we can use on ourselves too. We can prime ourselves to recall situations in our past where we felt in control and felt we had power, which will help reframe our present, think bigger picture and reduce stress.

This same feeling can also give us more agency. When we feel more powerful, we are more likely to act in beneficial ways and take risks that pay off. One study that allocated individuals positions of power found they were more likely to play a riskier version of blackjack. The researchers said it showed that 'possessing power in one context leads to action in a subsequent, unrelated context'.[35]

We all know that those who get ahead usually take risks to do so, because power can make them feel like they have more control over external events than they do. If you feel stressed or are facing an imbalanced relationship at home, use the knowledge that you have the power to change your own brain. We can reframe how we see situations, such as outdated societal expectations, to prevent excessive rumination, which frees us up to focus on situations we can control. If you are ready to push yourself that bit harder, research has shown that both exercise[36] and meditation[37] boost brain plasticity, and a combination of the two is even more potent. Studies looking at individuals with severe depression and anxiety have shown a remarkable improvement after only a brief mindfulness intervention.[38] It sounds simple, but even five minutes can feel long when left with no distraction (try it yourself below). And as for my brain hack? I am now certain that good brain health is key to a calm mind too.

## A MINDFULNESS EXERCISE:

- For five minutes, close your eyes and simply focus on breathing in and out.
- Focus on the feeling of your breath leaving your body and note where your chest rises and falls as you breathe.
- Don't worry if other thoughts pop into your mind, they undoubtedly will, but take stock of them and return your mind back to the breath. And back to the breath. And back to the breath.
- Mindfulness sounds simple, but it's surprisingly hard to sit still with nothing but your thoughts, especially when you are stressed, as your mind will be even busier.

Done? That was only five minutes, but note how many other thought processes popped in. Note just how busy your mind can be. In periods of stress, our minds cannot be still, they travel forwards to future events, focus on current stresses, and think about the past. No wonder it's exhausting, especially so when more negative thoughts can dominate. Evidence shows the better we are at bringing our minds back to our breath and letting go of some of the busy thoughts and feelings, the lower our stress levels will be.

## KEY POINTS:

- We need empathy to gain influence and power, but once in a position of power we begin to lose empathy because power can corrupt. This has been dubbed 'the power paradox'.

- We can counteract this corruption by reminding ourselves to think about how others feel, and by seeing power as a sense of responsibility over others rather than dominating others.
- We influence each other all the time, every single day, sometimes without realising it.
- We constantly compare ourselves to others, which can become stressful. We can easily learn to reframe how we see a situation in order to prevent excessive rumination.

## ACTION POINTS:

- Research has found that there are key personality traits that predict leadership: enthusiasm, kindness, focus, calmness and openness. Practise all of these to be effective.
- Kindness elevates, and nice people ultimately finish first. Being domineering may work in the short term but can quickly cause a loss of respect and ultimately lead to relationships breaking down, at work and at home.
- Our brains are constantly at work making predictions about the world based on previous events, and we can use that knowledge to prime our brains to feel more powerful. When we do so it helps increase abstract thought.

# 6

## A GLOBAL LOOK: WHEN POWER AND CULTURE INTERSECT

'Culture constitutes the unwritten rules of the social game.'
—Geert Hofstede

We are all products of our culture and cultural norms often shape behaviour. This gives us an interesting lens through which to view the different ways we respond to power imbalances, family life and workplace priorities. Imbalances manifest in numerous ways and interesting patterns emerge when power and culture mix. Culture is often defined as shared knowledge in a society that helps it to operate. The late Dutch researcher Geert Hofstede wrote that culture can be defined as 'the collective programming of the mind that distinguishes the members of one group or category of people from others'.[1]

Our culture is something we collectively learn as we grow up. Take the way the Dutch give three kisses as a greeting or when they say goodbye, or how the Japanese bow to show respect and gratitude, or that in the UK people will say 'We must meet for a coffee sometime', despite having no intention of meeting. These are all behavioural manifestations of cultural norms; being a social species, we share knowledge all the time, and as we do so, we learn from and copy each other.

Some cultures are more focused on the self and on achieving success, the individualistic cultures, where power is used to advance personal goals, sometimes at the expense of others. Individualistic cultures include the UK, the US and many European countries. Individualism is often confused with selfishness, but that's not necessarily the case; it can also be seen as how free we feel to make decisions. Dutch economist and social scientist Sjoerd Beugelsdijk explains it as follows: 'The example I always give to my students is, how free are you to pick the person you want to spend the rest of your life with or get married to? Is that a decision you can make yourself? Or is there a lot of pressure from parents or grandparents?' Answers vary widely depending on culture as well as religion, showing that even within countries there can be huge differences.

Countries in East Asia such as China, Japan and South Korea are often categorised as 'collectivist', where leaders are expected to take more responsibility for the behaviour of their group or team. In collectivist societies, group and community values are emphasised more than individual desires, and power tends to be defined as something that can be used to help others to advance collective goals. How this plays out in wider society has huge implications for leadership styles, company success and our attitudes to equality. Best of all, we can learn from countries that take a more nuanced approach to success that elevates the group more than the individuals. Our collective attitudes towards power shape country policies and even influence happiness. A culture that values work-life balance naturally has workers with more free time to devote to hobbies and social contacts, compared to a culture that values overwork and presenteeism, which is typically the case in South Korea and Japan.

To understand your attitude towards power, success and earnings, it will help you to know that we are all heavily shaped by our culture. If you come from an individualistic culture that values competition between individuals rather than first thinking of the success of your collective group, then you will better understand why you respond the way you do.

Over a decade ago, psychologists made a splash when they published research that showed that much of the most popular psychological literature focused only on WEIRD participants, that is: western, educated, industrialised, rich and democratic. The paper was titled 'The weirdest people in the world?' It showed that we in the West are outliers in many of the ways we think, and that numerous findings from the psychological literature cannot be extrapolated to the rest of the world.[2] It's now abundantly clear that not all countries have the same attitude towards dominance, power, gender inequality, work and the family. For those of us who grew up in the West, we can step outside of our inbuilt biases and learn important lessons about human nature.

How we fall between individualism and collectivism influences how we view success and pursue goals. Chinese students have been found to perform equally well on a test with or without rewards, whereas US students performed better when there were financial incentives.[3] This highlights that people from individualistic societies value personal success and expect to be rewarded for it; a culture that doesn't value effort unless there's a financial incentive isn't going to promote the greater good of the rest of the group. Individual power in those circumstances can be seen as self-serving rather than elevating, and a large reason it manifests in this way in the first place is due to peer pressure to keep up with others. We want to be the best and are conditioned to aim for it. It follows that people in WEIRD countries are more likely to describe themselves as better than average too – which has been dubbed the 'better-than-average-effect' and we'll hear more about later. This effect has been shown in numerous studies, including one where 94% of US professors rated their teaching skills as above average, which anyone with even a basic understanding of maths knows cannot be true.[4] It's not universal, though; participants from East Asia are more likely to underestimate their abilities and competence. While individualistic cultures prioritise self-esteem, which is often achieved by self-enhancing and a focus on individual success, collectivistic cultures prioritise 'saving face' and becoming a good person within the group. This is achieved through self-improvement, showing weakness and seeking validation from others.[5]

Many of us have experienced both situations. When trying to impress a new colleague we might amplify our strengths and focus on how we individually contributed to a particular success, but if someone compliments us in another setting – say, in my case, my cake-baking skills – we might play down our ability, so we don't appear boastful: '*I'm terrible at making cakes usually. This one turned out all right, but you should see what the icing is hiding.*'

The fact that we can pivot between individualistic and more self-deprecating mindsets shows that, with conscious awareness, we can push ourselves to reframe our focus on the needs of the group even if we are usually inclined to prioritise our own achievements. If you want a simple test, think of how you define yourself. Is it in relation to your own achievements or to the group you are part of? We can describe ourselves individualistically (*I am tall, incredibly charming and an excellent writer*), or collectively (*I am Dutch, a daughter, colleague and friend*).

Conveniently, being a bit more self-focused can help us get ahead. During a job interview the panel wants to hear about *your* achievements: not '*We* overcame this difficult challenge . . .' but what *your* role was in overcoming that sticky muddle. When we are in a stressful environment like an interview, it can be tempting to slip into a more collective mindset, acknowledging the group or team we worked with, especially if we feel a close affinity with them. This is important when talking about collaborating, but in certain situations it helps to demonstrate what *you* specifically did to lead a project or to overcome a challenge.

## ARE YOU HORIZONTAL OR VERTICAL?

Individualistic countries vary enormously but can be further categorised into whether they are horizontal or vertical. Vertical individualism is common in the US, the UK, Italy and France, but horizontal individualism is more common in Australia, New Zealand, Scandinavian countries like Sweden and Finland, and the Netherlands. All tend to focus on the self, but in a vertical culture the focus is on success within a hierarchy and individual achievements. Take an ambitious political leader who claims to be the best and wants to be recognised for it – we already learnt why this is so addictive, and the dopamine hits we chase on the hedonic treadmill only serve to strengthen this desire. Here, power is often used to advance an individual's agenda. Research that compared the US and Denmark showed that Americans were more inclined to talk about achievement and personal success than Danes, who are known for their 'horizontal' nature and tend to prioritise a more balanced approach to life. Unsurprisingly, Denmark also has a generous social welfare policy.[6]

On the other hand, horizontal societies still value success, but there is greater emphasis on fairness for all and it's more socially expected to use power to benefit the group. To complicate matters further, cultural frameworks can be used to describe groups within groups. In the West, for instance, men score higher on vertical individualism whereas women score higher on horizontal collectivism. However, this won't come as a surprise because women are socialised to anticipate needs.[7]

## POWER DISTANCES STILL DEFINE CULTURES

The differences between individualism and collectivism were famously described by Geert Hofstede as one of his six cultural dimensions in the 1970s. Another of his cultural dimensions he called 'power distance', which refers to how much a group accepts hierarchy. Individuals from countries that score high on power distance (measured on a scale between 0 and 100 called the Power Distance Index, or PDI) are most likely to conform to hierarchies and authoritative rule without question – this can be seen in countries like Russia and North Korea or institutions like the army. Countries with lower power distances include the United States, Sweden, Norway, the Netherlands and Iceland, where individuals generally expect greater equality and feel they can stand up to power. While inequality is prevalent in these countries too, it tends to be less accepted, as Hofstede explained very succinctly: 'There's always somebody who wants to take the position at the top if people at the bottom let her or him do it, but it is only if the people at the bottom *accept* it that this can be done.'[8] His theories offer an illuminating insight into how social norms shape our views of power and hierarchy from a young age. He noted that in high PDI countries, children are taught to value respect, whereas low PDI countries teach children to be independent. These values have a lasting influence into adulthood, in part because parents transfer cultural norms, habits and mindsets to their children.

While most countries fall somewhere in the middle of the power index, it is the high and low ends that are most revealing. In societies with a high power distance, inequality tends to be more prevalent. In low power distance countries, however, more people come from middle-income households and inequality is less prevalent. Subordinates expect to be consulted rather than instructed, whereas in high power-distance cultures, subordinates rarely challenge their superiors. Psychologist Robert Helmreich even equated a country's PDI rating with how pilots operate in the cockpit, and whether or not a co-pilot is likely to speak up if they disagree with a decision. He stated that in high PDI countries 'juniors do not question superiors'.[9] This shows that a lower power-distance culture is not only important for equality, but for the safety of the group as a whole.

## WHERE BEING AVERAGE IS FINE

Because culture defines a large part of our identity we can look to how society treats its citizens to understand group norms. In the UK, for instance, many employers expect regular overtime and even applaud it. This can foster an unhealthy work-life balance that those who have relatively little power cannot opt out of, and leaves behind those with caregiving responsibilities. Rest assured this isn't the case around the world. We can learn interesting lessons by looking at countries that place more value on work-life balance – where better to start than my country of birth?

The Netherlands is consistently rated among the top five happiest countries in the world. Whilst individualistic, it is also a typically horizontal culture. It's not socially acceptable to boast too much, which several idioms speak to. There is a *zesjescultuur*, which translates literally to a 'sixes culture', referring to the grade on an exam that is considered a pass. Students will be congratulated for having passed rather than on the grade they got. Then there's *Doe maar gewoon dan doe je al gek genoeg*, or 'Just act normal, that's already crazy enough', again reflecting the idea of maintaining a sense of modesty, humility and a need to stay grounded. These sayings reflect the fact that Dutch culture has deeply embedded views around equality, where it's seen as outlandish to act superior.*

Studies have shown a link between individualism and the likelihood of abusing power. The opposite is true for horizontal collectivist cultures.[10] This seems to suggest that horizontal cultures are better at correcting power imbalances. Consider this question: If you're stranded on a desert island with a group of people, what's the first thing you do? This question is part of a well-known game Sjoerd Beugelsdijk plays with his students to tease out their inbuilt sense of hierarchy. Dutch students, he says, will always start with finding a way to enable a system of democracy where everyone is equal and there's consensus with the plan of action. Many others will first pick a leader to be in charge.

This mindset translates into the business world too. Walk into a meeting in a Dutch organisation and it can be difficult to see who is leading the team. 'In the Netherlands, it's complete chaos. You need to be an insider to realise who's actually in charge,' laughs Beugelsdijk. You can see aspects of this horizontal culture in everyday communication too. If you've ever met anyone from the Netherlands you will have noticed how direct they are. Because this is expected, people don't take offence in the way they might

---

* For any Dutch people reading this, I am making huge generalisations that reflect a cultural trend – there are bound to be lots of individual discrepancies too.

do in the UK. If a Brit says 'I hear what you say', they could just as easily mean that they disagree. The Dutch would simply say that they disagree. With this in mind you can see why the Dutch would struggle with hierarchy. This directness then serves to make leaders more responsible to group feedback too.

Of course, the Netherlands is by no means a utopia; there are numerous social issues and a stubborn gender pay gap, but their happiness rating is not an accident. The Dutch are more well rested than other nations, and family life tends to be prioritised over work. Without a prevalent overtime culture, workers can be present for their family, and have more autonomy and power over their lives.* Women still do more at home, though the gap has narrowed and they spend *less* time on housework compared to a decade ago, while for men it's much the same.[11] Compared to other European countries the chore gap is lowest in the Netherlands, Norway and Finland. Men in the Netherlands, Spain and Norway also do more childcare than other European countries.[12]

## NOBODY SAYS 'WORKING FATHERS'

Along with the Netherlands, Sweden is on the list of countries that score high on egalitarianism – for good reason. It's often regarded as a utopia when it comes to equality and work-life balance, especially for parents. Couples expect more equality and this expectation helps them achieve it. The division of paid and care-work is more equal and childcare fees are heavily subsidised, meaning it is not financially crippling in the way it is in the UK and the US.

The expectations on women, while still heavily gendered, are not solely tied to mothering, which helps women pursue careers without the burden of the motherhood penalty. I was amused to discover that in Sweden women were confused when asked if they

---

* Fathers routinely take 'daddy days' and mothers tend to work part-time. The flipside here is mothers are often judged if they work full time, because the part-time norm is so expected.

were 'working mothers', simply because most mothers work so it's not a familiar term, just as nobody says 'working fathers' in the UK, because it's assumed men work.

It all starts with policy. Parents can take up to a total of 480 days' leave after the birth of a child. For the first 390 days they get 80% of their salary up to a monthly capped amount.[13] Three months are solely dedicated for fathers to take in a 'use it or lose it' approach; the rest can be split. As a result, parental-leave uptake by fathers has dramatically increased since 1995, so much so that dads are expected to take it. While we saw that in the UK fathers experience stigma when asking for time off, in Sweden it's the exact opposite – taking parental leave has become an essential part of being a good father.

Of course, this took time, but once a norm exists it's seen as strange for a dad to choose work over paid parental leave. That's why Swedish dads take the most parental leave in the EU.[14] When fathers take more paternity leave, mothers are more likely to re-enter the workforce in the first year after childbirth. When norms like this exist, companies quickly adapt too as most workers will take parental leave at some point. The same goes for when children are ill, when the Swedish state covers 80% of pay for any days missed by parents. Given that in many other countries it's often women who take days off when their kids are sick, you can see why they are judged for it and seen as less ambitious and less reliable. In Sweden nobody comes with such an obvious 'burden'. This has a noticeable impact and likely contributes to their high female employment rate, the highest in the EU.[15] Not only that, but it's been found that when Swedish fathers take paternity leave, it boosts women's earnings. For every month of leave a dad took, earnings for women increased by about 7%.[16] So fathers taking time off has the potential to minimise – and eventually even help erode – the motherhood penalty, as long as workplaces help encourage uptake. With support at home and work, an otherwise overwhelmed mother can spend time thinking about her professional life, without nappies, rashes and food prep infiltrating her thoughts as much.

This support translates into better mental well-being, a happier partner and a more loyal employee too. When Swedish dads were given flexible leave, it reduced the likelihood of their partners using medication for anxiety by 18%[17] and helped to reduce depressive symptoms.[18] A *New York Times* headline covering this research put it rather bluntly: 'Sweden finds a simple way to improve new mothers' health. It involves fathers'. Put like that it seems extremely obvious, but it needs pointing out because for so many that support simply isn't there.[19]

The greater the income equality, the higher trust there is too. Yet again the Nordic countries, the Netherlands and Switzerland score high on trust and income equality in Europe. This could be because in these more equal societies people are more likely to trust each other – whereas in an unequal society there are greater social divisions, making it harder to build trust. Another reason could be that when resources are scarce it increases competition between groups.[20]

Still, despite these egalitarian policies, women still earn less than men in all these countries, and when this norm is disrupted, it can have negative impacts, even in Sweden. A recent study found that when Swedish wives earned more than their male partners, these couples experienced decreased mental well-being. The men were 11% more likely to receive a mental health diagnosis – with their breadwinning wives 8% more likely.[21]

## USE IT OR LOSE IT

Another country with a 'use it or lose it' approach to parental leave is Iceland, and it shows again that this policy encourages fathers to take time off. Each parent can take six months of leave paid at 80% of their salary, six weeks of which can be transferred to the other parent. Like Sweden, most Icelandic dads take parental leave. Compare that to their Nordic neighbour Denmark, in which only 24% of dads take parental leave, even though Denmark is considered a country with generous policies that support family life.[22]

The benefits of parental leave go beyond helping women at work. Studies show that when fathers take leave, there's a greater likelihood that household chores will be shared. Norway's 'daddy quota' policy, which also reserves 15 weeks of leave for fathers, has led to positive changes in family dynamics. After twenty years, studies show that couples experience less stress around household chores, are more supportive of public childcare, and are more likely to share laundry duties.[23] These changes all add up. In the UK, there is extremely low paternity-leave uptake beyond the statutory requirement. When fathers do take leave, they have been shown to increase feeding and night-time support, and experience stronger bonds with their children even years later.[24] They are also more likely to view fatherhood as rewarding and to see themselves as more competent.[25] I know so many couples where the mother sacrifices her sleep because the father is going to work. When our second child was born I had the unfortunate predicament of being the only one who could feed him, so when he was waking up every hour of the night, my partner went to sleep in the baby's room while the baby stayed with me. We reasoned that it made no sense for us both to be sleep deprived as I could attempt to nap later. Childcare is also work, but it's become more socially acceptable for the mother to be sleep-deprived to protect the breadwinner. This is a bit of a dilemma, because a mother keeping herself emotionally well is crucial for a child's development in the future, and sleep deprivation has a negative impact on mental well-being.

Ingrained cultural norms can override even the most generous policy – showing it's not always the case that policy increases uptake. In Japan, the parental-leave policy is generous, but fathers barely take it. Japan is extremely hierarchical and workers are expected to show complete devotion to their employer. The gender pay gap there is high too, at 21.3%, though that figure obscures just how many women have dropped out of the workforce completely; in Japan only about 54% of women work, a figure that is showing slow signs of increasing, especially amongst the 25–54 age group.[26]

## A NEW NARRATIVE

The reason that policy to support parental leave is so vital is because female breadwinners who become parents cannot continue to prioritise their careers if there isn't support for them to do so. In countries with high support, women work more, whereas the longer they are out of the workplace, the less likely they are to advance in their careers.

While some companies in the UK are increasing leave for fathers, smaller firms cannot always afford to. If companies do not offer support for new parents, it can be prohibitively expensive for the man, usually the higher earner, to take leave. When there is little public support, it only serves to heighten existing power imbalances. If the next generation is to break the cycle, they need to have role models that show it's possible for either parent to have a successful career, and either parent to care – and for it to be a true choice, rather than one shaped by who has the highest earning power or by the cost of childcare. Shared parental leave could be a major driver for increasing equality at work, which could translate to more harmony and balanced power dynamics at home. It could even help countries with a dwindling population rate, given that so many couples choose not to have a first, second or third child because of exorbitant childcare costs and the risk to future careers. In subsequent decades, this will result in fewer young people entering the workforce, leaving a lasting effect on those countries' economies.

A major difference, then, between some of the Nordic countries and the US and UK is that the support comes from the state, rather than expecting individual solutions to these societal issues. Regardless of finances or your political beliefs, the countries that score highest in happiness are the ones that invest in high levels of support for their population. They may pay slightly higher taxes, but most people are happy to do so because they know it will benefit them, and the rest of society, in myriad ways.

## TRANSFERRING NORMS

Studies have shown that a parent's mindset influences their children's attitudes in the future. A recent study found that how your parents handle finances affects how you will too, even more than your partner's financial behaviour. Those who witness financial stress growing up tend to develop more cautious attitudes towards money later on in life.[27] Julie, a study participant, witnessed her grandmother take on the financial management in her home, which made her grandmother appear more powerful, but her grandfather 'powerless' and 'financially ignorant'. She now firmly believes that both in a couple should be responsible for financial management to avoid such an imbalance.

Fortunately, there's now greater awareness of intergenerational influence, which means that many adults consciously act in opposing ways to their parents, which could help counteract negative influences. This is the case for one female breadwinner I spoke to, Liz. She's a successful lawyer and earns most of the family income, while her partner, Jim, coaches rugby part-time at a nearby school. She witnessed her parents struggle financially, which served as a strong motivation not to expose her children to the stress of this insecurity, influencing her career choice: 'My kids will never *not* know where they're going to live next week. From when I was 11 onwards my parents basically just stopped paying attention. I'm very conscious that we are a lot more involved in their lives and are supportive and present.'

Liz and Jim are happy for their two boys to see her holding the positional power, and he is more than content doing the majority of childcare during the week. As Liz's salary is able to cover the household spending, it allows Jim to work in a role he is passionate about. While she is the higher earner, Liz acknowledges that he works harder at times, and understands how much work it takes to manage the house and childcare. I've heard from so many frustrated women who feel their labour at home isn't recognised as real work; we know it certainly isn't by society. Liz does appreciate Jim's contribution, and it makes for a happier union. Their relationship works because they communicate about all aspects of childcare and work together as a team. Jim hadn't built up a career the same way she had, so instead of letting this affect his self-esteem, he viewed the situation rationally and they allowed her economic power to influence who was at home more versus who spent more time working. Another key reason their relationship feels balanced, and Liz doesn't have to show 'gender display neutralisation', is because theirs was a conscious decision, so there's no resentment from Jim. Unlike some of the female breadwinners I spoke to, like Felicity, who felt their home lives were very imbalanced, Liz and Jim work hard to keep an even dynamic by having regular open conversations with each other.

How cultural norms are transferred is a crucial part of the puzzle that explains just how much our upbringing influences how we view power and how we are primed to act on it in our own relationships. When we recognise just how easily generational norms are passed down, it shows how much it affects how we divide tasks at home and may unlock something in our understanding. We can't undo our past, but we can understand that our childhood continues to shape us, which is a crucial step to helping us challenge any unhealthy dynamics and work towards more balance.

Given what we have explored in this chapter, the cultural context where we live makes a huge difference to how we behave, how we listen to others and how we feel supported at work and home. If policy-makers are serious about equality, we have a lot to learn from horizontal cultures. All this shows that systems can be put in place that nudge us all to share power more equally.

## KEY POINTS:

- Individualistic countries focus more on personal success, while collectivist countries emphasise the group or community.
- When fathers take a share of parental leave, it has numerous positive outcomes. Women are more likely to return to work, their earnings increase, and fathers become more involved in childcare and develop stronger bonds with their children.
- When men take parental leave it helps them feel like more competent fathers, which increases their involvement and can even contribute to a child's school success.

## ACTION POINTS:

- We can change our mindset from individualist to collectivist by reminding ourselves of our position within a group.
- If your company or team has a hierarchical, high power-distance culture, try to minimise the hierarchy by being approachable, listening and encouraging feedback, all of which will increase psychological safety (where you or your team feels free to take risks and admit mistakes).
- If your workplace allows it, share parental leave with your partner. If there is no allocation for men, campaign for it, citing the evidence from this chapter.

# 7

OVERPOWERED: WHY POWER IMBALANCES LINGER

'People are driven to believe that the world is just and fair, because, frankly, that makes it easier for us to get out of bed in the morning.'

—Pamela Smith

Pamela Smith grew up in a working-class neighbourhood in the suburbs of Detroit. Neither of her parents went to university. She was determined not to follow a similar path, even though statistics show that children are less likely to pursue higher education if their parents didn't. 'My parents vaguely expected me to go to college, but I do not remember us having extended conversations about it. I was a bright, overachieving kid, so the big push came more from various teachers. I also desperately wanted to get out of the town I grew up in, so much of the motivation was internal.'

A keen observer of social divisions around her, initially she believed she would never have any of the power that comes from the sort of career university graduates can pursue. But this very experience influenced where she would end up: studying psychology and creative writing at Michigan University. She became interested in studying how the influence of power affects us precisely because she had felt like an outsider at university. 'I was a little more aware of the dynamics going on because I couldn't take anything for granted. I had no idea how to do anything. And so there was just a point where I was very aware of all the power dynamics that went on like what it meant to relate to a professor.' She knew that her role as a research assistant meant she had relatively little power in comparison. She is now a professor herself at the University of California, San Diego, studying the very dynamics she had earlier felt she didn't understand.

Speaking with her, I was reminded about a phenomenon called 'educationism'. It's a subtle bias against those with lower levels of educational background or 'class status', and highly prevalent in class-obsessed societies like Britain and the US. We all intuitively know there are many indicators of both educational and class background, from the way we talk to the cultural references we use to the way we dress. It turns out the more educated are biased against the less educated. The French sociologist Pierre Bourdieu called it the 'racism of intelligence' that helps the upper classes justify their status.

This bias exists in higher education too, contradicting the belief that highly educated people are 'tolerant and morally enlightened'.[1] Worse, the lower educated are judged to be at fault for their lack of educational attainment, an unfair misconception that continues to divide society.

It was feeling like an outsider that inspired Smith to investigate power dynamics. She was surprised that most of the literature focused on power as being negative; that holding power corrupts us, that power makes people more selfish, lazy and mean. This didn't sit well with her, for how could anything ever get done if this was true?

This inspired Smith to better understand what power actually does to us, both those who hold it and those who don't, and also how it affects us in daily life, rather than those at extreme ends of it. She would show in her research that power isn't just for the privileged – most of us have access to varying forms of power. What's more, for many of us it changes throughout the day. One survey of over 2,500 people found that it was common to experience both low and high power simultaneously – for instance, someone can report feeling powerless in their personal relationship even if they are in a very senior position at work.[2]

In one study, Smith and her colleagues assigned individuals positions of either power or powerlessness. Those who were subordinate felt powerless and experienced reduced cognitive abilities such as impaired executive function. This is a crucial aspect of cognition involved in planning, problem-solving and making decisions. The participants with the least power also performed worst.[3]

Another study revealed that our perspective changes depending on our power status. Those who experienced low levels of autonomy tended to focus on details rather than the bigger picture.[4] I certainly noticed that when I was leading my team through organisational change. People would often ask me quite detailed questions rather than considering the end goals. Unsurprisingly, in uncertain times people look inwards at how change affects them personally instead of outwards to consider the bigger picture.

These results show that those in leadership positions should be mindful of how they communicate with more junior individuals. Understanding workloads and encouraging an open dialogue could reduce errors, improve their reasoning skills and therefore do wonders for productivity. Smith's research shows that we should take care to consider a person's seniority (or lack of) before judging their work too harshly. It's also worth understanding that it will benefit us all to empower those beneath us, as power improves cognitive function,[5] and helps individuals process information more efficiently.[6] And just as with cultural differences, workplaces can have varying levels of power distance, which can have a huge impact on psychological safety at work – that is, the extent to which you or your team feels free to take risks and admit mistakes. High power-distance companies or teams limit opportunities for junior employees to make suggestions, which can make them feel less valued. In the worst case, in a team with a bullying boss or an environment where people are worried for their jobs because they've seen colleagues lose theirs, it minimises the team's psychological safety and mental well-being, creating the perfect storm of toxicity and leaving little room to get the best out of employees. If you are worried about your job, it's not the best time to be creative or put forward your best ideas.

There are countless advantages when teams have high psychological safety. They come up with better ideas, feel more valued, are more engaged, motivated and even learn more.[7] Those who work in a less hierarchical team will feel freer to speak up when they disagree with others, whatever their level, meaning senior as well as junior colleagues can learn from feedback. High psychological safety has even been found to have a positive influence on diversity, as it empowers those from minority backgrounds to better express themselves.[8] Bringing your true self to work really has tangible benefits.

Social hierarchies therefore literally alter our cognition, just as we saw with the educationism bias. As Smith writes: 'It is not just differences in inherent ability, motivation or discrimination that lead to separation between the haves and the have-nots; the cognitive impairments associated with being powerless may also be an important contributor, leading the powerless towards a destiny of dispossession,' a paper by Smith and colleagues stated.[9] That's why it helps to have an awareness of the privilege and power we have, realising that tasks that seem easy to some may not be so for others.

## CHANGE IS SLOW BUT NOT STEADY

Workplace expectations are changing. Workers increasingly expect flexibility and if they don't get it, and feel they have been wronged, they speak out. In January 2024, the CEO of a baby clothing company was forced to issue not one, but two public apologies for her handling of the maternity leave of one of her staff members. Marissa Hughes was adopting a baby when something happened that no new parent wants to face – the baby was born prematurely. In order to spend time with the baby in hospital she requested remote working. Her request was denied, and the resulting fallout went viral. The leader of Kyte Baby, Ying Liu, said she would review the maternity policies, called herself 'insensitive' and 'selfish', and added that: 'I fully realise the impact of my actions'.[10] If Liu had shown more empathy initially, her company's reputation would likely be untarnished. It took public scrutiny to bring meaningful change, showing public attitudes strongly support just policies and can humble powerful decision-makers.

Even in day-to-day inequities, leaders can quickly get shamed. If they step too far from kindness and empathy, it can be catastrophic for their reputation and their business. Not many companies are subjected to public scrutiny to enforce change, but with citizen journalists able to publish social commentary instantly, many companies are aware they need to be more transparent and democratic to retain skilled employees. The pendulum is certainly shifting, though in many cases, not far enough.

When it comes to psychological traits, men and women are much more alike than different. 'The literature on gender differences shows that they are almost always much smaller than we think they are,' says Joris Lammers, a political psychology professor who researches attitudes around leadership and power. Despite this, there's a wide-held assumption that women are superior in lots of the softer skills now recognised as being important for leadership. These preconceptions are fuelling the idea that women make better leaders. This is indeed the case when you look at the hard data. Women do express more empathy and show decreased levels of dominance at work, which has been shown to be beneficial for companies, increasing psychological safety and therefore improving innovation and creativity. But as we heard, that's largely because women are conditioned this way, and these softer traits also mean women don't put themselves forward for leadership positions as frequently. Ironically this can create a defensive mentality, as well as a decreasing preference to hire women in leadership positions, as some believe they are being given an unfair advantage. Men might start to think that although they are the 'winners' now, soon they might be the losers, posits Lammers, even though men are usually in higher-paid roles. This kind of thinking reveals the mismatch in believing we have reached a turning point, versus the reality of how far we have yet to go. It's desirable for a company to show that it's taking diversity seriously, even if the statistics tell a different story.

In some cases, we're seeing a correction in the wrong way, with men feeling more marginalised and threatened by female power. In a European poll, when individuals were presented with the statement: 'Advancing women's and girls' rights has gone too far because it threatens men's and boys' opportunities', men were more likely to agree than women, the reasoning being that it's a competition, there's no space for both to get ahead, and that progress for one means a negative impact on the other.[11] This is unfounded – greater equality benefits men and women alike, as well as society as a whole. However, this view was more prevalent in countries with higher unemployment in recent years, just as it is out-of-work men that feel the most threatened by breadwinner women.

This attitude is interesting because, as mentioned in Chapter 1, younger men today feel less pressure to be the main breadwinners than older ones. There are clearly class and country differences, or it could be the case that younger men feel less pressure (because they *know* more women are providing adequately) but still feel threatened by it. We are a species of contradictions after all. In a 2022 survey by the charity Future Men, organised by YouGov, about half stated that they would feel emasculated if they could not provide financially, but only 37% felt society still expects them to 'be the breadwinner'.[12] However, the flipside of this is that half *don't* feel emasculated by their lack of breadwinning status.

Each family situation is unique, but a common thread I've seen in both the research and among those I've spoken to is that, because earnings are so closely tied to status for men especially, a diminished earnings harms their self-esteem. I spoke with one father of two, Adam, who earns the same as his wife but said his sense of status was tied to how well his business was doing, which his wife did not experience. As Noelle Chesley's work revealed, it's much harder for men to say they don't work than for women to say so. Steve, meanwhile, recalibrated his priorities to reflect that time with his children was more important than income. His status wasn't threatened as he was able to retrain into a career where he can control his own time.

This all ties into our idea of what masculinity represents. When participants were polled about what type of leaders workers would like to see, Lammers found that there was an increase in preference for 'female typical' traits in 2020 compared to 2010 – namely compassion, warmth and friendliness. Respondents still preferred typically male traits overall, such as seeming assertive, dominant and powerful.[13] Still, this shows that the stereotype of what makes a good manager is changing.[14]

Although we are moving in the right direction, change is slow. Sociologists even have a term for this gradual pace: 'structural lag'. The changes we are seeing will create a world where possibilities for higher-earning female breadwinners are more abundant than ever before, but we first have to navigate our attitudes towards money, work and power to get there.

## THE ILLUSION OF POWER

Many power imbalances only exist because they are created by society, one that favours wealth and success. And we've seen that how we are socialised plays a major role in shaping us. In dozens of studies, Deborah Gruenfeld noticed something she hadn't expected, nor was looking for: when participants were primed to feel power, there were no meaningful differences in how women behaved compared to men. Power distorted emotions, empathy and decision-making in the same way for both sexes.

In the real world, we do see differences in empathy, confidence and numerous other aspects because, Gruenfeld believes, women understand power more as a responsibility. 'It's kind of that intersection between what it means to be a woman and to, in a knee-jerk way, always be worried about taking care of people, and being in positions of power highlighting that even more,' Gruenfeld told me. She was thinking out loud as this was never part of an experimental test. But in any experiment researchers control for variables. 'Every time we did one of those studies there was a concern that we would get a gender effect, because that just complicates the story so much for us . . . And every time it was kind of like, Okay, phew! The men and women are acting the same way.' Clearly, then, gender differences largely occur *because* of power differences, rather than due to our biological sex. In a 2024 meta-study (a study of studies), Adam Galinsky and colleagues showed that 'gender differences can arise from and are reinforced through hierarchical structures'. Social power, the authors conclude, is one important factor that contributes to the differences between men and women, and under-appreciating this 'risks adding false credence to sex-gendered expectations for behaviour and reinforces inequality between men and women'.

Other studies reveal that this feeling of responsibility is not an innate gender difference, but is learnt – which should be good news for those of us willing to cultivate it. In the dozens of interviews I conducted with both men and women in same- and mixed-sex couples, a clear pattern emerged. Men who spent more time at home with their children also felt more responsible for many aspects of the home. As one dad, Martin Robinson, who stayed home with his kids for five years, wrote in the *Standard* newspaper, the ones who embrace it understand they need to put everything into it, to 'beat back the stereotypes, ditch the ego and do a damn good job – for the kids, for your partner, for yourself'.[15] Another dad who I spoke with told me he couldn't imagine having missed the early years when he was involved in every aspect of his child's life.

It's not only women who are prone to feeling more responsible power. Firstborn children, regardless of sex, have a similar tendency to feel more responsibility for others – they learn at a very young age that younger siblings have needs that are more important than their own. Statistics even show that firstborn men and women are more represented among political leaders.[16] These studies reveal that power should not be considered gendered, as it affects us all similarly. It's just that numerous gender imbalances occur *because* power has historically been associated with men, who tend to dominate political and leadership positions. At the same time, hierarchical norms and how we are socialised means we still expect certain traits to be more prevalent in power-holders, namely dominance and authority. It's our brains' 'expectation engine' coming into play once again.

From what we've learnt about kindness and the importance of responsibility and empathy, it suggests that because women are socialised to tap into their inbuilt empathy response, they should be better leaders to begin with, not because of innate talent but because expectations hone certain traits. There is some truth to that, as we'll see. If society and hiring managers were to begin to value empathy over dominance, we'd see a very different workplace.

Given all of this, you might wonder how those of us with less power can prevent ourselves becoming disempowered. Our expectations once again can come into play here, as can having support around us. In a 2018 study, 264 participants took part in several tasks and were then given a score that indicated whether or not they could be considered for a position of leadership, either 'likely leaders' or 'unlikely leaders'. Those who were told the latter reported lower ambition for leadership, whereas those told the former were found to be more ambitious and performed better in a subsequent task.[17] This shows that those around us play a crucial role in shaping our ambition. Simply being primed for leadership can be motivational.

## STATUS LEAKAGE

While men still hold more executive positions, women are increasingly being hired into positions of leadership, with positive outcomes for employees. Globally the figure is about 32%, but it is gradually rising.[18] Countries with female leadership experienced fewer deaths during the Covid-19 pandemic – Australia had 36 times more deaths than New

Zealand, with a population only five times greater. The author of a 2022 report stated that 'Female leaders tend to act promptly and decisively and are more risk-averse towards the loss of human life.' It could also have been because more progressive countries are more likely to hire women into positions of leadership in the first place. Nevertheless, the report stated that 'Perhaps male leaders could learn from their female counterparts and pay more attention to issues that matter to the health of the broader population and society.'[19]

Likewise, when women are on boards, companies have been shown to perform better and are more profitable. The same goes for ethnic diversity.[20] Businesses led by women increase organisational trust,[21] and when there are more women in the C-suite companies focus more on challenging the status quo and on innovative approaches.[22] For women to succeed in leadership, research shows that support at home is vital, and that support leads to more stable marriages too. One 2017 study looked to understand the potential impact of a woman's high-status job on her marriage, particularly when her job status is higher than her husband's. There were several findings, positive and negative. First, if a woman believed her lower-earning husband could affect her status, because she was embarrassed or resentful towards him, it could negatively impact the relationship. This was dubbed 'status leakage' and was a key driver for considering divorce. At the same time, this 'status spillover' didn't affect the male partners, unless the woman was vocally unhappy. This effect has been found in other environments too; actresses who win the Academy Award for Best Actress are 1.68 times more likely to divorce compared to those who are nominated but don't win, and it is therefore known as the 'Oscar curse'. It's not all bad news; for those who had partners who were very 'hands on' with housework, relationship satisfaction was high. As the authors write, 'We suspect that providing this type of tangible support not only allows wives to focus on their careers, but also denotes respect.'[23]

For Jim and Liz, neither is affected by Liz's higher-earning status. Jim feels a close bond to his children and takes pride in organising their schedule, while Carlos, another primary caregiving parent, enjoys being there for every school pick-up and is on the school PTA. He's the one who organises all the aspects of his child's schedule to enable his partner to focus on work. Mutual support and respect of roles, whether at work or at home, is clearly key for marital well-being.

It's also revealing that in times of crisis, women and people of colour are more likely to be promoted into leadership positions.[24] This is a phenomenon known as the 'glass cliff' – a term originated by sociologist Michelle Ryan and psychologist Alexander Haslam. The idea here is that you might reach the glass ceiling only to be presented with a cliff you can potentially stumble over.

Ryan told me she was inspired to study this phenomenon twenty years ago when a damning article in *The Times* reported that women were causing companies to crash. Ryan and Haslam took a closer look at the data and found that the correlation was the other way around – the companies were performing poorly *before* female leaders were appointed. It wasn't that companies didn't perform well because of women, it was that struggling companies needed a radical change, and therefore appointed a non-stereotypical candidate. There's no simple reason this phenomenon occurs, Ryan says, but a constellation of things, especially relating to gender stereotypes. Women are seen to have particular traits that might be useful in challenging times, such as being understanding, charismatic, tactful and courteous, which are different from traditional (male) leaders, where desirable traits include being assertive, adventurous and forceful. When it comes to leadership, stereotypically masculine traits tend to be rewarded more than feminine traits. Ironically, the possible reasons why women are not appointed as leaders as often in the first place is because of these very same soft skills. As a crisis typically involves confusion, uncertainty and stress, a warm and understanding leader certainly comes in handy.

The positive here is the belief that women can enact change when times are tough, and that they have the necessary traits to turn things around. However, there are also indications that women are sometimes set up to fail; board positions are not necessarily a good opportunity when there's a high risk of a crisis. As part of their research, Ryan and Haslam found instances of female stereotyping, lack of supportive networks, and women not being given enough time to complete tasks. One female middle manager said: 'I have been assigned projects which are failing with the belief that I can rescue these. The factors for the belief in my ability include that I am a woman and that this gives me some sort of advantage.' While commenting on a lack of social support, another said: 'I was placed on a project to manage that was the "project from Hell". Was I set up for failure? I don't know. But I know it would have been different if I was male. I would have been part of the old schoolboy network that they had going.'

In one research scenario, participants were asked to appoint a man or woman (both equally qualified) to a leadership position where fictional companies were performing either well or terribly. Invariably, participants chose women more often when company performance was poor.[25] This pattern has also been found among law students, where women were chosen for cases that looked harder to win.[26] Politics also has the glass-cliff problem. When asked to select male or female participants in safe or hard-to-win seats, women were chosen for the latter, which was borne out in real life in the 2005 UK general election, where women ran in harder-to-win seats. It's important to recognise and call out this phenomenon when it happens, so we can also value these positive traits when times are more stable, especially as so many companies talk about the importance of supporting women to reach leadership roles.

## THE BETTER-THAN-AVERAGE EFFECT

It's important to understand our own biases as we may miss out on opportunities if we under-estimate our abilities. Many of us have no doubt felt unqualified for a new job, but inspirational and helpful colleagues are key to progression when they help identify strengths and see potential. Many power imbalances could otherwise linger if we view ourselves as less competent than we really are. Add to this the finding that men overestimate certain abilities compared to women, such as how good they are at maths, while women under-estimate their abilities, and it's easy to see how the problem persists. Research has termed this the 'male hubris' and 'female humility' effect, and it persists despite decades of research showing that men and women are equally smart.[27] It is related to another well-known bias, the Dunning–Kruger effect, which is the unfortunate bias many people have of overestimating their competence, making them unaware of their incompetence. We've all met that person at a dinner party who is so convinced they are right, even when it's obvious to others they are speaking nonsense. The effect occurs because when you lack certain knowledge, you don't know what you're missing, so erroneously think you know more than you actually do. We can be 'unskilled and unaware of it', which leads to inflated self-assessments.[28] It works the other way around too; those who show talent in a certain area may mistakenly believe it was easy to acquire, so under-estimate just how skilled they are. If anything, it shows we need to learn to value and promote our own unique abilities and not assume everyone else can do the same.

There's also the lesser-known 'better-than-average effect'. Most of us can accurately rate someone else's ability, but have an inflated sense of our own. When asked, we are more likely to think we are above average than below. In the 1980s, one study found that 93% of US participants rated themselves as above-average drivers, when statistically this is impossible.[29] Couples are more likely to perceive their own marriage as better than others' – a useful bias to have for relationship satisfaction.[30] We also overestimate how generous we are compared to others.[31]

Taken together, these cognitive biases could be a recipe for disaster in the wrong hands, and certainly explain why incompetent leaders get ahead without realising their ineffectiveness, all the while thinking they are better-than-average, generous leaders. They aren't necessarily lying in job interviews – they literally think their skills are more advanced than they actually are. Knowing that many of us have these biases means we can learn not to take everything at face value. We can use this knowledge to influence more positive change and our above-average blind spot to psyche ourselves up for a job we otherwise feel unprepared for. Empathy, kindness, and compassion are all key for inspiring leaders. They aren't *female only* traits, but characteristics we can all harness in our lives to work towards becoming a respected leader who is not prone to corruption.

There's one hiccup in all of this which perhaps explains why kind leaders can sometimes be harder to find. Individuals with dominant, self-serving or narcissistic personality traits are particularly likely to seek positions of power, and once there, these traits are amplified because of the disinhibiting effects of power.[32] It could explain why we anecdotally hear more about horrible bosses than nice ones, even though most of us value the latter more. In a bit of a vicious loop, personality traits fuel the ambition for power, which in turn amplifies those same traits. Narcissists tend to be self-entitled, have an inflated sense of their own importance and are known to exploit others for personal gain, so a narcissist in power is particularly potent. Worse, it's been shown that if a group lacks a leader, a narcissist will be more likely to step in and take charge, even if they aren't up to the job.[33]

## RELATABLE LEADERS HELP SHARE POWER

It's clear that women face numerous structural issues preventing them from reaching leadership roles, but a hidden factor relates to the identities women have at work compared to at home. Expectations and stereotypes can become self-fulfilling, especially where women aren't as expected in positions of leadership, just as men aren't expected to be in lower-earning or homemaker roles. A survey of over 1,000 people found that work-life balance struggles for women may stem from feeling as though they can't be their true selves at work, due to a 'perceived lack of fit'. The survey also found that a woman's work identity did not align with her home identity. If you can't see a role model, then it's hard to imagine yourself in a comparable position.[34]

This is exactly what Michelle Ryan found at the Royal College of Surgeons. When asked to look at why female surgeons were underrepresented, one immediate issue materialised – the Royal College would bring out the most senior female surgeon as inspiration, which would backfire for more junior staff who couldn't easily compare their own roles to someone so senior. Just because there's a successful female surgeon doesn't mean that others can easily copy her success. It's then no wonder that comparisons to others can exacerbate a clash between work and personal identity. In my previous book, *The Motherhood Complex*, I found that a key reason for the clash between my motherhood identity and my work identity was because of the need to occupy two different selves that rarely aligned. Fortunately, Ryan's team found that exposure to relatable female leaders in attainable positions helped women to see themselves in those positions. Many companies aim to help by sending their employees on bias or allyship training, according to a 2024 McKinsey report,[35] but as the report states, 'The increase in training programs does not appear to be translating into greater awareness or action.' This shows that structural change is not there yet, and more needs to be done, namely changing the culture that values and rewards masculine traits, as well as nurturing and promoting more attainable role models.

Another often-presented solution is giving staff flexible work policies, which has become increasingly standard. This should be available for everyone and taken up equally – but it remains more common for women to work part-time and more flexibly, often doing so for childcare reasons. When they do this they can be judged as less committed or overlooked for promotions. Often, it's not a choice, and this constant juggle to fit work in around childcare contributes to parental burnout.[36] This exposes what Heejung Chung, a sociologist, calls the 'flexibility paradox'.[37] Women rely on flexibility for childcare needs, but often find themselves doing more housework and childcare because of it. She found that it's common for women to work from home more than men, creating a 'two-tier market' where women are doing more housework as well as paid work, but then getting judged and consequently penalised professionally for it. Add to this that men tend to see their roles as less flexible, meaning they show more 'facetime' in the office, which makes them more visible. Flexible policies may help retain women in the workplace but they do not help elevate women, making the pool of potential leaders even smaller. As we saw, women make good leaders, they simply face many more hurdles to be considered.

'If anything, what we need to do is get more fathers at home and managers to understand that fathers being involved in childcare and housework isn't necessarily antithetical to productivity,' Chung tells me. 'Men doing housework and childcare, and therefore having a better work-life balance, will benefit all workers.' We can perhaps take inspiration from the 'f\*\*k-it fathers' and see that flexible working can and should be taken by all as a default.

Of course, wider cultural change is more difficult to enact but small changes can make a big difference, such as company culture, quotas and targets for leadership. Then there are subtle things we can all do, including paying attention to who gets listened to in meetings, giving everyone a voice so it's not just those who speak the loudest that are rewarded. It's thinking about who gets promoted, who gets the bonuses. If bonuses are based on a culture of overwork, that automatically puts a large proportion of the workforce at a disadvantage, as anyone with caring responsibilities cannot work longer than their contracted hours. We shouldn't focus on those who are loudest and most arrogant, nor reward only those who give the most facetime, but focus on work done. We would all do well to think more closely about what good leadership looks like. Is it being pushy, arrogant or forceful, or being empathetic, kind, creative and motivational? I think we all know the answer.

Ultimately, the whole reason we have to look at gendered power structures is that a more equal workforce benefits men too. The very same men who feel judged for being lower earners would be judged less if it became routine for women to pursue power outside the home as much as men do.

## KEY POINTS:

- Social power is the major force that creates gender imbalances, but when in positions of power, it affects men and women alike.
- Individuals in subordinate positions feel more powerless, show reduced cognitive abilities, are less creative and less likely to think of the bigger picture.
- Unkind, hubristic leaders open themselves to public scrutiny which can lead to their downfall.
- Women are not innately more empathetic, but they have been conditioned by society to act on their emotions, which becomes self-fulfilling.
- Men who are unemployed often feel most threatened by female breadwinners, while younger generations of men experience less pressure to be primary earners.
- In groups with high psychological safety, people feel safer to share ideas and criticisms and it makes for a more creative, loyal team.

## ACTION POINTS:

- We can all find a relatable role model to learn from, rather than chase unattainable ideals.
- Be wary of failing upwards if promoted in precarious times.
- Hiring managers should prioritise candidates who show empathy over traditionally male characteristics like 'dominance' if they want to create kinder organisations.
- We can use the 'better-than-average' bias for good and to help convince ourselves we are right for a potential new job.

8

POWERFUL LOVE: WHEN LOVE OVERPOWERS,
AND THE MYTH OF MUTUALITY

'The future depends entirely on what each of us does every
day; a movement is only people moving.'

—Gloria Steinem

Exploring how power affects relationships is complex: while
someone might hold more influence in one area, like shared
finances, this doesn't always translate to complete control in other
domains, like social plans. This explains why there can be dissonance when one person in a relationship asserts more influence in
one area but not the other. A higher-earning spouse may have little
say on restaurant choices but be the authority on major decisions
like financial investments or where they live. As we've seen, even
if there's a clear imbalance of power, openly communicating about
how that power manifests means it doesn't have to lead to resentment. Doing so could also increase relationship satisfaction.

I spoke with Elisa, a tech-industry worker who is a case in point.
She has an extremely high sense of power in her relationship and
was able to instigate a move for her family from London to Abu
Dhabi when a career opportunity came up. As she earns more
than her partner, she has higher positional power, so he was the
one who gave up his sales role in London. She is a new mother,
and is aware that stepping back now would result in missed opportunities. After she communicated her desires to her partner, they
agreed to prioritise her career at this stage. In a few years' time

they plan to prioritise her partner's job again, and both feel that the balance of power will even out as they are both influencing each other in tandem. As Elisa says: 'It's harder for a woman with a child to get a job. [My husband] was understanding, he said, "I get it, you get the short end of the stick with motherhood", and we decided we were going to prioritise my career for the next couple of years. He's leaving his comfort zone quite a lot to allow me to take this opportunity.'

He does all the cooking, while her career-advancing role allows them to outsource childcare and cleaning during the week, meaning neither feels resentful when catching up on chores at the weekend. While initially he did feel emasculated due to no longer earning an income for the family, he rationalised it as an opportunity to work on career development for the future. Seeing their family as a team, where both can have a chance to pursue a higher-status role, has helped them shift who is able to prioritise their career. Without any extended family around to help out, being able to hire extra support has improved their relationship satisfaction.

Elisa and her partner's decision exemplifies the reality that in many relationships there's an ever-changing balance, a subtle push and pull of wants and desires, which sometimes align but are regularly in conflict. For every seemingly mutual decision, one person in a relationship may want a certain outcome more and so finds ways to influence the decision in that direction, and, if they can't, may feel resentful. If you've ever come to a crossroads where you had to compromise, see if you can recall why you did so, or whether you realised it at all. This constant negotiation of desires reveals what should now be apparent: all personal relationships require us to navigate power dynamics. If we are the ones who feel that tug and give in to our partner's demands, the imbalance can start to feel very uncomfortable.

Academics have long known that marital power manifests in several ways. In the late 1980s a researcher, Aafke Komter, noticed three distinct forms of power in a marriage:[1]

- **Manifest:** This is the most obvious and visible form of power, where one person's demands overpower the other. This could be an overt disagreement where one person overrules the other's interests (for example, an argument on which leisure activities to spend money on).
- **Latent:** This operates subtly; one partner might avoid raising an issue to prevent conflict. While there's no outward argument, the partner with less power may simmer with resentment, choosing silence over an inevitable rejection (for example, wanting to watch a movie instead of rugby, but knowing your suggestion would be overruled, leading to simmering resentment).
- **Invisible:** This is the most difficult form of power to see. It's where systematic inequalities between a couple are so ingrained they are seen as inevitable or natural to maintain the status quo (for example, prioritising one career over the other, accepting an unequal division of housework, or that one partner's desires hold less sway, but rationalising that as normal).

A new study has used these concepts as a framework to analyse dozens of interviews with heterosexual couples to understand power imbalances.[2] Sociologists Jaclyn Wong and Allison Daminger observed very little manifest and latent power but found that, even today, invisible power still dominated most relationships, despite couples intending to be balanced. Interestingly, Wong tells me, the couples didn't seem to be aware of it: 'We didn't see a lot of latent power. There was some resentment every now and then. But most people told us: "We agreed the whole time . . . we came to this decision together." Nobody felt like they had to hold back and not communicate with their partners.' While there were no obvious signs that couples overtly endorsed the male breadwinner/female homemaker arrangement, many fell into this pattern despite talking about how important the women's career was too. This led Wong and Daminger to propose that invisible power is constantly at play in modern relationships.

One couple, Steve and Lisa, each made decisions for the family but in specific domains. Steve, the sole earner, made all the financial decisions whereas Lisa organised travel and social plans. Meanwhile, Rebecca and Joseph compromised on a location when it was Joseph's turn to look for a job. Joseph appeared to have 'compromised' by looking for jobs only in areas where she also wanted to live, but it was for him they were moving at all; she had given up her job to do so. In their case, Rebecca helped him look for jobs too. Both of them worked to advance *his* goals, whereas *her* goals remained her own responsibility. His lack of cognitive labour in helping her find a job is a clear example of a 'gendered power imbalance in which both partners worked together to promote Joseph's interests'.

Couples were perceiving their decisions as mutual in order to keep their relationships feeling balanced. Ironically, invisible power was actually at play, keeping the power imbalanced, just less obviously. Wong and Daminger call this 'the myth of mutuality'. During interviews, most couples responded by emphasising the word 'us' when asked about decisions, but this proved to be the 'myth' – upon closer analysis, it was clear that one person was doing more of the mental work, with the more powerful person making the final decisions, though the interviewees seemed unaware this was the case. 'Because our couples believed so deeply that they were always working in collaboration with each other, they could overlook, or maybe didn't want to notice, when things were unequal, when someone was doing more of the legwork to make a pretty major decision,' explains Wong. Understanding hidden power is important on many fronts, especially because if a relationship or marriage doesn't work out, yet one career has been prioritised over the other, it leaves one person financially vulnerable. Take Shania, whose husband was unfaithful so she kicked him out. She has three children and is currently renting while her partner is between jobs: 'I am a full-time mum. I stopped working when my first son was born. My husband supported us all this time – he is a contractor and only works when he has a contract. He is spending all his money on his new "girlfriend" – how can he support me and the kids if he doesn't work? I don't have any income and I can't afford a lawyer. My whole world just collapsed and I don't know where to look for help.'

When Komter first came up with these concepts to explain the hidden power imbalances in a marriage, invisible power was more inevitable because it was then more common for men to be bread-winners and women to be homemakers. Today that's no longer the case, but invisible power lingers on. What is revealing about this study is that couples believed they had achieved mutuality, but in the process were not tracking whose needs were met and whose work it took to make it happen. This 'myth of mutuality', then, seems to hide the invisible power wielded by men.

## A LOW SENSE OF POWER REDUCES RELATIONSHIP SATISFACTION

If you need any further persuading that checking in on the power balance at home will be a good thing, it's abundantly clear that balanced dynamics create happier relationships. This may sound obvious, but the truth is that many of us don't necessarily think too much about what power we hold or lack, because the social structures we operate in are so ingrained and expected, and life often gets in the way of self-analysis. Recent research has shown that an individual's *sense* of power has more influence on having a positive relationship than their positional power.[3] In the study of 180 couples, most experienced a high sense of power and felt they were able to get their own way – meaning in this cohort the balance *felt* acceptable. Something intriguing was going on here, as we know many relationships have someone who has more influ-ence – but in this case both in the relationship felt they had a say. Of course, the couples who volunteered for this study tended to have no major relationship issues overall which goes some way to explaining these results. Still, this reveals that power can manifest in more than one way, and what's crucial is how you *feel* about what you can influence. Because having a high sense of power relates to self-confidence and higher instances of forgiveness during a conflict, it's clearly key to relationship satisfaction that each feels they have control and ownership to some degree.

Many relationships have certain imbalances and what's more critical is how we *feel* within that balance. We all have a basic need to express ourselves, feel understood and feel we have control, and when we do so we are happiest. A 2024 follow-up study cemented this idea further – in a large sample of participants, it wasn't equal or unequal power that increased happiness in relationships, but 'whether people feel that they exert influence'.[4] The point here is that as long as the power differences aren't too large, many of us are used to a varying degree of imbalance so it doesn't necessarily make us less happy, as long as the relationship on the whole is positive. Clearly it can depend on how you perceive these divisions and the consequences. If one in the relationship makes all the social plans, despite earning less and having lower financial power, they may feel quite happy as it ticks the 'sense of power' box.

Daminger and Wong's research explains why a 'sense of power' increases relationship satisfaction, and the reason is revealing. Having a sense of power isn't necessarily true power, but to avoid conflict, couples rationalise an imbalance as being mutual because they aren't always factoring in the mental work needed to get there. In a relationship where both partners have autonomy to make decisions, it creates a sense of both having control over a particular domain. While women and men have been found to be just as ambitious early on in their careers, decisions relating to the man's career are still often prioritised. This invisible power explains why so many power imbalances remain, despite society being much more progressive than a generation ago. 'When women get to call the shots in the household and regarding childcare, they're still calling the shots in the broader context of a capitalist society, where a person's power in society is determined by their economic means. And childcare and housework are all unpaid,' Wong says. Even if one person in a relationship oversees decoration, socialising, food and school decisions, under capitalism the person with more money or a higher-status job is the more powerful one from a societal standard, at least in the West. This again explains why breadwinner women challenge the status quo. If they are powerful both in the home and outside due to their higher earnings, it can create discomfort.

To rebalance a relationship that falls victim to 'the myth of mutuality', there are some tools we can employ. For instance, if you make a list together, both of you will take part in the planning aspect of the mental work more fairly. This could involve creating meal plans together or using a shared calendar. Wong mentions one couple who made systematic notes for each step of parenting, for example noting everything needed to get out of the house. This meant both could follow the list together rather than one taking on more of this work.

Another solution, which will take work before it takes effect, is for the person who bears most of the mental load to consciously step back and do less. You can start to do this by slowly handing over tasks. It has to be end to end, so taking kids swimming would require researching and then booking classes, and buying all the necessary gear. Mary in Chapter 1 felt she had to step back from the kitchen to avoid getting involved with all meals and creating more work for herself, as did I when handing over my son's birthday party planning to my partner. It was hard not to step in and send the invites because I knew he hadn't done it yet, but if I had, I would have been the one communicating all the details, collating RSVPs and sending updates, which takes time too. Even if it means your partner does things differently, letting go of that control means less work for you in the long run.

Similarly, consider whether you are the one planning all meals even if your partner does the actual cooking. Planning, purchasing and keeping track of the food in your house takes time. The end product, the meal, is only the final part of that labour. Taking ownership of meals from start to finish would remove the extra, often hidden, work and create habits beyond individual meals. The person cooking needs to make sure the ingredients are either already at home or are added to a shopping list and bought. Even better, that person learns how to improvise if they don't have all the ingredients for a recipe, which is only learnt by doing. This is something I've always routinely done, but it was only when my husband began cooking more often that he got used to identifying which ingredients could easily be tweaked. If that means a stir-fry has no garlic, or couscous is substituted for rice, so be it. It will still be nourishing and might even be tastier than the original plan.

The mental load matters when thinking about power dynamics because, traditionally, decision-makers have been viewed as the ones who hold most power. As we explored earlier, decisions at home can be a product of inequality outside it – and the fact that so many women perform most of the cognitive and mental labour in relationships can be *explained* by power imbalances. While decision-making may seem shared, the partner who shoulders more of the cognitive burden (anticipating, researching and planning) might actually hold less power, masked by the appearance of mutuality. If a couple tells you: 'We decided on this school for our child,' it hides the hours of research and school viewings that helped inform that decision. This isn't rare. Women often become the default household organisers – in part because of ingrained expectations of what women and mothers do at home. It's not that our partners don't want to or couldn't pick up some of this load (mine really does do a lot), it's more that women have been conditioned from an early age to do the bulk of what is typically considered 'women's work'.

## STABLE RELATIONSHIPS, BETTER BALANCE

The balance of power in a relationship matters to our identity precisely because it can shape our day-to-day choices, as well as the time available to pursue our goals. We heard in Chapter 5 about 'goal contagion', where an individual with lower power in their relationship starts to prioritise and adopt the hobbies and goals of their more powerful partner. This could be advantageous if both are fully invested in that goal, say if one person's fitness pursuits become a joint effort. It could also become detrimental and unfulfilling if someone completely loses sight of their own needs and desires that make up their identity.

This highlights a common relationship tension: balancing individual goals and shared pursuits. The ideal balance varies for each couple, but open communication is key to ensuring individual interests don't become too overshadowed by joint activities. I've seen this play out many times. A friend of mine started to enthusiastically follow her partner's football club even though she wasn't that interested in football. She now watches matches instead of the show she had preferred. It's a small adjustment but you can see how these changes can lead to larger ones if left unchecked. This also explains why so many couples end up prioritising the career goals of the higher earner, who often has greater financial power because the family is more dependent on their income.

Goal contagion can be positive – joint interests can bring a couple closer together – but when someone's interests and identity are overridden it can create lasting dissatisfaction. I've heard of too many instances where work and family are a barrier to pursuing hobbies. In many cases, the allocation of free time is far from equal. Take Jamilla, who lamented that her partner attends his hobby four or five times a week, and she has become so embroiled in parenting that she feels he is not equipped to responsibly watch their son who has additional needs:

In essence he expects me to stay home with the two babies while he's doing his hobbies several times a week. He says that's not what he expects but it obviously is because unless he cuts back on his hobbies, then me staying home alone with both babies is exactly what will happen. He suggests I join clubs too once the new baby is born . . . but actually he can't competently look after our own son alone now let alone a newborn too . . . Losing my mind going round in circles with him over this.

It is possible to address this early on, as Alya explains. She and her partner split everything when they are at home, and both have spent time being a stay-at-home parent. They have four hours each weekend to themselves to do as they wish, either hobbies or simply relaxing. Crucially, this expectation was consciously discussed early on: 'I always said I wouldn't have children if I had to parent alone. Last week I went for a massage and had a coffee by the beach. He went to see a morning movie and got lunch. The goal is always that we work together and face [any] problems or issues together.'

If there is an imbalance, without redressing it, couples are likely to continue to experience dissatisfaction. It's no wonder then that power imbalances affect both how long a relationship will last and how stable it is. In one study, researchers asked 114 participants about various relationships they had been in. In relationships that couples described as egalitarian, the experience was viewed as more stable and intimate, with less conflict and greater pleasure. However, women reported a relationship to be less stable if they felt subordinate to their partner, while subordinate men did not report a relationship to be less intimate and stable.[5] Curiously, both men and women were found to feel subordinate in their relationships in fairly equal numbers, but the differences appeared with how the women felt about it. When women had lower power, it was more toxic. Twelve were subject to domestic abuse, and two of these women were completely financially dependent on their partners. Looked at another way, power imbalances can affect anyone in a romantic partnership, but the stakes are higher for women. That's because 'relationships don't happen in a social vacuum', writes the author of the study, Laina Bay-Cheng.[6] Even where a man has less power at home, outside the home 'he's cushioned by a still-intact system of male privilege. Men are less likely to worry about the possibility of being assaulted or abused by a female partner.'

It has also been found that individuals with a higher socioeconomic status (SES) – which in turn gives them higher positional power – are worse at reading facial expressions and non-verbal behaviour. Just as power reduces empathy, it also reduces our understanding of body language. This means that if one person comes from money and continues to earn a high income, they may become less aware of their partner's wants and needs. To study this, a team showed participants pictures and videos and asked them which thoughts or feelings were being expressed. The people with higher incomes did not perform as well, whereas individuals from low SES backgrounds performed better at the task. The theory goes that individuals who have experienced scarcity often depend on the cooperation of the group, and so develop stronger social skills out of necessity. If you lack power, in other words, you get very good at reading the room – because your success depends on it.[7]

## WHEN RELATIONSHIPS TURN BAD

Whether you have unintentionally perpetrated a power imbalance or been subject to one, it's important to recognise how relationship dynamics affect us because the more obvious effects of power can mask subtle influences – which can be equally consequential. Following the #MeToo movement there is more awareness of power imbalances and age-inappropriate relationships than ever before, but despite this, imbalances remain everywhere, often in plain sight. It's important to understand what makes a good relationship, so we can immediately sense when something is toxic. To maintain a good balance, we need to recognise the warning signs of when power turns relationships sour. The journalist Amy Fleming wrote in the *Guardian*: 'I was deliriously happy' to get attention from older, good-looking men. '. . . when I was 15 and bursting with hopes of finding love and a place in the world outside of home and school. I thought I was streetwise because I avoided the obviously creepy old letches, but I was blissfully unaware of how ripe I was for being plucked from my own sense of teenage obscurity, instructed and moulded.'[8] She went on: 'Dating men as a girl must have been key in conditioning me for patriarchal life.'

I can relate. I once accepted a date with a 21-year-old when I had just turned 15, though I had told him I was 16. When I realised I didn't want to go on a second date as I felt rather uncomfortable about the whole thing, I fessed up to my age – but he still sent me flowers and said he'd like to take me out again because I seemed mature for my age. I was 15!

## RISKY MASCULINE 'IDEALS'

We heard about how power can corrupt and that consequently leaders lose the very traits that helped them rise. In personal relationships there is often more at stake. In a detailed meta-analysis with a total of 19,000 participants, it was shown that conforming to traditional masculine traits (such as desiring power over women, pursuing status or acting promiscuously) causes mental health problems among men.[9] The authors wrote that 'Sexism is not merely a social injustice, but also has deleterious mental health-related consequences for those who embrace such attitudes.' If a man goes into a relationship with a sexist attitude, it negatively affects his partner and causes additional stress to both. In addition, men who conform to more stereotypically masculine views are known to take greater health risks generally.[10] This analysis reveals that it would benefit us all to redefine masculine ideals, which could have the dual effect of reducing sexism and increasing mental well-being.

This is especially important when considering the link between power and status. In a 2017 study, Melissa Williams and Deborah Gruenfeld wanted to understand the effect power had on harassment, as there is some evidence that perpetrators attack women when they feel disempowered. As they put it, 'Chronic powerlessness fosters a desire for power.' Being low status can make people feel insecure and can even cause people to feel shame. Scarily, it also seems that this could trigger harassment.

In the first part of their study, they asked men to read a scenario that was intended to trigger feelings of hostile sexism. The story involved a woman, 'Kate', playing hard to get. She is reportedly sexually promiscuous, spends an evening dancing, flirting and drinking with a man, and agrees to share a taxi with him. However, she declines his invitation to come home with him. After reading this the men were asked how they felt about Kate to see whether the story triggered either benevolent or hostile sexism. They were asked to rate Kate after reading statements that included: 'Kate tries to gain power by getting control over men', and: 'Once Kate got a man to commit to her, she would probably try to put him on a tight leash'. The study primed individuals who typically defined themselves as having low power to feel more powerful. Interestingly, it was this group who displayed the most hostile sexism. Because being primed to feel more powerful also reduces empathy, this is a particularly potent mix, as these individuals are likely to 'feel less constrained by social norms' and sexism gives these men an 'outlet for their frustration'.

A follow-up study showed similar results. Men who generally felt disempowered in daily life but were temporarily given a feeling of power acted with more hostility towards a fictional attractive colleague who was described as being either unavailable or available. In the unavailable condition the woman was described as 'tired of college guys', whereas in the available condition she was described as 'interested in meeting new people'. This was despite the fact that the example was in a professional setting and the fictional colleague was described as more junior to the participant.[11]

It's worth pointing out the more positive findings too. The men well used to having power and influence showed decreased hostile sexism. This could be due to what we heard earlier, that those in power sometimes feel responsibility for others, whereas those at the lower end of a hierarchy might grab on to power and opportunistically intimidate others to maintain their status. The experimental findings resonate with real-world experiences. Feelings of hostility have been shown to increase the likelihood of harassment.[12] This is not a rarity either, as high rates of harassment have been reported, in some cases up to 88% of those asked. Me too.

To explore these power dynamics further, Williams and Gruenfeld included both female and male participants. Again, they showed that low-status participants who were temporarily given power acted vindictively. Participants were asked to imagine a romantic interest at work that went unrequited. Then participants were asked if they would support this individual with a good reference for a potential new role or provide a bad one – meaning they likely wouldn't get the role and could therefore still be a colleague. They found that the low-status individuals who were temporarily placed in a power position were more likely to write a bad reference.

There's lots going on here. If someone goes through life without feeling they have much influence on others and that they aren't taken seriously, it can easily cause resentment and a feeling of injustice. Given a chance to wield power, then, these individuals prioritise immoral goals. They feel entitled to do what they want because they have been unable to exercise control for so long, Williams explains. Those who feel they lack power can then quickly become entitled, and reason that they 'deserve more than what I have, and it's my turn now'. Power gives individuals the drive to pursue goals, positive or negative – and in this case it can contribute to the objectification of others rather than seeing them as equals, as well as putting their own needs before those of others.

## THE ALLURE OF STATUS

Consider a past or present relationship and think about what drew you to your partner. Was it a complementary trait to your own, or something you lacked? A study by Joris Lammers and colleagues shows that individuals who have chronically low levels of control value status in a partner, even at the expense of love and attraction. In the study, involving a simulated dating scenario, the low-power individuals preferred high-status characteristics, including having a well-paid job and good financial prospects, as well as the sense that someone 'can connect me to other people' and 'has a good reputation', instead of other traits such as attractiveness, sexual compatibility, sparking curiosity, and '[making] me feel warm and fuzzy'.[13] Unfortunately, we all know that the allure of someone's wealth can fade quickly if the basis for a relationship lacks love.

This can make such partnerships especially vulnerable when women are breadwinners and their partners feel as though they have a lower status as a result. Taken together, you can see why a cycle of abuse, unhappiness and even the risk of divorce can be exacerbated when individuals feel undervalued due to their lower status.

Looking at relationship dynamics is so interesting because in the home, power manifests in different ways to the outside world. In consenting sexual relationships, interesting patterns can emerge. A 2019 study featuring participants from four countries found that high-power men and women showed more sexual assertiveness and esteem.[14] It was the feeling of power that changed things, not their gender. This suggests that the differences we see in society do not stem from innate gender differences but are due to power imbalances that come from societal expectations. We know that women are socialised to act more submissively, but this study shows that when they are free to act outside these norms, they no longer do so. The findings show once again that power disinhibits us, and that 'Gender differences in sexuality may eventually be attenuated or even disappear when women gain an equally dominant position in society as men.' Fascinatingly it's in the most private areas of life where power also has a disinhibiting effect on us. The power research we've explored so far on cookie-eating bosses and rude expensive car drivers clearly also applies to personal relationships.

## WHEN POWER MAKES US SUSPICIOUS

Those with higher incomes and therefore higher positional power have been found to be more suspicious of a potential partner's ulterior motives, are less likely to commit to a relationship, are less trusting and less thankful. This shows that a large earnings gap can tangibly affect commitment or prevent relationships from forming in the first place. As you can imagine, lower commitment reduces trust. You can see how power imbalances can quickly become unhealthy and why couples with a large earning gap face extra hurdles.[15]

It's logical, then, that having high power increases the desire for what psychologists refer to as 'social distance'. By this they simply mean the degree to which people feel close to others. Powerful people seek more distance and are therefore less overtly needy, which in some cases could be linked to the mistrust of others we just heard about. Powerful people live in an environment where others need their attention, but they don't need it to be reciprocated, reinforcing the distance. Think of it like a dance; powerful people move and other people follow, and so they have to move again to maintain an optimal distance.[16] You can see how this would increase desirability, as they are forever out of reach. It's perhaps also why playing 'hard to get' keeps a potential partner interested, because that very act creates an imbalance of power. If you've ever purposely waited a few days before texting back someone you've been on a date with, you know what I mean. I've certainly had this done to me and returned the 'favour'. The surge of power this incited, I'm now sorry to say, was palpable.

As it's human nature to want what we can't have, it follows that high-power people are more likely to be unfaithful – again an effect found in men and women alike. This was shown in a study of individuals with real power at work, either in upper, middle or lower management. The higher up they were, the more likely they were to have been unfaithful, and even if they hadn't been unfaithful yet, they were more likely to predict that they would consider being unfaithful in the future. For women the effect was slightly stronger, showing once more the disinhibiting impact of power. It seems to release individuals from societal restraints, which is especially impactful for women, who tend to be judged more harshly for cheating.[17] At the same time, powerful people feel more confident (though we know that those with more dominant personalities are more likely to seek power, enhancing the confidence they already exhibit). This influences their decision-making and increases the likelihood of taking risks, making it all the more important to understand the consequence of these risks.

Then there's the added complex interplay of emotional involvement. The person who feels most committed to a relationship has been found to have less power overall. Think of the old trope of being needy – it gives the less committed person more power, precisely because that person has less to lose if the relationship ends. They can therefore make demands with little cost. This phenomenon even has a term, 'the principle of least interest', and is ripe for creating an unhealthy dynamic. A person more vested in the relationship would be more likely to follow the desires of their love interest than the other way around, which is exactly what we saw with goal contagion and creating social distance.

This can be problematic when there are serious imbalances, as we've seen in many real-world cases. When a powerful person is less committed to a relationship, they are more likely to bully or manipulate their spouse, an effect that has been found in both homosexual and heterosexual men and women. It can be subtle too. In one study, six different types of 'influence' were found, including what researchers called 'weak influencing factors' such as manipulation and supplication (pleading, crying or acting ill); 'stronger factors', including direct bullying and autocracy (insisting, claiming better knowledge), and lastly, 'neutral methods' such as disengaging and bargaining.[18] If you recognise any of these types of influence, consider when it occurs and who instigates it. Does it stem from power inside or outside the home? Clearly the most detrimental effects in a relationship are the stronger factors, which include bullying, whereas disengaging and bargaining surely resonate with many of us. Given the fact that even non-verbal social dominance has been shown to negatively affect romantic relationships,[19] we would all do well to take stock and assess how much a partner is disengaging, bargaining or even manipulating us.

Taken together this research reveals that it's *because* men and women have different access to resources that can cause complicated dynamics at home. When it comes to our relationships, how people influence and even control their partners varies depending on how much power they have. In an ever-continuing cycle, the less power we have, the more cognitive labour we do in a relationship. If we all learn to recognise the triggers that make us vulnerable, we will be at less risk of feeling overpowered. If you are reading this and realise you are the more powerful person at home or in your own relationship, then use this status for good, recognise the pitfalls of power but also the strengths of increased confidence and a willingness to take risks. Take on more cognitive labour at home, and you will be sure to increase relationship satisfaction in the process.

## KEY POINTS:

- Different types of power affect relationships: positional, relating to income or class; and subjective, relating to our ability to subtly influence others.
- The myth of mutuality exposes the idea that invisible power guides relationships, meaning we attribute decisions as mutual even when they serve one person more than the other.
- Both men and women who have more positional power state that they are more likely to be unfaithful.

## ACTION POINTS:

- To avoid one person in the relationship becoming the 'household manager' consider creating a list, meal plan or schedule for both partners to follow.
- If home life is imbalanced, the person who does more can consciously step back and hand over tasks end to end to encourage lasting habits.
- Take note of the type of influence someone in a relationship has over you and whether it occurs because of power outside the home.

# 9

## SHOWING YOUR TRUE SELF: HOW OUR EMOTIONS INFLUENCE OTHERS

'I don't want to be at the mercy of my emotions. I want to use them, to enjoy them, and to dominate them.'

—Oscar Wilde

Our emotional responses can transcend cultures, countries and personal connections – and, most importantly of all, we cannot easily control how we feel. That's why advertisers use positive storytelling to encourage us to feel good about their products. Modern medicine recognises emotional power too: we know that adverse emotions can cause physical symptoms and stress can make us physically ill. But what is now better understood is that our emotional state is contagious; it influences others too.

How we feel can shape our world-view as well as our view of others, but what might surprise you is how pervasive as well as subtle this can be – especially as people can be unaware of how they come across; understanding this plays a huge role in how we are seen, and how we can influence others. In Chapter 5 we heard how our brains are incredibly good at making emotional predictions based on what we see, hear and feel, and which can be impaired once we are in power. In this chapter, we'll explore how we can use an awareness of our emotional state to overcome some of the cognitive biases that come with power – and how we can improve our well-being in the process.

## EMOTIONAL CONTAGION

Our emotional senses can be so powerful that we instinctively imagine what others are feeling. Emotions can be contagious too. Think about a time when you walked into a room and noticed tension. How did you notice this? Was it a facial expression, body language, or both? How did it make you feel? Or how about a time when you were feeling extremely low but had already committed to a dinner, so you attended anyway. The mood is jovial, everyone is smiling, and shortly after you arrive, you are too. It's our brains' predictive power at play again – the brain is constantly trying to predict the future. When thinking about someone's current mental state, the brain also aims to anticipate their thoughts, feelings and emotions. This is important because successful and meaningful social events require us to anticipate others' mental states.[1]

How we respond to others is emotional contagion in action. It happens at work too; leaders have been shown to influence their team positively if they have a positive mood themselves, resulting in more cooperation and better performance.[2] When you become aware that this ripple effect exists, you will start to notice it everywhere. Try smiling at a stranger and see what happens. We can influence the emotional lives of others to help form deeper connections.

We mirror emotions from an extremely young age. Parents will smile at their babies for weeks and babies eventually start smiling back, which makes us smile more too. If someone near us looks angry, it can automatically trigger a similar feeling. It's why one person's bad mood in a group can sour relations. Smiles elicit smiles and warm body language can make us feel closer to others. We all mimic body language with people we trust and want to form a connection with.

Now consider empathy, our ability to understand the thoughts and feelings of others. It's an extremely powerful emotional response that helps others feel understood. It's also a potent cohesive glue that facilitates bonding and teamwork. Those who show high empathy are known to be more effective at working together. In one experiment, participants were divided into groups to tackle several tasks including 'solving visual puzzles, brainstorming, making collective moral judgments, and negotiating over limited resources'. The groups with participants who asked more questions, listened and were in tune with others' emotions performed best at the tasks. The greater the 'social sensitivity of group members' who took the thoughts and experiences of others into account, the more seamlessly they worked together.[3] Intriguingly, the more women there were in a group, the greater the performance was overall, which is no surprise as women are socialised to be more empathetic.

Harnessing our empathic response is a hidden superpower. Children and adolescents with high levels of empathy have more friends, do better in exams, are less anxious and happier. Those with high empathy make better leaders, tend to be good employees and show the potential to rise. To maintain influence in all parts of life, clearly, we need to be empathetic.[4] Equally, if we are empathetic to our partner's stressors at work or at home, it can lead to a more harmonious relationship.

The brain–body connection is so strong that the brain responds similarly when we experience something painful and when we witness someone else in pain. This was shown by the neuroscientist Tania Singer, who scanned the brains of lovers as they witnessed each other experience pain. When they did so, the same areas of the brain were active as when they were in pain themselves.[5]

Of course, this can be useful in real life; if we see our loved one hurt, we instantly want to help, showing that the emotional and physical are intricately tied together. Our empathy response is known to be stronger with members of our own group. For better or worse, we have a well-understood in-group bias, which also explains why some people respond with apathy to a distant conflict involving individuals we don't immediately relate to. We are more sympathetic to those who are most similar to us.

Another experiment found that our emotional state can affect this process. First the experimenters tested participants' brain responses when they were feeling pain to see if it was similar to when they witnessed someone else in pain. (Under full agreement, this person had a probe attached to their leg that gradually increased in temperature until it felt painful.) Then the participants were made to feel bad by watching a negative movie clip from *The Shining*, and subsequently watched someone else in pain. Now the empathy response in their brain was reduced, revealing that a negative mood can negatively affect judgements. Conversely, if they were lucky enough to watch a clip from *When Harry Met Sally* they were *more* empathetic when watching someone else in pain.[6] Similarly, if we are in a bad mood, real pain intensifies, but if we are in a good mood it can act as an analgesia to pain. A child is less likely to cry from a fall when having fun, whereas a grumpy child might howl at the slightest bump. Adults are much the same.

## POWER REDUCES EMPATHY FOR PAIN

We know power diminishes empathy and we've just seen that our negative emotions can reduce it further, but emerging work now shows that the way those in power experience the pain of others is far from what we might expect. In one study participants were primed to recall a time when they felt powerful, while others were asked to recall when they felt powerless. They were then shown a picture of a finger being pricked by a needle (the pain condition) or by a cotton bud (the neutral condition) while the electrical activity in their brain was monitored. Here's where the interesting changes emerged. While both groups showed a similar *initial* emotional response to pain, only the higher-power individuals showed a response in the area that *evaluates* the response a moment later – the 'thinking about thinking' part of the brain.[7]

While we've explored numerous other studies that show those in power can be less empathetic, when specifically asked to watch a painful scenario, the powerful people showed a heightened response too. It doesn't mean they would act on this empathy as a result, but the part of the brain processing others' pain is working as it should – showing we can all tune in to this crucial skill when reminded to do so. Sukhvinder Obhi, who led the study, explains that while the mirroring research we heard about earlier showed that high-power people mirror less, when individuals are specifically told what to focus on, it can change the response. The perspective-taking and empathy deficits found in those with power could well disappear if you give powerful people a goal, as they are clearly good at marshalling their resources when needed. Whilst this was a lab-based study, the implications are relevant at home, just as they are at work. Everyone can tune into a beneficial emotional response, it just costs more cognitive energy to do so, which explains why many people may unknowingly take shortcuts to avoid it. We all know that creating a balanced and satisfied relationship takes work, but knowing that we can activate our empathic response with a little extra work should be useful for us all.

Successful relationships depend on our ability to empathise with others and understand their perspectives, especially when power dynamics are at play. In professional environments, if we aren't mindful of how we come across, toxic power dynamics may well persist if a person in power lacks empathy for those who are less powerful. Those in positions of power have been found to be less attuned to the emotions of others compared to those who lack power.[8] At the same time, the powerless need to witness others carefully because their lives can easily be affected by those in power, making them remarkably good at reading emotional responses. As we heard, those from lower class backgrounds are better at reading others' mental states. If your life depends on others more powerful than you, it benefits you enormously to understand their emotions, which could lead to a greater sense of control.

When it comes to personal relationships, we can train ourselves to become more empathetic, which could help prevent us falling prey to the power paradox. If we want to benefit from power, we also have to learn how to remain empathetic and compassionate. One way to do so is to ensure that once we reach power, we continue to feel responsible for others, and we can do so by better understanding how others feel.

## RESPONSIBLE POWER

Annika Scholl, a psychologist, has done research on exactly that. She found that it's crucial for leaders to feel responsible for their subordinates. People in power get tempted to misuse it precisely because it encourages more focus on the self than on others. This made Scholl question how feeling responsible could change matters, so she set out to discover which conditions would help leaders to step away from self-centred temptations of power to feel more responsible. She found three interesting preconditions that helped keep those in power in check.

The first depends on how much the leader identifies with people in the group. This has to do with the concept of 'social identity theory' which is the now well-understood notion of how our self-identity links with how we fit into several groups. In my case I identify with other journalists, runners and basketball players. My husband has instant affinity with other football fans (specifically Arsenal) and filmmakers. We identify with groups who share our values, interests and even characteristics. In the study, participants were either given a managerial role or an assistant's role, where the manager oversaw the distribution of bonuses as well as the evaluation of the assistant's work. The team manipulated the levels of identification participants had with the group by highlighting certain factors about themselves and asking the 'managers' to remember positive and negative associations of being in that group. When a participant in power identified with those they had power over, it created the feeling of being a collective team and in turn resulted in feeling greater responsibility for them too.[9]

Scholl then showed that power-holders feel more responsible when attention is drawn to others, especially when taking someone else's perspective, meaning the focus is away from the self.[10] The work showed how influential the idea of the team being represented as 'us' and 'we' rather than 'you' and 'I' was. The old saying 'We're all in it together' is worth uttering as it reinforces group cohesion and takes away the tendency for those in power to put themselves first.

Her third condition was to do with proximity. Being in the room with someone else helped the leaders feel more responsible. Something interesting happens when there's greater physical distance between leaders and their subordinates. If a leader anticipates holding a virtual meeting, they are much more likely to be out of touch than if it is face to face. Out of sight is literally out of mind and shows the importance of face-to-face meetings for difficult conversations. We learn so much from others simply from body language and can bond over small talk. Depersonalisation through virtual meetings can strip away that key part of human social connection, and as the work shows, has a real impact in diminishing responsibility. It shows why large companies increasingly fire their staff digitally. Without the instant feedback of those in the room, they won't feel as accountable, and if they do care, doing it virtually can save them from feeling bad, though the company reputation will be at risk. Group virtual firings of employees have been rising in recent years, and these heartless practices tend to quickly spread on social media and might deter the very talent such companies want to attract in future.[11]

## EMPATHIC DISTRESS

It's also important to understand that while empathy can be a hidden superpower that helps us connect with others, there's a crucial skill we need to develop to avoid becoming overly empathetic, at which point empathy can become distressing. If we are witnessing prolonged suffering or pain, we can start to feel depressed or helpless, something called 'empathic distress'. This feeling is so strong that it can result in fatigue and complete withdrawal from the situation, which prevents us from helping someone who may need us.

One evening, my daughter burst into tears at bedtime and when asked what was wrong, said she felt so sorry for me because I had hurt myself and she couldn't stop thinking about it. I realised it was my job as a parent to help protect her from her heightened feelings of empathy, which can cause her to have such an intense and upsetting emotional response. Adults have similar responses and get better at controlling it, but seeing someone we care about in distress can cause us pain too. And because these feelings are painful, we find coping mechanisms to protect us. While empathy is crucial for healthy relationships, our own emotional state can significantly impact our ability to empathise with others. If we're constantly stressed or unhappy at work and we bring this negativity home, it may be difficult for our partner to continue to be empathetic longer term as it can become emotionally exhausting. It's worth understanding that while we can and should be able to lean on our partners for support, prolonged negativity can hinder empathic support and even lead to conflict.[12]

Empathic distress and the subsequent withdrawal blunts our ability to feel suffering as a self-protective mechanism. We saw this at play during the Covid-19 pandemic. Intense news interest spiked then tailed off as people experienced distress from reading about the scale of suffering. This same process explains why bosses can seem cold-hearted when you come to them with a problem – they simply don't have the time or resources to empathise with each new issue, because they have targets to hit, a strategy to implement and a large team to manage. Feeling overly empathetic would stop them getting the job done, especially because feeling empathy takes a lot of mental effort.

To avoid veering into empathic distress we can still be helpful, kind and understanding towards others by turning to compassion, characterised by showing warmth and concern for others. I recently had a dangerous complication which resulted in emergency abdominal surgery. The two days before the operation, I was in the most excruciating pain of my life – the type even morphine couldn't dampen. My husband sprang into action to get me the help I needed. Feeling overly empathetic might have reduced his help-fulness.

Compassion can protect us from empathic distress, whilst still showing we care. Rather than cause us negative feelings, compas-sion can help us become more prosocial, whilst still understanding what others are going through. If we feel compassion, we can sympathise instead of feeling sad ourselves and are therefore more likely to help others. One study found that individuals who had been trained in compassion were more likely to help strangers in a computer game. The more they had practised compassion, the more they helped. Crucially the brain also looks different during a compassionate response versus an empathy response. After compassion training, areas important for positive emotions were more active.[13]

The benefits of compassion training are plentiful: it helps us understand other cultures, religions and races. Even a short stint of compassion training teaches individuals to understand others without the associated distress. It's the difference between feeling sad when others are sad, versus concern and warmth towards them, making us more inclined to want to help.

The reason there's such a difference between two seemingly similar traits is because they are represented in different parts of the brain.[14] Leadership courses often have sections on listening skills as well as tuning in to others' feelings and perspectives, precisely because showing compassion has so many upsides. If you feel like you could benefit from increasing your compassion, be reassured that we can all do so, becoming better partners, parents and colleagues in the process – everyone likes to feel understood, after all.

The real-world implications are vast, especially because of our in-group bias. Clearly this same process applies when some-one in power views themselves as superior. If an individual in a relationship feels their career elevates them into a perceived superior position at home, especially if they earn more money, it can cause real conflict in a relationship. A charity worker earning a lot less than their lawyer partner might still want to further their career, but need the active support of their higher-earning partner to do so, especially if they have children. By being mindful of these patterns, we can prevent resentment building.

This can play out positively in relationships. Fran has always been the higher earner in her relationship. She works in recruitment and her partner used to work in retail. As they now have one child, her husband left his retail job as he worked long hours, and now works in an admin role from home that is much more flexible. He submitted a flexible working request to do so – which in the UK, as of 2024, employees can request from day one. This ensured his start time allowed him to drop their child off at school. They have invested in a cleaner to avoid squabbles over the load. Through communication and understanding, they have a system that helps to allow Fran to have the mental energy for her job. Understanding each other's needs has been crucial for them to get to this balance:

> My husband does almost all cooking and tidying up afterwards, all laundry, all gardening, any cleaning needed between the cleaner coming. Child sick days don't automatically fall to me; we decide based on who has less on that particular day. We have after-school care two to three days per week. I have the flexibility to pick my son up, but it was exhausting trying to do it five days a week and still get my work done (and also causing resentment that my husband could just work and not worry about it). When either of us start to feel resentful we know we need to review our situation, try to pinpoint what's causing it, and come up with a plan to address it. We don't pool finances completely – we started off contributing 50:50 to household bills then we moved to me contributing more.

Their relationship shows that by understanding each other's needs, Fran and her partner are able to achieve a balance in both their emotional and financial lives. The flexible work policies they rely on tend to improve employee satisfaction, as we can see in the Nordic countries, which are well known for labour laws that support flexibility and work-life balance. Many countries have followed suit to varying degrees – Germany, for instance, offers laws that protect part-time work, job shares and working remotely.

## EMOTIONAL SUPPRESSION

Given what we've learnt so far, it's clear that someone's emotional state shapes how we see them, even if it's not reflective of reality. Take our mood; when someone is happy we are more likely to perceive them as being both dominant and socially competent, whilst a person who looks sad or scared comes across as less dominant. Anger, however, makes someone appear less social but highly dominant. Of course, if we are enraged it's not possible to feign happiness, but being aware of how we come across is important. An awareness of how others react to our mood is also crucial. Our facial cues are so telling that even lowered eyebrows will make us look angrier (and dominant, which could be useful in certain situations). We should also bear in mind the phenomenon of the 'attractiveness halo', where attractive faces are judged as more powerful, more intelligent and healthier. The reason we respond this way to emotional expressions has an evolutionary basis – we have been primed to avoid angry people but to approach happier ones.[15] Again this goes to show that our emotional power is surprisingly potent, and one we can harness for good. While we can't force ourselves to feel happy if we are feeling angry, know that simply putting on a happy face can change our internal state too. This is called the 'facial feedback hypothesis', when a fake smile can cause a real, positive change in our mood. The old saying, 'Fake it till you make it' seems to apply to our emotional state too.[16]

\* \* \*

We've now seen how important our emotions are for reading others as well as how others perceive us. However, the irony is that when we lack power it leads us to suppress our true emotions. When we feel powerless, we are more prone to masking how we truly feel. This is a protective mechanism, so that we avoid any negative repercussions, but if it's a regular occurrence it causes an extremely toxic dynamic.

During conflicts between romantic partners, emerging research has shown that there are certain times we are more likely to suppress emotions than others. Those with lower power have been found to suppress their emotional responses but *only* if they felt their partner was unresponsive. On a more positive note, if their partner was responsive – that is, they showed signs of compassion, understanding and validation of their feelings – then the lower-power individual did not suppress their emotions. This is revealing and shows that power imbalances in a relationship can significantly affect how much of our true selves we show. And power imbalance diminishes when individuals feel that their partner genuinely understands and cares for them.[17] In cases where individuals did suppress their emotions, it was for self-preservation. If they felt genuinely misunderstood, as signified by a socially unresponsive partner, they would not feel safe to share their true feelings.

Take a scenario where you know you have been wronged. Perhaps your partner told you they would be home at six, but they only appeared at eight. If you felt you had lower power you might be less likely to express your anger, whereas if you had higher power you might explain how displeased you were – or even better, have laid out expectations early on to avoid any future conflict. Precisely because power-holders are the ones who can withhold or grant certain rewards, those with less power don't want to upset the balance and so suppress emotions. Clearly this can be hugely detrimental to a relationship because understanding each other is key for a balanced life. This is regularly apparent in cases of domestic violence. Rather than confront their partner, victims retreat in on themselves, learning to mask their emotions so as not to antagonise their abuser.

Understanding how our emotional response varies depending on whether or not we feel supported can help identify pain points in a relationship. If you consistently cannot express your true feelings, it's a clear indication that the power balance within your relationship is unhealthy and would benefit from being redressed. However, if you feel you are the more powerful one, think about how your position affects your partner; do they adapt to your lifestyle rather than put themselves first? Are they pursuing your goals more than their own – the goal contagion phenomenon we heard about earlier? If you think they are, check in with them, ask which aspects of themselves are tied with your identity versus their own. Unlocking our emotional response to our position of power at home is a quick way to check how our power, or lack of it, is affecting us emotionally. Try it and see what happens.

## KEY POINTS:

- Our emotional state affects how much empathy we feel with others. If we are in a negative state, we care less about others' pain, but if our empathy response is working well it can strengthen relationships.
- Our emotions are contagious and can easily affect others. This can be positive or negative as our emotions can cloud how we view others.
- Leaders who express positive emotions to their team tend to have more cooperative staff who perform better.

## ACTION POINTS:

- Train yourself to feel compassion by tuning in to how others feel. Responsible leaders tend to be more empathetic, and we can encourage responsibility by thinking of ourselves as part of the team.

- Don't assume your emotions are felt by your partner too or assume they understand what you are feeling.
- Consider how the power you have over others can mask what emotions they express. If you have high power, you are less likely to be attuned to the emotions of those beneath you, while those who feel powerless are more likely to hide their true feelings.

# 10

## POWERFUL LEADERS: WHY KIND LEADERS FINISH FIRST

'What greater wisdom is there than kindness?'

—Jean-Jacques Rousseau

If having power helps us influence others, we can do spades of this in the workplace, whatever level we are at. It's common for more junior staff to feel anxious and to worry about saying the right thing whilst also trying to impress. I recall this most vividly as a 23-year-old in a morning newsroom meeting, pitching stories to appear on national news. The editor would discuss the top news stories of the day and the team was encouraged to suggest story ideas. Worried about coming across as ignorant, initially I rarely pitched anything. Later on in my career I had the confidence and experience to frequently offer suggestions even if I didn't feel like an expert. When I read about 'pluralistic ignorance' I realised this may have been at play. This is where we mistakenly believe others think differently to us, when actually we may be thinking the same thing – others in the newsroom may have been just as nervous as me. Awareness of my own skills (and knowledge gaps) completely changed the way I approach conversations. Instead of being worried about how I come across, I'm curious about what the other person says.

There are studies which may help you not to worry about looking stupid in front of others: it's been shown that we overestimate how much others judge any errors or social mishaps.[1] Most people like other people and don't think too deeply about an innocent social faux pas. I remember profusely apologising twice when I had called someone the wrong name. In reality, they probably didn't really mind, just as I don't mind if someone admits they've forgotten my name – unless it's a repeated occurrence, of course.

What this reveals about power dynamics is that while we may worry about speaking up about a complicated task, because we think we will be judged, it's better to admit we need help than spend hours agonising and consequently delivering a project late. The very power dynamics at play that prevent us from asking for help are actually the same ones that mean we'd be judged more harshly for being slow and 'failing' if our boss isn't aware of our workload in the first place. As we heard, people in power are prone to thinking of the bigger picture rather than considering the details. We can teach our superiors to see our perspective by over-communicating the details involved, and each time we do so, we'll learn more and need help less often.

## SURVIVORSHIP BIAS

If we want to understand how leaders think, it helps to first consider common flaws in our perception, especially when it comes to defining success.

It was the early 1940s and the Second World War was in full swing, with catastrophic casualties occurring on the ground and in the air. It created an urgent need to rapidly advance aircraft technology, so that the latest versions could be deployed to bomb the enemy. Of course, as is the nature of war, many were still shot down and many lives were lost.

To understand more about what makes a plane vulnerable, a statistician named Abraham Wald was tasked by the US military with figuring out improvements. His team looked at returning planes to see which parts had the most damage and could do with being reinforced in later models. The theory was that damage exposed a weakness that could be improved. Wald looked at the problem differently. He figured out that the damaged planes that returned were not the ones that showed weaknesses – in fact, these planes had managed to return despite significant damage from bullet holes. He reasoned that his team should instead focus on the planes that didn't return. These planes might have been hit at the exact areas that made them weak, whereas the planes that made it back were the survivors. He had realised that to see the full picture, it's the missing data that's the most important. And in this case the missing data was lost with the planes behind enemy lines.

Only looking at success without considering the hidden failures along the way is a phenomenon known as 'survivorship bias'. If we only consider the survivor, we are missing all the failures. It's a common cognitive shortcut we use when considering successful people, and it's a bias that leaders have too. It's tempting to try and learn how successful people made it and attempt to emulate their success. If we didn't try, we wouldn't stand a chance, but it's also worth remembering that the chances of reaching the top in many fields is rare. This is important to understand when considering power dynamics in the workplace because it highlights that we are bad at judging the path to success. If we don't look at the whole picture, it could hinder the very progress we are trying to make. We can look at someone like Bill Gates, who didn't finish university, and think it shows that being a college drop-out can lead to success, when the reality is there are many more college drop-outs who won't ever come close to being an entrepreneur. Even when we are aware of survivorship bias, those in power have an alluring effect on us and we might mistakenly try to copy them and think we'll achieve similar success.

## POWERFUL BOSSES, POWERLESS STAFF

To avoid being overpowered, we need to understand the common power dynamics at play at work. Let's start with a simple scenario: if you've ever had an email from a manager asking for a 'quick catch-up' meeting, but without a topic to discuss, you'll know the resulting whirlwind of feelings you can experience. If your role is going incredibly well, you might think you're finally getting the recognition you deserve. At other times, you might wonder whether you've done anything wrong; did you pay close enough attention to detail on that last report? Small events suddenly start looming as potential for criticism. It's what the psychologist Adam Galinsky calls the 'leader amplification effect'. A quick catch-up sounds benign to a leader, but can be amplified in the employee's mind to any number of things. Galinsky explains:

> Leaders are often unaware that they are on a metaphorical stage. They overlook the fact that what they say and how they say it – their casual glances, their incidental shifts in posture – are intensely scrutinised and analysed. They are blind to their outsized impact in shaping the psychological experience of others. In short, bosses think they are whispering, when their workers experience them as shouting.[2]

It works the other way around too: to get the most out of your own leaders, be clear about what you want in a catch-up. By managing upwards in this way, it gives us more power over the choices we present, and managers usually respond well to proactive suggestions and ideas. If they like to have the final say, suggest options that work well for you too. They have so much to think about that they can't always create individualised, detailed action plans.

## DON'T INTERRUPT BUT DO LISTEN

Now take another scenario. Consider how often you've been in a social interaction where it's hard to get a word in, or where you feel constantly interrupted. Maybe you are the one who talks more. Maybe you are the interrupter (if so, take stock at a next team meeting and perhaps count to three before speaking). In many conversations there is often one person who dominates. This can be subtle – such as body posture – or more overt – time spent talking. The most obvious forms of conversational dominance is interruption. We are such social creatures and conversation is an important part of bonding, meaning we are particularly sensitive to being interrupted as it can stop a conversation in its tracks, which can impede social connection.

Think about how effortless it is to talk to your best friends, and how well they listen. The best managers also tend to be good listeners. Many studies show this link: for instance, good leaders who have high emotional intelligence are also active listeners,[3] and listening creates more satisfied employees, resulting in lower employee turnover and higher engagement.[45] The reasons are fairly simple: humans like being heard and valued, and by actively listening we can get to the bottom of any concerns or stresses before they escalate further. Listening is a sign that we are paying attention to what's important. A conflict or stress might sound like no big deal to you, but for someone more junior it might be occupying their mind after work hours too. If you want to create a harmonious relationship, listen to each other.

Similarly, managers: if you want to retain your talent, be sure to listen to your staff. If they don't have much to say, think about asking some more open-ended questions. 'How are you doing?' could open the floor to much more than 'How is your project going?' They can choose to answer about work, or perhaps something else that is on their mind that's preventing them from performing at their best. A particularly good manager I had, used to open with 'What's on your mind?' meaning I felt able to talk about work stresses or anything else that was affecting me. Even though I hesitated to share anything personal, I knew that if I did, I would be listened to.

## THE BABBLE EFFECT

Conversations are often guided by social norms: we are much more likely to interrupt a friend than someone in a more obvious position of power. However, if we are on equal footing and someone asserts more conversational power, problems can begin. If you've ever spoken to a friend or colleague who goes on and on in a rambling monologue, it can feel very one-sided and you start to wonder when you might get a word in. It's a hugely frustrating experience because in conversations that flow, people tend to take turns. Psychologists call it 'conversational rule breaking' when someone regularly interrupts. It can be benign, but it can also be a form of dominance or control. And the latter often occurs when a leader is out of touch with their audience. It's even been found that people who speak the most are more likely to be promoted to leadership positions, rather than those who are most competent, the so-called 'babble hypothesis', where we are prone to misjudging people's conversational dominance as competence.[6] So listen to colleagues and leaders around you, and consider whether they are elevating the needs of the group or simply speaking the loudest and most often.

As well as kindness, clear communication is crucial in leadership, but what else makes the most effective and powerful leader without veering into the more negative aspects of power we heard about? The first aspect, which has been shown repeatedly, is likeability. When I first started managing a small team, I worried about shifting from a colleague and friend to manager, thinking I had to become more distant and authoritative to lead a team effectively. One aspect is true: it's hard to maintain the same friendships with colleagues if you are managing them, because the power balance has so obviously shifted. While being authoritative can be useful at times, it doesn't mean being unapproachable, mean or strict. A manager can be both kind and commanding. In one analysis of over 50,000 leaders based on 360-degree feedback data, being unlikeable was found to be detrimental. While you can be unlikeable and be an effective leader, it's improbable; only 27 of the *least likeable* were found to be effective leaders.[7] People won't necessarily know whether or not they are liked, and many under-estimate their own likeability, as we've heard, but there are methods we can all employ to become more likeable. This is especially important for leaders, because the liking gap doesn't seem to be at play for the most powerful, as leaders were found to rate themselves as more likeable than they were rated by colleagues. The authors noted that when leaders ask for advice and feedback, they become more effective. If you ask your subordinates what you could improve on, they'll feel heard and appreciated. If you listen to them, they will likely also show more loyalty and feel more invested in the project overall. Other aspects that increase likeability include:

- Positive emotional interactions with others.
- Showing integrity.
- Working and cooperating with colleagues.
- Being available to coach and mentor your team.
- Inspiring your team (leading by example).
- Focusing on the future and showing bigger-picture thinking.

This tallies with other leadership research. A study led by the psychologist Jonathan Haidt found that when leaders were perceived to be fair and showed self-sacrifice (by prioritising their teams' interests over their own) their employees showed more 'moral elevation' – meaning warmth and admiration. It gets better too: simply by being exposed to this feeling of moral elevation after watching a video, individuals focused more on others than themselves and reported wanting to be a better person and perform acts of kindness for others. We heard in Chapter 5 that nice people finish first, and the same can be said of leaders. Kindness in leadership is not only inspiring, but self-perpetuating. It could even be hormonal – when we feel morally good, oxytocin, the feel-good hormone, increases.[8] Without kindness, a powerful leader quickly alienates themselves.

## WHEN LEADERS SACRIFICE

The self-sacrifice could be something simple; it might be the editor taking the blame for an error on an article, rather than pointing out which employee made the mistake, or worse, publicly shaming them. The person at fault will know it and appreciate feeling protected. It could be something bolder, like a company owner taking a pay cut. The benefits are clear, an inspiring leader can lead to greater job satisfaction and more productivity as a result.

Take Tim Reeves, the ex-CEO of a small rural hospital in Pennsylvania, Bucktail Medical Center. The hospital had faced years of financial difficulties, and in one drastic moment Reeves dipped into his personal savings to provide an interest-free loan of $50,000. Without his loan, critical services would have been at risk due to lack of funds. He documented the concerns about his hospital's finances on the popular podcast 'This American Life', broadcast at the start of December 2023. It was his style of leadership that intrigued me. Reeves tells me he was the type of CEO who didn't dress in a suit or tie, he was approachable, and proud to serve his small community of around 3,000 people. As for his $50,000, he reckons he might never get it back but had been prepared for that scenario. He speaks about it pragmatically; if he hadn't done it, would his staff have been paid? He isn't sure. What's clear is that the responsibility he felt for his team and for the community took a toll on his health and he resigned shortly before we spoke. We heard about how responsible leaders are more at risk of stress precisely because they care, and Reeves is a case in point of that playing out. He cared so much it ultimately cost him his job. 'I certainly understood the risks better than anyone else, but I also believe in the commitment the staff had demonstrated to do what was necessary to keep the facility moving forwards. It needs to be here, if it's not here, people are going to die.' Self-sacrifice can come at a cost, but can also bolster a person's status.

## DO NICE LEADERS FINISH LAST?

If kindness is inspirational and gets the most out of staff, I struggle to reconcile the anecdotal instances of kind people coming last and of being overlooked for promotion because of being 'too nice'. Many workplace cultures still value what are seen as stereotypically masculine traits that many people, men and women alike, don't have. It's also true that those with dominant personalities are more likely to seek positions of power in the first place. We've all heard about women being passed over for promotion, but I've also heard of instances where men were overlooked for being 'too nice', despite being extremely competent. Even though kindness can get the best out of employees, leaders often believe they have to act more authoritatively. In a recent poll of over 4,500 people, about half said they would quit their job if they didn't like their manager, and over a third said they would stop feeling motivated to work productively.[9] Bad managers are terrible news all round. Toxic workplaces lead to disgruntled staff and can exacerbate the risk of burnout. The stress individuals feel at being at the bottom of a hierarchy can be so detrimental it can contribute to heart disease,[10] while positive workplaces have more productive and happier staff.[11]

It's not surprising that many power-holders act in their own self-interest when you consider that many of us are primed to desire status and power. The very act of drawing someone's attention to their achievements can then suppress their helpfulness, and bosses on the hedonic treadmill become less helpful as a result. Whilst we know that kindness matters, dominant, authoritative bosses find it harder to enact this trait. However, if you highlight their benevolence, helpfulness goes up.[12]

In a culture that heavily values achievement, it's no wonder that individuals can become more self-serving, and the seed for this is sown early on. A study of Dutch children revealed that those who showed narcissistic traits were more likely to be leaders in their class and to perceive themselves as superior, though their leadership was not particularly effective. We see similar results in adulthood too.[13] There are some slight cultural variations, though, as narcissism scores are higher in individualistic cultures compared with collectivistic cultures. One recent study looked at the impact of cultural differences on narcissism and self-esteem in Germany. It compared individuals who grew up in former East Germany (more collectivistic) and West Germany (more individualistic). West Germans had higher levels of narcissism than East, while also having lower self-esteem.[14] The reason for these differences could be because 'narcissistic self-focus may be viable during economically prosperous times (West Germany) and tempered by economic recession'.

## THE SECRET TO LIKEABLE LEADERS

There is a way for all of us to act with more kindness, especially if we find ourselves drawn to power or dominance. If we see power as responsibility, it can change everything. It triggers an awareness that, in any power tussle, someone is responsible. Parents feel responsibility for their children, which regularly prompts them to put their children's interests above their own, and bosses who feel responsible for the well-being of their employees will think about their staff more than those who don't.

The same goes for when communication breaks down in a marriage. Both sides are responsible for fixing a problematic power dynamic, but unfortunately, thinking about power as responsibility is not easy given that power can corrupt. Still, feeling responsible remains crucial for effective leadership, and will in turn create a more cohesive team. On the other hand, being an ambivalent supervisor leads to higher stress and exhaustion among staff.

Frustratingly, being a responsible leader is more stressful. One study found that leaders who see power as having 'responsibility' compared to the more self-serving idea of opportunity, are more stressed.[15] The risk of burnout, especially for middle managers, remains high. They aren't senior enough to be out of touch but are exactly the type who have to ensure the well-being of those beneath them, making them more predisposed to burnout.[16]

So, kindness and feeling responsible can clearly elevate leaders and their staff, but what else? How can we change the narrative to encourage the sort of power that inspires, rather than that which dictates? It helps to remember that we can influence the power balance in many situations. Think about the last person who inspired you. Now think about someone who made you feel angry. What was it about those two opposing influences that either makes you smile, or feel angry to this day? This is the leader amplification effect in action. Because leaders are in a position of power, how they speak and behave has more influence than they are aware of. 'The attention they receive, coupled with the power they wield, means their actions have an immediate and amplified impact on their employees,' writes Galinsky.[17] The worst effects are when leaders shout, issue threats or utter derogatory comments, all of which affect employee performance. We heard earlier how our own mindset can change how we experience the world. Couple this with emotional contagion and it goes some way to explaining the amplification effect. A leader's mindset can influence how we experience day-to-day life, precisely because their actions and attitude are amplified.

Early in my career, as a junior employee in the live TV newsroom, editors would frequently bark commands at junior producers. Shouting at a junior staff member won't magically make an interviewee appear faster. The editors I remembered most fondly were calmer and tended to think of other solutions – the bigger-picture view, I now realise. Galinsky found that most bosses aren't aware of how their words, and even their posture, cause so much impact. That shouting editor was probably shouted at when they were starting out too. But as stressed employees tend to be less creative and motivated, shouting at them doesn't benefit anyone. Galinsky found that the most inspiring leaders are generous, courageous and see the bigger picture, while infuriating leaders are the exact opposite: selfish, cowardly and can become stuck in the weeds. If you've ever dealt with a micromanager this will likely resonate. To inspire others, we have to empower them in the first place, be likeable and feel responsible.

The best advice I got when I started leading a team was to consider how to influence my superiors with 'upwards management'. Do the tasks you anticipate need doing, or present options, which means your boss needs to exert less mental energy when it comes to delegating work. I always made sure I had several interesting projects on the go that I believed my boss would approve of, so they wouldn't instruct me to work on topics that were less appealing. To do this successfully first requires figuring out priorities and goals to make sure you are delivering what is expected. In my case, it worked. When I had no formal workplace power, I created my own, which gave me more job satisfaction and meant I worked hard to maintain the autonomy I had carved out for myself. With that autonomy I delivered stories I was passionate about.

There's another way to influence upwards. Being kind to your superior can make them more helpful towards you too. When supervisors feel appreciated, they also experience higher job satisfaction, are more optimistic and in turn, helpful. This can apply at any level, whether you are a leader yourself or are still relatively junior.[18] This can then become a sort of kindness loop, where kindness begets kindness.

## THE POWER TANGO AND HUBRISTIC LEADERS

Researching the ways people can learn to be kinder, more inspiring and more influential, one thing stood out for me. What about the individuals who use their positions of power for illicit personal gain, or the misconduct that gets shrugged aside, or the misogynistic remarks that don't seem to have consequences? It is surprisingly common for those in power to overstep boundaries and leverage their power for their own immoral gains. Researchers call this the 'power tango'. As people are transformed by having power, they can become intoxicated by it, meaning they are more likely to take risks and break rules, even to the point of defying social norms (like the wealthy car drivers we heard about). But just as people become intoxicated by their own power, other people become entranced by those in power. Our tendency to admire those who are more powerful can lead us to overlook both minor misdemeanours and more serious illegal activities.

For instance, it's well established that people in power feel more able to cheat and take what is not theirs. In one cunning study there was a bowl of sweets outside the experiment with a sign indicating they were for children. Many people will sneak a sweet from a jar if they can get away with it. However, the participants who had rated themselves as wealthier (a proxy for power) took double the amount of sweets after they walked out of the study compared to those who scored lower on power. Even my six-year-old knows it's wrong to take someone else's things, but that moral compass can clearly easily be corrupted.[19]

Of course, it can seem as though some powerful individuals can get away with abusing power for years. That may be so, but only up to a point; their influence cannot endure. One analysis looking at US presidents and UK prime ministers over a 100-year period called the type of corruption that comes from bad leadership 'hubris syndrome', characterised by 'exaggerated pride, overwhelming self-confidence and contempt for others'.[20] Worse, the analysis suggests the very trigger of 'hubris syndrome' is power, and in many cases, declining power, especially if the individual had limitless power for many years. Many dictators neatly fit this bill. The analysis, which was aptly co-authored by ex-politician Lord David Owen, reported that anyone who gains power can be affected. Take the hubris of those who contributed to the 2008 financial crash. They were certainly taking more risks with other people's money without carefully considering the consequences.

While those affected by abuses of power may be unlikely to seek help or retribution, others around them can. With enough action, there are consequences. Several Enron leaders served prison time, Harvey Weinstein was convicted of historical sexual offences, and Jeffrey Epstein and Ghislaine Maxwell were imprisoned for sex trafficking. So, while power affords some protection for bad behaviour, when power corrupts absolutely, a consequent downfall becomes increasingly likely.

Fortunately, views around leadership are evolving. It was once defined by dominance, assertiveness and micromanagement, but in many places that is outdated. If you are lucky, good leadership consists of regular communication, empathy and understanding. If demands by staff are changing, it should level the playing field with regards to who can be elevated into a leadership position. And while the will is there, and public attitudes are changing, other barriers need to be knocked down too. We need to untangle workplace needs and leadership assumptions, and reduce how much we value competitive self-interest at work, as well as realise that workers have commitments outside the office. We also need to understand that group norms influence how likely we are to act. If we are working for overly dominant or controlling bosses, we may say nothing if we think others respect them. People misperceive how others view a bad boss unless enough people speak up too.[21] Hopefully everything you've read in this chapter will help you speak up when needed in order to hold those in power to account.

## KEY POINTS:

- Looking only at the most successful people risks us forgetting all those who failed on the way. We need to consider the whole picture so as not to fall victim to 'survivorship bias'.
- The leader amplification effect means that leaders can become blind to their impact and under-estimate how closely their words

and actions are scrutinised.

- Leaders who ask for honest feedback and who listen to their employees will have more loyal and happy staff and will even become more likeable.
- Influencing upwards is a powerful technique to get ahead when you have relatively little power. You can do this by being kind to your superiors as well as anticipating the tasks that need doing before being asked.

## ACTION POINTS:

- Listen to those around you, especially if they are more junior, and ask them for feedback.
- Appreciate your supervisors; showing gratitude can make them more helpful towards their employees.
- Don't interrupt people, especially if you are in a greater position of power. Men especially, do take note when female colleagues are interrupted, call this out and give everyone a chance to speak equally.

# 11

## BREATHE, RELAX, EMPOWER: PUSHING FOR CHANGE IN AN UNEQUAL WORLD

'All animals are equal, but some are more equal than others.'
—George Orwell

Mary M has just had her third baby. She's tired, as most parents are, but she feels energised about her career. She featured at the start of this book and her story highlights that it takes effort and conscious awareness to make home dynamics more equal. This can pay off. She was aware of the issues that female breadwinners face but ensured that invisible power did not push her into doing more caring at home, despite being the primary breadwinner. For her this included stepping back in the kitchen, educating herself about the mental load, and communicating her needs to her partner.

We've now heard from several people who, like Mary, have consciously come to terms with imbalanced power as higher earners. Some employ strategies that improve their relationships while others experience stress, resentment and an increased workload at home. The common factors that increase well-being in these cases include a strong emphasis on communication, understanding mutual goals, and chasing autonomy.

I've condensed the findings from this book into 10 key guiding principles that can help you foster better dynamics in your personal and professional lives, hopefully inspiring the next generation in the process. Some may sound simple, but in our busy lives it's easy to overlook the basic tools we can use to confront obvious imbalances and make meaningful change. Awareness isn't enough, it needs to result in action too.

Here are 10 tools you can use to empower yourself at work and home:

1. Over-communicate
2. Harness empathy and compassion
3. Undo assumptions and don't blindly imitate
4. Be aware of stereotypes
5. Value care-work
6. Share the mental load
7. Understand our inbuilt sense of fairness
8. Know your own goals
9. Prime your brain to be less stressed
10. Understand what drives power

## 1. OVER-COMMUNICATE

Katty Kay, the well-known BBC news presenter, is the primary breadwinner in her relationship, but it wasn't always the case. She started earning more about 15 years ago, in her mid-40s. Both she and her partner had already established their careers by this point. They have four children, the youngest of whom was then three. Kay was in a high-profile role that required regular travel to interview public figures. This meant her career had to be put first. When she wasn't able to pick up sick children from school, she was still called first, a common experience among breadwinner women. Something had to change, but she wasn't sure how to begin. Their working patterns had changed gradually but without vocalising the stress points, meaning she started to feel resentment:

> Our kids were still quite young, and for the first months of a year we didn't really have a conversation about it, about what this meant for my schedule and his schedule and what that meant to me in terms of expectations at home. That was a

real mistake. My advice to anybody who finds themselves in this situation would be [to] talk about it as soon as it happens, because otherwise it kind of creeps up on you and resentment and confusion builds up.

As she hadn't communicated what she needed, her husband, Tom, thought he was already doing more than his fair share. He came from a family where his dad had never organised a playdate, called a doctor or packed a lunchbox, meaning 'he had no role model for being a partner who didn't earn more than their spouse'. Kay needed him to do more than 50% because her role took her out of the house more. After discussions, there were noticeable improvements. It wasn't all plain-sailing, she recalls, but he quickly took on all the organisation around school, including homework, attending plays and going to parents' evenings. It's harder, she says, when couples start out more traditionally, but then the female partner becomes more successful and starts earning more, giving her a higher status outside the home. 'I really have a lot of empathy for men in this situation and for how incredibly hard it is for them to get out of the very narrow lane that they are cast into.'

For these reasons, acknowledging and discussing the resulting changes are crucial for relationship satisfaction, as well as showing compassion and empathy to your partner, communicating when things get hard, and *why* they feel hard. After all, it's socially accepted for women to be stay-at-home mothers, part-time workers, career-focused or anything in between, in a way that it is not for men. It's why Kay describes men like her husband as the 'sandwich generation', who sit between their very traditional parents and a generation of men who are becoming more likely to earn less than their partners, and where it's slowly becoming more accepted for them to work flexibly and prioritise family life without judgement.

We should see a real shift soon, with men caring more as the rise of female breadwinners continues. When men are doing, as Kay says, the 'boring daily organisation of children's lives', children will grow up seeing that their dads are fully capable of organising and running a household and will hopefully expect nothing less if they have children themselves. In the previous generation there was even less acceptance of men being anything but breadwinners, but today's sons of stay-at-home dads will grow up with role models who show that caring can be a part of a man's identity just as it can for women.

Evidently, certain traits we model do transmit to the next generation. Children of stay-at-home fathers who actively partic-ipate in caregiving and playtime, and who respond warmly to their emotions, have been shown to have positive parent–child relationships with strong bonds.[1] This is linked to the fact that dads are spending more time with their children compared to 50 years ago, making fatherhood increasingly central to a man's identity.[2]

To communicate effectively, don't try to make a change in the heat of the moment when a conflict arises, but do so in advance. Divide tasks, understand compromises, and understand what role personality might play. Extroverts tend to be more dominant and forceful, for instance, and may not realise they are exerting power over others. We should also remember that dominant personality traits tend to seek greater power, so understanding the role of personality in communication styles will also help.

## 2. HARNESS EMPATHY AND COMPASSION

Building on the first principle of communication, a key part of understanding what and how to communicate is knowing how someone is feeling in the first place. That's why we can all benefit from honing our empathy skills and harnessing compas-sion, and when we do, we're more likely to feel responsible for the outcome. We've heard a lot about how power reduces empathy, meaning that those of us in positions of power risk losing sight of what matters to others. Those with higher earn-ings – which intersect with power – can also show reduced empathy, as shown in the study where higher earners were worse at accurately interpreting facial expressions compared to lower earners.[3] This is problematic because the higher earners tend to have the most power. If we know how our partner or colleague is feeling, we will better be able to anticipate their needs. If we feel affinity with a team we manage, we will feel more responsible for their well-being, which makes for a more compassionate leader. As we heard in Chapter 9, we can train ourselves to cultivate compassion. This is vital whether in a professional or personal setting. Responsible leaders are more likely to take on unpleasant tasks,[4] and prioritise team and community goals over personal ones. If you are already an 'other orientated' person, power enhances this trait and you will likely feel more responsibility too. Another factor, which we can also self-enhance, is the degree to which you identify with the organisation or group. The more you identify with others, the more compassionate you will feel.

Discussing responsibility early on matters too. One study found that when CEOs didn't mention responsibility in a job interview, they were seen by employees as despotic leaders who prioritised their own interests.[5] Individuals who naturally gravitate towards responsibility, as well as those with early exposure to it – say from looking after young siblings – tend to channel power more positively. Feeling responsible has also been shown to lessen some of power's negative effects, including risky decisions.[6]

And crucially, we've seen that physical proximity matters. We are more likely to feel empathetic and responsible for those we can physically see. This is important to understand, given that many of us work in hybrid roles with less facetime, meaning we take part in less office chit-chat and, as a consequence, are less likely to learn about each other's lives.

## 3. UNDO ASSUMPTIONS AND DON'T BLINDLY IMITATE

We are an extremely impressionable species. Our ancestors survived by adopting the traits and habits of those around them because life was precarious and dangerous. Today we still do this, we conform to group norms and ideas, even if our own intuition says otherwise. Take the famous experiment from the 1950s where Solomon Asch influenced participants to say a line was of equal length to the line beside it, even though it was obviously a different size. Individuals conformed to group answers rather than believing their own eyes. This happens in much more subtle ways every day, as we are prone to multiple cognitive blind spots that affect how we see reality. The many biases we've explored occur precisely because everyday decisions are heavily influenced by group norms and stereotypes. We see this play out in assumptions around female breadwinners, financial divisions and intergenerational norms. These assumptions have real-world impacts. A 2023 US poll found that only 2% of respondents support the idea that children are better off with fathers at home and mothers at work, while one in five (19%) said it's best for fathers to work and mothers to focus on the home. The majority (77%) supported both parents working.[7]

Female breadwinners are still not as socially accepted as male breadwinners, but the positive here is that most support both parents working, which wasn't the case a few decades ago. As recently as 2014 a survey found that just over half the respondents' believed children were better off if their mother stayed home.[8] This shows that, as family dynamics change, so can attitudes. In another decade that 2% support for fathers at home is bound to rise.

Just as we value power outside the home, we need to recognise and value it inside too. We can and should enable women to prioritise breadwinning and support men to lean out. We need to stop criticising men and devaluing their effort at home, but instead divide and conquer the mental load so that women don't continue to have 'faux power' at home. In turn, we need to stop assuming that women are better at managing the home – something male managers have said of their female partners despite project management being a core part of their own careers. If someone can manage complex projects involving multiple stakeholders, detailed research and regular communication, then they can research party favours, dental practices and dry-cleaners, all the while anticipating when tasks need doing rather than being reminded. Both intrinsic motivation and external expectations are crucial to make this a reality. The assumption of who does what needs to be discussed earlier on to avoid imbalanced patterns that fuel resentment. And remember, nobody is especially good at multitasking. Our brains can literally only focus fully on one task at hand. Anyone who looks like they are multitasking is simply doing many things in short succession, often at the expense of something else such as job hunting or updating their CV.

If we were to take everyone we meet at face value, rather than comparing them to outdated expectations, we wouldn't be subject to as many of the negative attitudes towards lower-earning men or higher-earning women. If we were to make our own rules about how to live rather than conform to group expectations, we'd feel more powerful too. We'd smoke less, not be swayed by extreme ideologies, we'd believe scientific facts and know when to query data that doesn't look right, and ultimately, we'd be more in control of our own minds.

## 4. BE AWARE OF STEREOTYPES

We've explored how to be a good partner, friend and leader, as well as which aspects we can control. Gender shouldn't affect who holds power, but because of how we are socialised, it does, in a vicious cycle, with power causing many gender and racial imbalances. It's therefore important to acknowledge the role stereotypes play, especially as we are instantly judged based on our appearance as well as our gender, race and culture.

Women are judged on their appearance more than men and one consequence is that how we look impacts upon our perceived leadership potential. Attractive individuals are often seen as more employable, rated as smarter, and have higher lifetime earnings.[9] People with baby faces are seen as more trustworthy and warm, but also as less authoritative.[10] When it comes to leadership positions, one study found that attractive men, but not women, were seen as trustworthy, loyal leaders, meaning that attractive women can be penalised simply for how they look.[11] Meanwhile, a study comparing the faces of Fortune 500 company CEOs to other comparable faces, found that the facial profile consistent with leadership was a white 'competent looking' man.[12] To pinpoint the absurdity of a lack of representation at the top, in 2018 my colleagues took the top 100 CEOs from the Fortune 500 companies and compiled them into one composite image, which looked like, you guessed it, a white male.[13] Clearly we are stereotyped for leadership simply based on how we look, but how we look is not necessarily linked to our competence. As Susan Fiske showed with her work on stereotypes, how we pigeonhole individuals is not only harmful, but can be discriminatory.

Diversity in the top 500 companies *is* improving, but our biases need to play catch-up. To ensure we don't fall into this facial-appearance bias, we should objectively consider experience. We all have implicit biases, but taking a moment to check that our stereotypes aren't overriding a person's character or influencing our interpretation of their behaviour can be a first step to overcoming them. Second, an awareness of the many biases we have will help find better candidates, and not favour a subgroup unfairly just because they look more confident than others or are part of our in-group, which might activate our affinity bias, our hidden tendency to favour those most like us.

Another empowering message to understand about many of the cognitive biases we've discussed is that we can use this understanding for our own benefit. We can train ourselves to appear more competent than we actually feel. Our mind's predictive process will then start to make us act and feel more confident too. Whilst it's infuriating to learn that we are judged on aspects of ourselves we cannot control, everything you've read so far should help arm you to override erroneous first impressions.

## 5. VALUE CARE-WORK

We've heard about how we are primed to compete with others, and that those with dominant personalities are more predisposed to seek leadership positions. That said, it is men, not women, who are expected to act more dominant, priming them with a double whammy of 'predisposed breadwinner' and competitive norms – an expectation that harms female breadwinners as well as men who aren't the main earners.

Unfortunately, many of us are taught to act competitively at work, which could be a key reason why we value certain professions over caring. When we compete in the workplace it can elevate our status and give us more power, resulting in pay rises and promotions. There are no such obvious rewards for care-work. 'It is easy to figure out who won the deal, the lawsuit, the sales contract and compensate the winner accordingly. It is much harder, as teachers and education reformers both know, to measure learning outcomes,' writes Anne-Marie Slaughter.[14] Although we can measure performance with tests, socioemotional skills do not fit neatly into boxes that can be studied. It's sensitive caregiving and a balanced relationship that leaves an important impression on children. It's even been proposed that children who experienced an insecure (anxious or avoidant) attachment growing up, later have an unhealthy predisposition to seeking power, and are more prone to self-serving behaviours, while those with secure attachments are more likely to use power to help others.[15] It's not that sensitive caregiving isn't possible if one parent is working late, but solo parenting is more stressful so the one at home may have depleted mental resources.

On a societal level, until we value care-work as something both parents do, it will continue to be deprioritised financially and socially. If we equate masculinity with caregiving, it will be a more positive experience for stay-at-home dads, and they won't continue to be held to outdated standards. Nobody acts surprised if a woman scales down her career for her children, and until our children see both parents caring, these stereotypes will persist.

To change that mindset we need action, and it's starting slowly. My colleague Dan was one of the early adopters of taking fully paid paternity leave when his second child was born. For his firstborn, a daughter, his wife found it very isolating in the early days – he took two weeks' leave with two weeks' statutory pay, not enough time, he felt, to bond.

When his son was born, the BBC had implemented paid parental leave of 18 weeks. The difference was monumental. Dan was able to bond with his son as well as taking a more active role in his daughter's care. Supportive leadership made him feel able to step away from work with no repercussions. At home, childcare is a lot more equal too, though he acknowledges tasks are still very gendered – he does repairs and his wife does more housework. Perhaps most importantly, and a key reason he wanted to be more present, is the bond he's noticed with his five-year-old. He's therefore keen to continue to be as present as possible even when he returns to work:

> I want to make sure I still have that time, both with [my daughter] and [my son], where I have a bit of just me-and-them time. I feel really strongly that everyone who has the opportunity to take parental leave should do it for numerous reasons. You cannot get that time back when they're so small, and they go through so many changes and grow so much every single month of that first six months of their life, that if you get an opportunity not to miss that and to be part of that, you know it's only going to benefit you as a dad, you as a family and your partner.

Lots of men may want to take more leave but policy hasn't caught up, and unless it does, it's women picking up the slack, often at a detriment to their careers. If we want to live in a world where it's acceptable for men to demand more flexibility at work, to take paternity leave and be welcomed into parenting groups, we need to value caregiving roles in men and women equally, and at the same time, support higher-earning women. If this happens, we'll slowly be able to uncouple male self-esteem from the pressure to be the sole provider as stay-at-home dads Alex and Steve have done.

Men taking on care-work not only redistributes labour at home but can affect their idea of what masculinity means. So, check your work policies, demand change if nothing exists, and call to mind examples to convince your employer to follow suit. Retaining good staff is vital to a company, and employees who have a positive work-life balance are likely to remain more loyal too.

## 6. SHARE THE MENTAL LOAD

Women still do more housework than men, despite the fact that a survey of over 6,000 UK respondents found that the majority felt that it should be equally shared.[16] On the plus side, only 9% agreed with the outdated idea that 'A man's job is to earn money and a woman's job to look after the home', compared to 48% in 1980. This survey exposes that, while attitudes have changed, housework roles remain stubbornly gendered.

Another survey put some more damning figures on it. In the UK women do more housework than men in most households, a staggering figure of 93%. Well done to the 7% of you who do share household tasks equally.[17]

What makes this more difficult to equalise is that much of the work around household organisation is invisible. Even handing certain tasks over is difficult because a lot of this work is hard to monitor and it takes more mental labour to hand over. I can't delegate meal prep without also handing over shopping lists and my mental tab of what we are running low on. In addition, for mothers, women are judged on their homes and how they parent in a way that men are not, meaning we spend more time internalising and thinking about all the admin needed for parenting.

The mental load is now being increasingly recognised by scientists and sociologists, who understand that studying it will go some way to validating and then redistributing the unequal division of labour in the majority of heterosexual households. Experts say that this hidden work comes in three overlapping categories. There's 'cognitive labour' – which is thinking about all the practical elements of household responsibilities, including organising play-dates, shopping and planning activities. There's 'emotional labour', which is maintaining the family's emotions; calming things down if the kids are acting up, or worrying about how they are managing at school. Third, the 'mental load', is the intersection of the two: preparing, organising and anticipating everything, emotional and practical, that needs to get done to make life flow. There are several key stages of the mental load – anticipation, planning, research and deciding – with only the latter being shared more equally.

Just as we value power outside the home, we need to recognise and value it inside the home too, especially the 'invisible power' that we heard about, which fosters the myth of mutuality. When there is greater equality at home, then women will carry less of the mental load into their paid working lives, which will help level the playing field.

So how can we learn to reduce it one step at a time and alleviate some of the more hidden stressors of family life? We can all expect and support women to prioritise breadwinning and then support men to lean out. Don't view women as better at managing the home. There needs to be an intrinsic motivation to share housework equally, combined with the expectation of both doing so. That's why handing over tasks end to end is so important. If a task remains shared, both of you still have to spend mental energy on reaching the desired outcome, or one becomes the commander, the other the footsoldier.

## 7. UNDERSTAND OUR INBUILT SENSE OF FAIRNESS

Although I have interviewed many couples with positive experiences, we shouldn't gloss over the fact that inequality at home can harm relationships, contributing to marital stress as well as divorce.

Tatjana Greil Castro has always had a successful career in the financial industry, managing a large team and huge financial assets. She has four teenage children, and her partner was a stay-at-home dad for much of that time. Ten years ago she was interviewed by the *Financial Times* as a pioneering example of a successful breadwinning woman who had tried to ensure her husband didn't feel 'unmanned' by handing over all financial responsibilities at weekends to him and encouraging him to have an equal say in the household finances.[18] Except, what she didn't reveal at the time was that at home things were far from balanced. She earned all the money but still organised the house and childcare. Gradually resentment increased. In their case they couldn't find a solution, their relationship broke down, and they now co-parent from two different households. Despite being the sole earner, Greil Castro took on most of the care at home too. She recalls being frustrated and resentful, as her partner didn't contribute at work or at home, resulting in conflict. It was unfair at home, but this was the model they had both grown up with. Today she says she's happier as a divorcee than she would have been had she stayed married, and hopes to model this for her children too.

This highlights that some dynamics are too problematic to fix, and if children continue to see an unfair distribution of work at home, they might later expect the same. That's why fairness is key for achieving balanced power dynamics. We heard how many anthropologists believe that fairness and cooperation have been key to our success as a species. Even children do their utmost to avoid inequity, preferring to forgo a treat in lieu of an unfair distribution of rewards.

Understanding our inbuilt sense of fairness matters as it helps us to understand why imbalanced power dynamics affect us so negatively. Using the principles explored so far – communication, empathy, and challenging and avoiding stereotypes – will help us to build more balanced connections. As for leaders, listening, speaking up and being kinder will go a long way to rectifying a conflict, unfair situation or power imbalance, and help build better psychological safety in the process too.

## 8. KNOW YOUR OWN GOALS

It's empowering to know what goals you want to achieve, so real-ising that a more powerful partner's goals can override yours should be concerning. It's natural to want to build connections with loved ones and find common interests, but when we are time-poor, have a family and a busy job, one person's goals can quickly get prioritised over the other's.

We've heard that those in power can use that power to pursue their own goals, and that the more dominant person in a relation-ship tends to set and prioritise their own goals.[19] Given that power is also linked to confidence, and a lack of it reduces self-esteem, you can see how easy it is for the powerful person to continue prioritising their own interests – unless goals are explicitly agreed upon and time to pursue them is protected. We've heard already that there's a huge gulf in leisure time at home between fathers and mothers. To correct that we can each note down how much leisure time we have per week and, if it is unfair, divide accordingly. With that in mind, we can discuss which pursuits are mutual and benefit the whole family. Write down what you want to achieve and what time you may need to do it, and then set boundaries. My Saturday mornings are always protected so I can join a local 5k run at 9 a.m., whilst my husband has his weekly football game on Saturday afternoons. This comes from communication and a mutual understanding of the importance of our hobbies. This doesn't just apply to personal relationships, as studies show that focusing on shared goals is beneficial for both employees and the employer,[20] whereas self-focus can sour relations.

## 9. PRIME YOUR BRAIN TO BE LESS STRESSED

The many power dynamics we are subject to in daily life can be stressful. Losing power reduces our self-esteem, and can lead to chronic stress and reduced creativity. Continued stress elevates the hormone cortisol, and that impairs the very social connections we need to reduce it. However, when we feel empowered, we can cope with stressors better. Using the brain's prediction engine can help us trick ourselves into feeling less stressed. We've heard how psychologists use priming to incite power in individuals by asking participants to recall a time they felt powerful. It really works, and we can use a similar trick ourselves. If we feel as if a situation is becoming unmanageable, we can take a step back and recall a time when we felt empowered. It can be something simple, like the time we oversaw a day out with friends, or a PTA event. Memories of this power can boost confidence and assertiveness in the present moment.

We've heard many of the benefits that subtle forms of power and influence can give us. We can use these insights in all areas of our lives. Feeling empowered helps us speak out, rather than staying quiet, which if we want to enact meaningful change is vital. We need to shout about our inequities at home and in society. Have you ever sat at the worst table in a restaurant that was right next to the bathroom and said nothing? Or how about being uncomfortably cold due to air conditioning? These are minor inconveniences, but we can similarly speak up against bullies and terrible bosses.

If you did say something, think about what made you feel confident enough to do so. A friend recently told me he'd rather eat uncooked food and pretend it was fine than embarrass someone else by complaining and inconveniencing the staff. It's quite common to stay silent when we feel aggrieved, but it's handy to know we can prime ourselves to speak up. I have definitely (apologetically) asked for a more optimal seat in a restaurant because I knew my experience would be more enjoyable. Equally I've suffered in silence in a far-too-cold office.

Deborah Gruenfeld was inspired to study whether people could be encouraged to speak out from an unlikely experience. Once, on a flight, an important-looking business executive next to her changed the air-conditioning settings so that the cold air blew directly on her. He might not have realised what he had done but it took her half an hour before she did anything about it. This scenario later influenced her research. Remember the blackjack experiment, where feeling empowered in one scenario made individuals take more risks in card games? In a follow-up to this study, researchers wanted to understand how power could lead to action in an uncomfortable situation. First participants were primed to recall when they felt power over someone else. They then took part in tasks to enhance this feeling, and it was at this moment the experimenters set out to annoy them by placing a fan exactly where they were asked to sit. It was loud and far too close for comfort, but there were no instructions indicating that they could move the fan or switch it off.

The results showed that the very people who had been primed to feel more powerful were also more likely to act and move the fan.[21] Most of us have witnessed a similar real-world scenario, where someone demands to move seats on a plane or someone complains loudly about service. These scenarios can result in favourable actions, and this kind of influence can create more opportunities or a more comfortable life. So now you know: move the fan, change the temperature, ask for support. If you do it politely and aren't demanding an action at the expense of others, then speaking out can make you feel more powerful and less stressed too. Life's too short to sit in front of a cold fan, after all.

## 10. UNDERSTAND WHAT DRIVES POWER: OVERCOMING THE PARADOX TO FIND TRUE AUTONOMY

We've seen in countless ways that power is a constant force that shapes our interactions, from small everyday exchanges to life-altering meetings, from the boardroom to the bedroom. People seek it to have more autonomy, control and agency. Groups or individuals seek leaders who have a vision and can help the group enact certain outcomes – and so we legitimise power in others, hoping it will serve the group, and use it to advance our own agenda.

Having power can improve our health and well-being, and even give us more access to prized resources. In a book about power dynamics, it's tempting to conclude that power-hungry individuals want more influence over others to advance their own goals, often at others' expense. But you've got this far so will know that doesn't tell the whole story. Of course there are some bad players – despotic leaders, bullies and narcissistic bosses – but research suggests that, for the most part, our desire for power stems from a need to have autonomy over our own lives, not to control or influence others.[22] From a series of studies, Joris Lammers and team concluded that 'the desire for power is born not of a desire to be the master of others, but to be master of one's own fate and domain.' When we don't get autonomy, it affects us in multiple ways. We saw, for instance, that when individuals lack control, they seek higher-status partners at the expense of other desirable traits.[23]

Understanding the motivations for power will hopefully help you to look differently at those who are in more powerful positions than you, as well as those who you have power over. A child mid-temper tantrum isn't out to personally annoy you, they want autonomy, even if to them autonomy means wearing a sparkly princess dress with no coat in the pouring rain. A moaning colleague isn't necessarily being difficult, they want clarity and ownership. Viewing power this way should hopefully unlock a whole new way of looking at those around you and allow you to empathise with their situation and see the true motivation behind power plays.

It's also worth uncoupling power from individual traits to under-stand why some in power use it to manipulate others. We heard how we can harness power for the greater good, and that kindness helps elevate. It's therefore very pleasing to know that if you take individuals who tend to be more communal in their outlook, and give those people more power, they become more disinhibited and liberated by power, helping to enhance these communal traits.[24] This also means that selfish people with power behave more selfishly, precisely because power gives us freedom from constraints and the ability to do more of what we set out to do. Melissa Williams explains it to me as follows: 'Inherent to power is the ability to make your own choices and to not have goals placed on you or consequences that would follow from your behaviour. What that means is that people with power tend to behave a little bit more in line with their own dispositions, their own personal goals, their own personal values.'

This is all very well if we are good-natured, but if power is in the wrong hands, it can be problematic. We've heard about how power changes how we feel and act, but there's something else at play. Our personality traits affect who seeks power and how we act when we gain it. There tend to be greater abuses of power among dominant individuals, showing that the link between power and corruption depends on the person in power as well as their culture. This could also occur because those who score high in dominant personality traits are more prone to seeking power in the first place, meaning dominant narcissists are overrepresented in powerful positions. Think about a terrible boss alongside a bad politician and consider if they have common traits. As these traits are magnified once an individual reaches power, it can be a particularly potent mix. Because of the better-than-average effect, these individuals will also *think* they are superior.

All this shows that we need to be vigilant when choosing who we help empower, whether elected or appointed to leadership positions. In our personal life we can consciously select partners with similar values to us and learn to recognise personality traits of those who are more likely to be power-hungry, as well as understand the impact of positional power outside the home. A relationship contract may be one step too far for many of us, but aligning goals and discussing how finances will be shared early on can help resolve potential conflicts and earning disparities more easily. If we understand each other's desires and pressure points, it will allow us to better react to any of the negatives and, even better, enhance the positives.

For those of us who are passionate about creating a better world, it is not in our nature to accept an unjust one where inequality persists. Fortunately, we can shift and challenge subtle influences and expectations in many areas of our lives. The fact that we can do so is illuminating. Each time we correct an unhealthy power game, we are paving the way for societal as well as generational change. As women increasingly become primary breadwinners, we are witnessing how traditional power dynamics are changing in real time. As these female breadwinners increase, it could be the driving force for tipping the scales of household inequality, which so far has been difficult to correct. And finally, a key aspect of how all this research ties into real life is an awareness of the dynamics that exist in the first place, knowledge which you are now armed with. We can and should all see it as our responsibility to use this understanding to inspire change, both in our personal lives and in the world at large.

# ACKNOWLEDGEMENTS

As with any such project, there are so many people behind the scenes who have been crucial to making this book happen – first and foremost my husband, Stephen, who not only understands my ambition but knows how to be an equal partner and therefore helped me to carve out writing time. It's fitting to be writing a book about power dynamics when a balanced home life has been so crucial for me to hit my deadlines alongside family commitments, raising our two beautiful children.

The team at Canongate, with their vision and support, have made the process not only rewarding, but fun – whether it's bouncing ideas around, restructuring, or working on publicity, you are a fantastically collaborative team, championing both me and the idea. Thanks to Helena Gonda – I still remember our first meeting from which I came away buzzing with enthusiasm – and to Jenny Fry, Claire Reiderman, Caitriona Horne, Aisling Holling, Leila Cruickshank, Charlie Tooke, Jessica Neale, Phyllis Armstrong and Jamie Byng. Let this be the first of many! And to my agent, Catherine Cho, the one who first took me on, thank you for everything and continuing to support me, as well as sharing my long-term vision. To my friend and colleague David Robson – who is always ready to share advice about the writing process and indeed introduced me to his Canongate editor – thank you for your crucial role in making this book happen. And to my fellow science journalists and colleagues, Richard Fisher, Amanda Ruggeri, Catherine de Lange, Zaria Gorvett, Richard Gray, Camelia Sadeghzadeh, Griesham Taan, Pierangelo Pirak: shared ideas and the joint pursuit of sharing evidence-based insights has helped me enormously throughout my career. To my supportive managers past and present – Matt Walker, Jonathan Fildes, Mary Wilkinson and Cassian Harrison – modelling inspiring leadership has taught me a lot, and helped me in my own leadership role.

This book couldn't have happened without all the contributors who generously took the time to share their stories, as well as the academics who explained their insights to me. You know who you are and I remain ever grateful to the dozens of people who spoke with me so openly and answered my questions, some of them quite personal, and to the researchers who clarified their scientific findings throughout the process.

Finally, to my parents, who raised me to believe I could pursue the goals I set my mind to, and who brought me up with well-balanced power dynamics at home, meaning I expected the same for my own relationship too.

# FURTHER READING

Bregman, Rutger, *Humankind: A Hopeful History*, Bloomsbury, 2020

Chung, Heejung, *The Flexibility Paradox: Why Flexible Working Leads to (Self-)Exploitation*, Policy Press, 2022

Grant, Adam, *Think Again: The Power of Knowing What You Don't Know*, WH Allen, 2021

Gruenfeld, Deborah, *Acting with Power: Why We Are More Powerful Than We Believe*, Profile Books, 2020

Kay, Katty, and Claire Shipman, *The Power Code: More Joy. Less Ego. Maximum Impact for Women (and Everyone)*, Harper Business, 2023

Robson, David, *The Expectation Effect: How Your Mindset Can Transform Your Life*, Canongate, 2022

Sieghart, Mary Ann, *The Authority Gap: Why Women Are Still Taken Less Seriously Than Men, And What We Can Do About It*, Black Swan, 2022

Slaughter, Anne-Marie, *Unfinished Business: Women, Men, Work, Family*, Oneworld Publications, 2015

Storr, Will, *The Status Game: On Human Life and How to Play It*, William Collins, 2021

# NOTES

## Introduction

1 Gruenfeld, D. (2021). *Acting with Power: Why We Are More Powerful Than We Believe.* Profile Books.
2 Keltner, D. (2007, December 1). The power paradox: True power requires modesty and empathy, not force and coercion. Greater Good Science Center.
3 Keltner, D., Gruenfeld, D. H., & Anderson, C. (2003). Power, approach, and inhibition. *Psychological Review*, 110(2), 265–284.
4 Galinsky, A. D., Magee, J. C., Inesi, M. E., & Gruenfeld, D. H. (2006). Power and perspectives not taken. *Psychological Science*, 17(12), 1068–1074.
5 Russell, B. (1938). *Power: A New Social Analysis.* Allen & Unwin.

## 1: Subverted Power

1 Daminger, A. (2019). The cognitive dimension of household labor. *American Sociological Review*, 84(4), 609–633.
2 Bishop, K. (2022). Women breadwinners: Why high-earners compensate at home. BBC.
3 Waldersee, V. (2018). Four in ten men in heterosexual relationships feel responsible for earning most of the household income. YouGov.
4 Fry, R., Aragão, C., Hurst, K., & Parker, K. (2023, April 13). In a growing share of U.S. marriages, husbands and wives earn about the same. Pew Research Center.
5 Glass, J. L., Raley, R. K., & Pepin, J. R. (2021). Children's financial dependence on mothers: Propensity and duration. *Socius*, 7.
6 Office for National Statistics (2023). Families and households in the UK: 2023.
7 Glynn, S. J. (2016). *Breadwinning mothers are increasingly the U.S. norm.* Center for American Progress.

8   Klesment, M., & Van Bavel, J. (2017). The reversal of the gender gap in education, motherhood, and women as main earners in Europe. *European Sociological Review*, 33(3), 465–481.

9   Hu, Y. (2019). What about money? Earnings, household financial organization, and housework. *Journal of Marriage and Family*, 81, 1091–1109.

10  Bittman, M., England, P., Sayer, L., Folbre, N., & Matheson, G. (2003). When does gender trump money? Bargaining and time in household work. *American Journal of Sociology*, 109, 186–214.

11  Syrda, J. (2023). Gendered Housework: Spousal relative income, parenthood and traditional gender identity norms. *Work, Employment and Society*, 37(3), 794–813.

12  Chesley, N. (2017). What does it mean to be a 'breadwinner' mother? *Journal of Family Issues*, 38(18), 2594–2619.

13  Wrohlich, K., & Bünning, M. (2020). Undoing gender with institutions: Lessons from the German division and reunification. *The Economic Journal*, 130(629), 1445–1481.

14  Hochman, O., & Lewin-Epstein, N. (2023). What if she earns more? Gender norms, income inequality, and the division of housework. *Journal of Population Economics*, 45, 1–20.

15  Simister, J. (2013). Is men's share of housework reduced by 'gender deviance neutralization'? Evidence from seven countries. *Journal of Comparative Family Studies*, 44(3), 311–325.

16  Hofmarcher, T., & Plug, E. (2022). Specialization in same-sex and different-sex couples. *Labour Economics*, 77, 101995.

17  Eurostat (2004). Labour Force Survey 2004. Gender statistics: Labour market. European Commission.

18  Hu, Y. (2021). Divergent gender revolutions: Cohort changes in household financial management across income gradients. *Gender & Society*, 35(5), 629–657.

19  Chesley, N. (2017). What does it mean to be a 'breadwinner' mother? *Journal of Family Issues*, 38(18), 2594–2619.

20  US Bureau of Labor Statistics (2024). Families with own children: Employment status of parents by age of youngest child and family type, 2021–2022 annual averages. US Department of Labor.

21  Fry, R. (2023, August 3). Almost 1 in 5 stay-at-home parents in the U.S. are dads. Pew Research Center.

22  Fatherhood Institute (2022). Closing the gap: UK fathers doing 18% more childcare since pre-pandemic.

23  Jones, C., Foley, S., & Golombok, S. (2022). Parenting and child adjustment in families with primary caregiver fathers. *Journal of Family Psychology*, 36(3), 406–415.

24 Mascaro, J. S., Hackett, P. D., & Rilling, J. K. (2014). Differential neural responses to child and sexual stimuli in human fathers and non-fathers and their hormonal correlates. *Psychoneuroendocrinology*, 46, 153–163.

25 Kelland, J., Searle, N. & Brown, A. (2024). Fathers at work – Forfeits, deficits and disregarding discourse. *Gender, Work & Organization*, 10.1111/gwao.13199.

26 Fry, R., Aragão, C., Hurst, K., & Parker, K. (2023). In a growing share of U.S. marriages, husbands and wives earn about the same. Pew Research Center.

27 Fry, R. (2023). Almost 1 in 5 stay-at-home parents in the U.S. are dads. Pew Research Center.

28 Di Nallo, A., Lipps, O., Oesch, D., & Voorpostel, M. (2021). The effect of unemployment on couples separating in Germany and the UK. *Journal of Marriage and Family*, 83(5), 1340–1358.

29 Eriksson, S., Rooth, D. O. (2004). Do employers use unemployment as a sorting criterion when hiring? Evidence from a field experiment. *American Economic Review*, 104(3), 1014–1039.

30 Hall, R. (2021, March 3). Girls doing more housework in Covid lockdown than boys. *Guardian*.

31 Kowalewska, H., & Vitali, A. (2024). The female-breadwinner well-being 'penalty': Differences by men's (un)employment and country. *European Sociological Review*, 40(2), 293–308.

32 Blom, N., & Hewitt, B. (2019). Becoming a female-breadwinner household in Australia: Changes in relationship satisfaction. *Journal of Marriage and Family*, 81(1), 192–208.

33 McMunn, A., Bird, L., Webb, E., & Sacker, A. (2020). Gender divisions of paid and unpaid work in contemporary UK couples. *Work, Employment and Society*, 34(2), 155–173.

34 DeRose, L. F., Goldscheider, F., Brito, J. R., et al. (2019). Are children barriers to the gender revolution? International comparisons. *European Journal of Population*, 35(4), 987–1021.

35 Seedat, S., & Rondon, M. (2021). Women's wellbeing and the burden of unpaid work. *BMJ*, 374, n1972.

36 Sánchez-Mira, N. (2021). (Un)doing gender in female breadwinner households: Gender relations and structural change. *Gender, Work & Organization*, 31(4), 1196–1213.

37 Álvaro, J. L., Garrido, A., Pereira, C. R., Torres, A. R., & Barros, S. C. (2019). Unemployment, self-esteem, and depression: Differences between men and women. *Spanish Journal of Psychology*, 22, 28, E1.

38 Gulliford, J. (2014). Research indicates that men are more likely to suffer adverse health consequences as a result of being unemployed

than women. LSE British Politics and Policy. Retrieved October 5, 2024.

39 Glass, J. L., Raley, R. K., & Pepin, J. R. (2021). Children's financial dependence on mothers: Propensity and duration. *Socius*, 7.

40 Parker, K. (2021, November 8). What's behind the growing gap between men and women in college completion? Pew Research Center.

41 Klesment, M., & Van Bavel, J. (2017). The reversal of the gender gap in education, motherhood, and women as main earners in Europe. *European Sociological Review*, 33(3), 465–481.

42 Kelland, J., Lewis, D., & Fisher, V. (2022). Viewed with suspicion, considered idle and mocked – working caregiving fathers and fatherhood forfeits. *Gender, Work & Organization*, 29(5), 1578–1593.

43 Rice-Oxley, M. (2017, November 21). The 'masculine mystique': Why men can't ditch the baggage of being a bloke. *Guardian*.

44 Van Bavel, J., Schwartz, C. R., & Esteve, A. (2018). The reversal of the gender gap in education and its consequences for family life. *Annual Review of Sociology*, 44, 341–360.

45 De Hauw, Y., Grow, A., & Van Bavel, J. (2017). The reversed gender gap in education and assortative mating in Europe. *European Journal of Population*, 33(4), 445–474.

## 2: Money Talks

1 Heggeness, M., & Murray-Close, M. (2019). Manning up and womaning down: How husbands and wives report earnings when she earns more. Opportunity and Inclusive Growth Institute, Working Paper 28. Federal Reserve Bank of Minneapolis.

2 Rheinschmidt, M. L., & Mendoza-Denton, R. (2014). Social class and academic achievement in college: The interplay of rejection sensitivity and entity beliefs. *Journal of Personality and Social Psychology*, 107(1), 101–121.

3 John-Henderson, N., Jacobs, E. G., Mendoza-Denton, R., & Francis, D. D. (2013). Wealth, health, and the moderating role of implicit social class bias. *Annals of Behavioral Medicine*, 45(2), 173–179.

4 Cho, M., Impett, E. A., Campos, B., Chen, S., & Keltner, D. (2020). Socioeconomic inequality undermines relationship quality in romantic relationships. *Journal of Social and Personal Relationships*, 37(5), 1722–1742.

5 Engstrom, H. R., Laurin, K., Kay, N. R., & Human, L. J. (2024). Socioeconomic status and meta-perceptions: How markers of culture and rank predict beliefs about how others see us. *Personality & Social Psychology Bulletin*, 50(9), 1386–1407.

6    Laurin, K., Engstrom, H. R., Alic, A., & Tracy, J. L. (2024). Is being elite the same as living an easy life? Two distinct ways of experiencing subjective socioeconomic status. *Journal of Personality and Social Psychology*, 127(4), 822–845.

7    Latu, I. M., Mast, M. S., Bombari, D., & Lammers, J. (2019). Empowering mimicry: Female leader role models empower women in leadership tasks through body posture mimicry. *Sex Roles*, 80(1–2), 11–24.

8    Brosnan, S. F., & de Waal, F. B. M. (2003). Monkeys reject unequal pay. *Nature*, 425(6955), 297–299.

9    Warneken, F. (2015). Precocious prosociality: Why do young children help? *Child Development Perspectives*, 9(1), 1–6.

10   Kanngiesser, P., & Warneken, F. (2012). Young children consider merit when sharing resources with others. *PloS One*, 7(8), e43979.

11   Shaw, A., & Olson, K. R. (2012). Children discard a resource to avoid inequity. *Journal of Experimental Psychology: General*, 141(2), 382–395.

12   Camerer, C. (2003). *Behavioral Game Theory: Experiments in Strategic Interaction*. Princeton University Press.

13   Sanfey, A. G., Rilling, J. K., Aronson, J. A., Nystrom, L. E., & Cohen, J. D. (2003). The neural basis of economic decision-making in the Ultimatum Game. *Science*, 300(5626), 1755–1758.

14   Isoda, M. (2021). Socially relative reward valuation in the primate brain. *Current Opinion in Neurobiology*, 68, 15–22.

15   Slaughter, A.-M. (2015). *Unfinished Business: Women, Men, Work, Family*. Random House.

16   Burgess, A., & Goldman, R. (2021). Lockdown Fathers: The untold story (executive summary). Contemporary Fathers in the UK series, Fatherhood Institute.

17   How motherhood hurts careers: A new study measures its impact on women's employment worldwide. (2024). *The Economist*.

18   Munsch, C. L. (2015). Her support, his support: Money, masculinity, and marital infidelity. *American Sociological Review*, 80(3), 469–495.

19   Killewald, A. (2016). Money, work, and marital stability: Assessing change in the gendered determinants of divorce. *American Sociological Review*, 81(4), 696–719.

20   Perel, E. (2013). Rethinking infidelity: A talk for anyone who has ever loved. TED.

21   Haerpfer, C., Inglehart, R., Moreno, A., Welzel, C., Kizilova, K., Diez-Medrano J., Lagos, M., Norris, P., Ponarin, E., & Puranen, B. (eds) (2022). World Values Survey: Wave 7.

22 Carlson, D. L., & Soller, B. (2019). Sharing is more fun for everyone? Gender attitudes, sexual self-efficacy, and sexual frequency. *Journal of Marriage and Family*, 81, 24–41.

23 Maas, M. K., McDaniel, B. T., Feinberg, M. E., & Jones, D. E. (2018). Division of labor and multiple domains of sexual satisfaction among first-time parents. *Journal of Family Issues*, 39(1), 104–127.

24 Doepke, M., Hannusch, A., Kindermann, F., & Tertilt, M. (2022). The economics of fertility: A new era. NBER Working Paper 29948. National Bureau of Economic Research.

## 3: Hetero Norms

1 Library of Congress US Reports: Price Waterhouse v. Hopkins, 490 U.S. 228 (1989), at 234.

2 Eyal, T., Steffel, M., & Epley, N. (2018). Perspective mistaking: Accurately understanding the mind of another requires getting perspective, not taking perspective. *Journal of Personality and Social Psychology*, 114(4), 547–571.

3 Lazarus, A., & Mandel, H. (2023). The allocation of housework in same- and different-sex partnerships: Recent evidence from the U.S. *Sex Roles*, 89(5–6), 394–408.

4 Brewster, M. E. (2017). Lesbian women and household labor division: A systematic review of scholarly research from 2000 to 2015. *Journal of Lesbian Studies*, 21(1), 47–69.

5 Bashe, P. M., & Skinner, N. (2022). Exploring power dynamics in same-sex marriage. Department of Psychology, University of Cape Town.

6 Van der Vleuten, M., Evertsson, M., & Moberg, Y. (2023). Joint utility or sub-optimal outcomes? Household income development of same-sex and different-sex couples transitioning to parenthood in Denmark, Finland, Norway, and Sweden. *Journal of Family Issues*, 45(8), 2049–2076.

7 Andresen, M., & Nix, E. (2022). What causes the child penalty? Evidence from adopting and same-sex couples. *Journal of Labor Economics*, 40(4), 971–1004.

8 Kurdek, L. A. (2007). The allocation of household labor by partners in gay and lesbian couples. *Journal of Family Issues*, 28(1), 132–148.

9 Eriksson Kirsch, M., & Evertsson, M. (2022). Taking turns: lesbian couples' decision of (first) birth mother in Sweden. *Journal of Family Studies*, 29(4), 1865–1883.

10 Wilson, B. D. M., & Bouton, L. J. A. (2024). LGBTQ parenting in the US. UCLA Williams Institute.

11  Fergusson, B. (2020, July 18). 'Mum's day off, is it?': What adopting as a same-sex couple taught us. *Guardian*.

12  Ruppanner, L., Brandén, M., & Turunen, J. (2018). Does unequal housework lead to divorce? Evidence from Sweden. *Sociology*, 52(1), 75–94.

## 4: Caring Can Be Masculine

1  LoBue, V., & DeLoache, J. S. (2011). Pretty in pink: The early development of gender-stereotyped colour preferences. *British Journal of Developmental Psychology*, 29(3), 656–667.

2  Mondschein, E. R., Adolph, K. E., & Tamis-LeMonda, C. S. (2000). Gender bias in mothers' expectations about infant crawling. *Journal of Experimental Child Psychology*, 77(4), 304–316.

3  Johnson, K., Caskey, M., Rand, K., Tucker, R., & Vohr, B. (2014). Gender differences in adult-infant communication in the first months of life. *Pediatrics*, 134(6), e1603–e1610.

4  Mascaro, J. S., Rentscher, K. E., Hackett, P. D., Mehl, M. R., & Rilling, J. K. (2017). Child gender influences paternal behavior, language, and brain function. *Behavioral Neuroscience*, 131(3), 262–273.

5  Population Health Monitoring Group (2024). Suicides in England and Wales: 2023 registrations. Office for National Statistics.

6  Connor, S., Edvardsson, K., Fisher, C., & Spelten, E. (2021). Perceptions and interpretation of contemporary masculinities in western culture: A systematic review. *American Journal of Men's Health*, 15(6), 15579883211061009.

7  Ratliff, K. A., & Oishi, S. (2013). Gender differences in implicit self-esteem following a romantic partner's success or failure. *Journal of Personality and Social Psychology*, 105(4), 688–702.

8  Hawkins, H., Lesick, T., & Zell, E. (2021). Implicit self-esteem following a romantic partner's success: Three replications and a meta-analysis. *Personal Relationships*, 29(1).

9  Smith, S., & Inhorn, M. C. (2016). Emergent masculinities, men's health and the Movember movement. In Gideon, J. (ed.), *Handbook On Gender and Health*, Edward Elgar, 436–456.

10  Caruso, A., & Roberts, S. (2018). Exploring constructions of masculinity on a men's body-positivity blog. *Journal of Sociology*, 54(4), 627–646.

11  Brandth, B., & Kvande, E. (2018). Masculinity and fathering alone during parental leave. *Men and Masculinities*, 21(1), 72–90.

12  Trades Union Congress (2016). Fathers working full-time earn 21% more than men without children, says TUC.

13 Correll, S. J., Benard, S., & Paik, I. (2007). Getting a job: Is there a motherhood penalty? *American Journal of Sociology*, 112 (5), 1297–1338.

14 Forbes, S., Birkett, H., & Smith, P. (2021). What motivates employers to improve their shared parental leave and pay offers? Government Equalities Office (Gov.uk).

15 Sethna, V., Perry, E., Domoney, J., Iles, J., Psychogiou, L., Rowbotham, N. E. L., Stein, A., Murray, L., & Ramchandani, P. G. (2017). Father-child interactions at 3 months and 24 months: Contributions to children's cognitive development at 24 months. *Infant Mental Health Journal*, 38(3), 378–390.

16 Parkes, A., Riddell, J., Wight, D. and Buston, K. (2017) Growing up in Scotland: Father-child relationships and child socio-emotional wellbeing. Discussion Paper. Scottish Government, Edinburgh.

17 Weale, S. (2023, September 20). Fathers have unique effect on children's educational outcomes, study finds. *Guardian*.

18 Abraham, E., Hendler, T., Shapira-Lichter, I., Kanat-Maymon, Y., Zagoory-Sharon, O., and Feldman, R. (2014). Father's brain is sensitive to childcare experiences. *Proceedings of the National Academy of Sciences*, 111, 9792–9797.

19 Lynch, K., Lyons, M., and Cantillon, S. (2009). Time to care, care commanders and care footsoldiers. *Affective Equality: Love, Care and Injustice*, Kathleen Lynch, John Baker and Maureen Lyons (eds). Palgrave Macmillan, 132–157.

20 Warrier, V., Toro, R., Chakrabarti, B., et al. (2018). Genome-wide analyses of self-reported empathy: Correlations with autism, schizophrenia, and anorexia nervosa. *Translational Psychiatry*, 8, 35.

21 Zimmermann, D. H., & West, C. (1996). Sex roles, interruptions and silences in conversation. *Amsterdam Studies in the Theory and History of Linguistic Science Series 4*, 211–236.

22 Mast, M. S. (2002). Dominance as expressed and inferred through speaking time. *Human Communication Research*, 28(3), 420–450.

23 Snyder, K. (2014, August 14). Boys learn to interrupt. Girls learn to shut up. *Slate*.

24 Miller, D. I., Nolla, K. M., Eagly, A. H., & Uttal, D. H. (2018). The development of children's gender-science stereotypes: A meta-analysis of 5 decades of U.S. draw-a-scientist studies. *Child Development*, 89(6), 2061–2076.

25 Carli, L. L., Alawa, L., Lee, Y., Zhao, B., & Kim, E. (2016). Stereotypes about gender and science: Women ≠ scientists. *Psychology of Women Quarterly*, 40, 244–260.

26 Elliott, K. (2015). Caring masculinities: Theorizing an emerging concept. *Men and Masculinities*, 19, 240–259.

## 5: Understanding Power

1 Keltner, D. (2016). *The Power Paradox: How We Gain and Lose Influence*. Penguin Random House.

2 Judge, T. A., Bono, J. E., Ilies, R., & Gerhardt, M. W. (2002). Personality and leadership: a qualitative and quantitative review. *The Journal of Applied Psychology*, 87(4), 765–780.

3 Boehm, C. (1999). *Hierarchy in the Forest: The Evolution of Egalitarian Behavior*. Harvard University Press.

4 Richardson, D. R., Vandenberg, R. J., & Humphries, S. A. (1986). Effect of power to harm on retaliative aggression among males and females. *Journal of Research in Personality*, 20, 402–419.

5 Schwartz, J., Riis, J., Elbel, B., & Ariely, D. (2012). Inviting consumers to downsize fast-food portions significantly reduces calorie consumption. *Health Affairs*, 31(2), 399–407.

6 Schoppe-Sullivan, S. J., Brown, G. L., Cannon, E. A., Mangelsdorf, S. C., & Sokolowski, M. S. (2008). Maternal gatekeeping, coparenting quality, and fathering behavior in families with infants. *Journal of Family Psychology*, 22(3), 389–398.

7 Stevenson, M. M., Fabricius, W. V., Cookston, J. T., Parke, R. D., Coltrane, S., Braver, S. L., & Saenz, D. S. (2014). Marital problems, maternal gatekeeping attitudes, and father–child relationships in adolescence. *Developmental Psychology*, 50(4), 1208–1218.

8 Chung, H. (2021). Shared care, fathers' involvement in care and family well-being outcomes: A literature review. Gov.uk.

9 Post, C. (2015). When is female leadership an advantage? Coordination requirements, team cohesion, and team interaction norms. *Journal of Organizational Behavior*, 36(5), 627–644.

10 Van Bommel, T. (2021). The power of empathy in times of crisis and beyond. Catalyst.

11 Croom, S. (2021, June 6). 12% of corporate leaders are psychopaths. It's time to take this problem seriously. Fortune.

12 Galinsky, A. D., Magee, J. C., Inesi, M. E., & Gruenfeld, D. H. (2006). Power and perspectives not taken. *Psychological Science*, 17(12), 1068–1074.

13 Laurin, K., Fitzsimons, G. M., Finkel, E. J., Carswell, K. L., vanDellen, M. R., Hofmann, W., Lambert, N. M., Eastwick, P. W., Fincham, F. D., & Brown, P. C. (2016). Power and the pursuit of a partner's goals. *Journal of Personality and Social Psychology*, 110(6), 840–868.

14 Tan, K., Li, N. P., Meltzer, A. L., Chin, J. L. J., Tan, L. K. L., Lim, A. J., Neuberg, S. L., & van Vugt, M. (2022). Effects of economic uncertainty and socioeconomic status on reproductive timing: A

life history approach. *Current Research in Ecological and Social Psychology*, 3, 100040.

15 Dickerson, S. S., & Kemeny, M. E. (2004). Acute stressors and cortisol responses: A theoretical integration and synthesis of laboratory research. *Psychological Bulletin*, 130(3), 355–391.

16 Hogenboom, M. (2003). How I rewired my brain in six weeks. BBC Future.

17 McLaughlin, K. A., & Sheridan, M. A. (2016). Beyond cumulative risk: A dimensional approach to childhood adversity. *Current Directions in Psychological Science*, 25(4), 239–245.

18 Chetty, R., Jackson, M. O., Kuchler, T., et al. (2022). Social capital I: Measurement and associations with economic mobility. *Nature*, 608, 108–121.

19 Flashman, J. (2012). Academic achievement and its impact on friend dynamics. *Sociology of Education*, 85(1), 61–80.

20 Christakis, N. A., & Fowler, J. H. (2008). The collective dynamics of smoking in a large social network. *New England Journal of Medicine*, 358(21), 2249–2258.

21 Boothby, E. J., Cooney, G., Sandstrom, G. M., & Clark, M. S. (2018). The liking gap in conversations: Do people like us more than we think? *Psychological Science*, 29(11), 1742–1756.

22 Robson, D. (2024). *The Laws of Connection: 13 Social Strategies That Will Transform Your Life*. Canongate.

23 Sandstrom, G. M., & Dunn, E. W. (2014). Is efficiency overrated?: Minimal social interactions lead to belonging and positive affect. *Social Psychological and Personality Science*, 5(4), 437–442.

24 Siegel, E. H., Wormwood, J. B., Quigley, K. S., & Barrett, L. F. (2018). Seeing what you feel: Affect drives visual perception of structurally neutral faces. *Psychological Science*, 29(4), 496–503.

25 Hatfield, E., Cacioppo, J. T., & Rapson, R. L. (1994). *Emotional Contagion*. Cambridge University Press.

26 Pessoa, L. (2008). On the relationship between emotion and cognition. *Nature Reviews Neuroscience*, 9(2), 148–158.

27 Hogeveen, J., Inzlicht, M., & Obhi, S. S. (2014). Power changes how the brain responds to others. *Journal of Experimental Psychology General*, 143(2), 755–762.

28 Naish, K. R., & Obhi, S. S. (2015). Self-selected conscious strategies do not modulate motor cortical output during action observation. *Journal of Neurophysiology*, 114(4), 2278–2284.

29 Lupien, S. J., McEwen, B. S., Gunnar, M. R., & Heim, C. (2009). Effects of stress throughout the lifespan on the brain, behaviour and cognition. *Nature Reviews Neuroscience*, 10(6), 434–445.

30 Martinez, D., Orlowska, D., Narendran, M., Slifstein, M., Liu, F., Kumar, D., & Broft, A. (2010). Dopamine type 2/3 receptor availability in the striatum and social status in human volunteers. *Biological Psychiatry*, 67(3), 275–278.

31 Anderson, C., Hildreth, J. A. D., & Howland, L. (2015). Is the desire for status a fundamental human motive? A review of the empirical literature. *Psychological Bulletin*, 141(3), 574–601.

32 Bailey, D., & Geary, D. (2009). Hominid brain evolution. *Human Nature*, 20, 67–79.

33 van Vugt, M., & Tybur, J. M. (2015). The evolutionary foundations of status hierarchy. In *The Handbook of Evolutionary Psychology*, D. M. Buss (ed.). John Wiley.

34 Zugman, A., Alliende, L. M., Medel, V., & Crossley, N. A. (2023). Country-level gender inequality is associated with structural differences in the brains of women and men. *Proceedings of the National Academy of Sciences*, 120(20), e2218782120.

35 Galinsky, A. D., Gruenfeld, D. H., & Magee, J. C. (2003). From power to action. *Journal of Personality and Social Psychology*, 85(3), 453–466.

36 Hötting, K., & Röder, B. (2013). Beneficial effects of physical exercise on neuroplasticity and cognition. *Neuroscience and Biobehavioral Reviews*, 37(9 Pt B), 2243–2257.

37 Wheeler, M. S., Arnkoff, D. B., & Glass, C. R. (2017). The neuroscience of mindfulness: How mindfulness alters the brain and facilitates emotion regulation. *Mindfulness*, 8, 1471–1487.

38 Winnebeck, E., Fissler, M., Gärtner, M., Chadwick, P., & Barnhofer, T. (2017). Brief training in mindfulness meditation reduces symptoms in patients with a chronic or recurrent lifetime history of depression: A randomized controlled study. *Behaviour Research and Therapy*, 99, 124–130.

## 6: A Global Look

1 Hofstede, G. (2001). *Culture's Consequences: Comparing Values, Behaviors, Institutions, and Organizations Across Nations* (2nd edn). Sage.

2 Henrich, J., Heine, S. J., & Norenzayan, A. (2010). The weirdest people in the world? *The Behavioral and Brain Sciences*, 33(2–3), 61–135.

3 Gneezy, U., List, J. A., Livingston, J. A., Qin, X., Sadoff, S., & Xu, Y. (2019). Measuring success in education: The role of effort on the test itself. *American Economic Review: Insights*, 1(3), 291–308.

4 Cross, P. (1977). Not can, but will college teaching be improved? *New Directions for Higher Education*, 17, 1–15.

5   Heine, S. J., & Hamamura, T. (2007). In search of East Asian self-enhancement. *Personality and Social Psychology Review*, 11(1), 4–27.

6   Nelson, M. R., & Shavitt, S. (2002). Horizontal and vertical individualism and achievement values: A multimethod examination of Denmark and the United States. *Journal of Cross-Cultural Psychology*, 33(5), 439–458.

7   Dabiriyan Tehrani, H., & Yamini, S. (2022). Gender differences concerning the horizontal and vertical individualism and collectivism: A meta-analysis. *Psychological Studies*, 67(1), 1–17.

8   10 minutes with (2014, November 18). 10 minutes with Geert Hofstede . . . on power distance. YouTube.

9   Helmreich, R. (2004). Culture, threat, and error: Lessons from aviation. *Canadian Journal of Anesthesia*, 51(1), R1–R4.

10  Torelli, C. J., & Shavitt, S. (2010). Culture and concepts of power. *Journal of Personality and Social Psychology*, 99: 703–723.

11  Roeters, A. (2017). Household and care. In *Time Use in the Netherlands: Edition 1*. The Netherlands Institute for Social Research.

12  Eurostat (2019). How do women and men use their time – statistics. Eurostat Statistics Explained.

13  Savage, Maddy. (2024, February 1). Sweden: Where it's taboo for dads to skip parental leave. BBC.

14  Fahlén, S., & Duvander, A.-Z. (2023). Fathers who do not use parental leave: A register-based analysis of Swedish fathers to children born between 1994 and 2017. ISF.se.

15  Eurostat (2020, March 6). Women's employment in the EU.

16  Johansson, E.-A. (2010). The effect of own and spousal parental leave on earnings. Institute for Labour Market Policy Evaluation.

17  Persson, P., & Rossin-Slater, M. (2019). When Dad can stay home: Fathers' workplace flexibility and maternal health. *American Economic Journal: Applied Economics*, 16(4), 186–219.

18  Heshmati, A., Honkaniemi, H., & Juárez, S. P. (2023). The effect of parental leave on parents' mental health: A systematic review. *Lancet Public Health*, 8(1), e57–75.

19  Miller, C. C. (2019, June 4). Sweden finds a simple way to improve new mothers' health: It involves fathers. *New York Times*.

20  Ortiz-Ospina, E., Roser, M., & Arriagada, P. (2016). Trust. OurWorldInData.org.

21  Getik, D. (2024). Relative income and mental health in couples. *The Economic Journal*, 134(664), 3291–3305.

22  Shand, T. (2018, February 21). The need for fully paid, non-transferable parental leave: Leaving inequality behind and giving our children the care they need. Background paper for the European Parliament.

23  Kotsadam, A., & Finseraas, H. (2011). The state intervenes in the

battle of the sexes: Causal effects of paternity leave. *Social Science Research*, 40(6), 1611–1622.

24 Knoester, C., Petts, R. J., & Pragg, B. (2019). Paternity leave-taking and father involvement among socioeconomically disadvantaged U.S. fathers. *Sex Roles*, 81(5–6), 257–271.

25 Petts, R. J., & Knoester, C. (2018). Paternity leave-taking and father engagement. *Journal of Marriage and Family*, 80(5), 1144–1162.

26 World Bank (2023). Japan. Gender Data Portal, World Bank Group.

27 Bendall, C. (2022). A family affair: The role of intergenerational norm transfer in shaping finances in adult relationships. *Journal of Social Welfare and Family Law*, 44(2), 144–168.

## 7: Overpowered

1 Kuppens, T., Spears, R., Manstead, A. S. R., Spruyt, B., & Easterbrook, M. J. (2018). Educationism and the irony of meritocracy: Negative attitudes of higher educated people towards the less educated. *Journal of Experimental Social Psychology*, 76, 429–447.

2 Smith, P. K., & Hofmann, W. (2016). Power in everyday life. *Proceedings of the National Academy of Sciences*, 113(36), 10043–10048.

3 Smith, P. K., Jostmann, N. B., Galinsky, A. D., & van Dijk, W. W. (2008). Lacking power impairs executive functions. *Psychological Science*, 19(5), 441–447.

4 Smith, P. K., & Trope, Y. (2006). You focus on the forest when you're in charge of the trees: Power priming and abstract information processing. *Journal of Personality and Social Psychology*, 90, 578–596.

5 Yin, Y., & Smith, P. K. (2020). Power and cognitive functioning. *Current Opinion in Psychology*, 33, 95–99.

6 Overbeck, J. R., & Park, B. (2001). When power does not corrupt: Superior individuation processes among powerful perceivers. *Journal of Personality and Social Psychology*, 81(4), 549–565.

7 Newman, A., Donohue, R., & Eva, N. (2017). Psychological safety: A systematic review of the literature. *Human Resource Management Review*, 27(3), 521–535.

8 Singh, B., Winkel, D. E., & Selvarajan, T. T. (2013). Managing diversity at work: Does psychological safety hold the key to racial differences in employee performance? *Journal of Occupational and Organizational Psychology*, 86(2), 242–263.

9 Smith, P. K., Wigboldus, D. H. J., & Dijksterhuis, A. (2008). Abstract thinking increases one's sense of power. *Journal of Experimental Social Psychology*, 44(2), 378–385.

10 Solé, E. (2025, January 30). Kyte Baby employee denied remote work after infant hospitalized in NICU. *NBC News*.

11 Off, G., Charron, N., & Alexander, A. (2022). Who perceives women's rights as threatening to men and boys? Explaining modern sexism among young men in Europe. *Frontiers in Political Science, 4*.

12 Future Men Survey 2023 (2022). Research reveals more than half of UK men feel pressure and anxiety due to societal expectations.

13 Feenstra, S., Stoker, J. I., Lammers, J., & Garretsen, H. (2023). Managerial stereotypes over time: The rise of feminine leadership. *Gender in Management, 38*(6), 770–783.

14 Powell, G. N., Butterfield, D. A., & Jiang, X. (2021). The 'good manager' over five decades: Towards an androgynous profile? *Gender in Management: An International Journal, 36*(6), 714–730.

15 Robinson, M. (2023, January 12). Stay-at-home dads should be celebrated – not shamed. *Evening Standard*.

16 Steinberg, B. S. (2002). The making of female presidents and prime ministers: The impact of birth order, sex of siblings, and father-daughter dynamics. *Political Psychology, 23*(4), 703–722.

17 Steffens, N. K., Fonseca, M. A., Ryan, M. K., Rink, F. A., Stoker, J. I., & Nederveen Pieterse, A. (2018). How feedback about leadership potential impacts ambition, organizational commitment, and performance. *Leadership Quarterly, 29*(6), 637–647.

18 Amar, S. (2023). Why everyone wins with more women in leadership. *Forbes*.

19 Chang, D., Chang, X., He, Y., & Tan, K. (2022). The determinants of COVID-19 morbidity and mortality across countries. *Scientific Reports, 12*(1), 5888.

20 Hunt, V., Dixon-Fyle, S., Prince, S., & Dolan, K. (2020). Diversity wins: How inclusion matters. Report, McKinsey & Company.

21 Joshi, M. P., & Diekman, A. B. (2021). My fair lady? Inferring organizational trust from the mere presence of women in leadership roles. *Personality and Social Psychology Bulletin, 48*(8).

22 Post, C., Lokshin, B., & Boone, C. (2021). Adding women to the C-suite changes how companies think. *Harvard Business Review*.

23 Byrne, A., & Barling, J. (2017). When she brings home the job status: Wives' job status, status leakage, and marital instability. *Organization Science, 28*(2), 177–192.

24 Ryan, M. K., & Haslam, S. A. (2005). The glass cliff: Evidence that women are over-represented in precarious leadership positions. *British Journal of Management, 16*(2), 81–90.

25 Haslam, S. A., Ryan, M. K. (2008). The road to the glass cliff: Differences in the perceived suitability of men and women for

leadership positions in succeeding and failing organizations. *Leadership Quarterly*, 19(5), 530–546.

26 Ashby, J., Ryan, M. K., & Haslam, S. A. (2007). Legal work and the glass cliff: Evidence that women are preferentially selected to lead problematic cases. *William and Mary Journal of Women and Law*, 13(3), 775–794.

27 Reilly, D., Neumann, D. L., & Andrews, G. (2022). Gender differences in self-estimated intelligence: Exploring the male hubris, female humility problem. *Frontiers in Psychology*, 13, 812483.

28 Kruger, J., & Dunning, D. (1999). Unskilled and unaware of it: how difficulties in recognizing one's own incompetence lead to inflated self-assessments. *Journal of Personal and Social Psychology*, 77, 1121–1134.

29 Svenson, O. (1981). Are we all less risky and more skillful than our fellow drivers? *Acta Psychologica*, 47, 143–148.

30 Rusbult, C. E., Van Lange, P. A., Wildschut, T., Yovetich, N. A., & Verette, J. (2000). Perceived superiority in close relationships: Why it exists and persists. *Journal of Personality and Social Psychology*, 79(4), 521–545.

31 Epley, N., & Dunning, D. (2000). Feeling 'holier than thou': Are self-serving assessments produced by errors in self- or social prediction? *Journal of Personality and Social Psychology*, 79(6), 861–875.

32 Zeigler-Hill, V., & Beigi Dehaghi, A. M. (2023). Narcissism and psychological needs for social status, power, and belonging. *Personality and Individual Differences*, 210, 112231.

33 Brunell, A. B., Gentry, W. A., Campbell, W. K., Hoffman, B. J., Kuhnert, K. W., & Demarree, K. G. (2008). Leader emergence: the case of the narcissistic leader. *Personality and Social Psychology Bulletin*, 34(12), 1663–1676.

34 Morgenroth, T., Ryan, M. K., Rink, F., & Begeny, C. (2021). The (in)compatibility of identities: Understanding gender differences in work–life conflict through the fit with leaders. *The British Journal of Social Psychology*, 60(2), 448–469.

35 McKinsey & Company and LeanIn.Org (2024). Women in the workplace 2024: The 10th-anniversary report.

36 Cook, R. (2024, January 10). Mothers are more likely to work worse jobs – while fathers thrive in careers. *The Conversation*.

37 Chung, H. (2020). Gender, flexibility stigma and the perceived negative consequences of flexible working in the UK. *Social Indicators Research*, 151(2), 521–545.

## 8: Powerful Love

1 Komter, A. (1989). Hidden power in marriage. *Gender & Society*, 3(2), 187–216.

2 Wong, J. S., & Daminger, A. (2024). The myth of mutuality: Decision-making, marital power, and the persistence of gender inequality. *Gender & Society*, 38(2), 157–186.

3 Körner, R., & Schütz, A. (2021). Power in romantic relationships: How positional and experienced power are associated with relationship quality. *Journal of Social and Personal Relationships*, 38(9), 2653–2677.

4 Körner, R., & Schütz, A. (2024). Power balance and relationship quality: An overstated link. *Social Psychological and Personality Science*.

5 Bay-Cheng, L. Y., Maguin, E., & Bruns, A. E. (2018). Who wears the pants: The implications of gender and power for youth heterosexual relationships. *Journal of Sex Research*, 55(1), 7–20.

6 Bay-Cheng, L. (2017). Who wears the pants in a relationship matters – especially if you're a woman. *The Conversation*.

7 Engstrom, H. R., & Laurin, K. (2024). Lower social class, better social skills? A registered report testing diverging predictions from the rank and cultural approaches to social class. *Journal of Experimental Social Psychology*, 111, 104577.

8 Fleming, A. (2023). My babyface, so obviously underage: What I learned about men and power before I could consent. *Guardian*.

9 Wong, Y. J., Ho, M.-H. R., Wang, S.-Y., & Miller, I. S. K. (2017). Meta-analyses of the relationship between conformity to masculine norms and mental health-related outcomes. *Journal of Counseling Psychology*, 64(1), 80–93.

10 Courtenay, W. H. (1999). Better to die than cry? A longitudinal and constructionist study of masculinity and the health risk behavior of young American men. *Dissertation Abstracts International Section A: Humanities and Social Sciences*, 59(8-A), 3207.

11 Williams, M. J., Gruenfeld, D. H., & Guillory, L. E. (2017). Sexual aggression when power is new: Effects of acute high power on chronically low-power individuals. *Journal of Personality and Social Psychology*, 112(2), 201–223.

12 Begany, J. J., & Milburn, M. A. (2002). Psychological predictors of sexual harassment: Authoritarianism, hostile sexism, and rape myths. *Psychology of Men & Masculinity*, 3, 119–126.

13 Lammers, J., & Imhoff, R. (2021). A chronic lack of perceived personal control increases women and men's self-reported preference

for high-status characteristics when selecting romantic partners in simulated dating situations. *Social Psychological and Personality Science*, 12(7), 1345–1357.

14 Lammers, J., & Stoker, J. I. (2019). Power affects sexual assertiveness and sexual esteem equally in women and men. *Archives of Sexual Behavior*, 48, 645–652.

15 Inesi, M. E., Gruenfeld, D. H., & Galinsky, A. D. (2012). How power corrupts relationships: Cynical attributions for others' generous acts. *Journal of Experimental Social Psychology*, 48(4), 795–803.

16 Liu, Z., Luan, M., Li, H., Stoker, J. I., & Lammers, J. (2024). Psychological power increases the desire for social distance but reduces the sense of social distance. *Journal of Experimental Social Psychology*, 110, 104528.

17 Lammers, J., & Maner, J. (2015). Power and attraction to the counter-normative aspects of infidelity. *Journal of Sex Research*, 53, 54–63.

18 Howard, J. A., Blumstein, P., & Schwartz, P. (1986). Sex, power, and influence tactics in intimate relationships. *Journal of Personality and Social Psychology*, 51, 102–109.

19 Ostrov, J. M., & Collins, W. A. (2007). Social dominance in romantic relationships: A prospective longitudinal study of non-verbal processes. *Social Development*, 16(3), 580–595.

## 9: Showing Your True Self

1 Thornton, M. A., Weaverdyck, M. E., & Tamir, D. I. (2019). The social brain automatically predicts others' future mental states. *Journal of Neuroscience*, 39(1), 140–148.

2 Barsade, S. G. (2002). The ripple effect: Emotional contagion and its influence on group behavior. *Administrative Science Quarterly*, 47(4), 644–675.

3 Williams Woolley, A., Chabris, C. F., Pentland, A., Hashmi, N., & Malone, T. W. (2010). Evidence for a collective intelligence factor in the performance of human groups. *Science*, 330(6004), 686–688.

4 Keltner, D. (2016). *The Power Paradox: How We Gain and Lose Influence*. Penguin Random House, p.82.

5 Singer, T., Seymour, B., O'Doherty, J., Kaube, H., Dolan, R. J., & Frith, C. D. (2004). Empathy for pain involves the affective but not sensory components of pain. *Science*, 303(5661), 1157–1162.

6 Qiao-Tasserit, E., Corradi-Dell'Acqua, C., & Vuilleumier, P. (2018).

The good, the bad, and the suffering. Transient emotional episodes modulate the neural circuits of pain and empathy. *Neuropsychologia*, 116(Part A), 99–116.

7  Galang, C. M., Jenkins, M., Fahim, G., & Obhi, S. S. (2021). Exploring the relationship between social power and the ERP components of empathy for pain. *Social Neuroscience*, 16(2), 174–188.

8  Uskul, A. K., Paulmann, S., & Weick, M. (2016). Social power and recognition of emotional prosody: High power is associated with lower recognition accuracy than low power. *Emotion*, 16(1), 11–15.

9  Scholl, A., Sassenberg, K., Ellemers, N., Scheepers, D., & de Wit, F. (2018). Highly identified power-holders feel responsible: The interplay between social identification and social power within groups. *The British Journal of Social Psychology*, 57(1), 112–129.

10  Scholl, A., Sassenberg, K., Scheepers, D., Ellemers, N., & de Wit, F. (2017). A matter of focus: Power-holders feel more responsible after adopting a cognitive other-focus, rather than a self-focus. *The British Journal of Social Psychology*, 56(1), 89–102.

11  Lufkin, B. (2022, July 1). Zoom firing: Are virtual layoffs the future? BBC Worklife.

12  Geiger, E. J., Pruessner, L., Barnow, S., & Joormann, J. (2024). Empathy is associated with interpersonal emotion regulation goals in everyday life. *Emotion*, 24(4), 1092–1108.

13  Leiberg, S., Klimecki, O., & Singer, T. (2011). Short-term compassion training increases prosocial behavior in a newly developed prosocial game. *PLoS One* 6(3), e17798.

14  Klimecki, O. M., Leiberg, S., Lamm, C., & Singer, T. (2013). Functional neural plasticity and associated changes in positive affect after compassion training. *Cerebral Cortex*, 23(7), 1552–1561.

15  Zebrowitz, L. A., & Montepare, J. M. (2008). Social psychological face perception: Why appearance matters. *Social and Personality Psychology Compass*, 2(3), 1497–1517.

16  Coles, N. A., March, D. S., Marmolejo-Ramos, F., et al. (2002). A multi-lab test of the facial feedback hypothesis by the Many Smiles Collaboration. *Nature Human Behaviour*, 6, 1731–1742.

17  Alonso-Ferres, M., Righetti, F., Valor-Segura, I., & Expósito, F. (2021). How power affects emotional communication during relationship conflicts: The role of perceived partner responsiveness. *Social Psychological and Personality Science*, 12(7), 1203–1215.

## 10: Powerful Leaders

1   Savitsky, K., Epley, N., & Gilovich, T. (2001). Do others judge us as harshly as we think? Overestimating the impact of our failures, shortcomings, and mishaps. *Journal of Personality and Social Psychology*, 81(1), 44–56.

2   Galinsky, A. (2023). Bad bosses forget one simple thing. *Business & Society*.

3   Goleman, D., Boyatzis, R., & McKee, A. (2002). Primal leadership: The hidden driver of great performance. *Harvard Business Review*, 80(12), 42–51.

4   Bregenzer, A., Milfelner, B., Šarotar Žižek, S., & Jiménez, P. (2020). Health-promoting leadership and leaders' listening skills have an impact on the employees' job satisfaction and turnover intention. *International Journal of Business Communication*.

5   Lloyd, K. J., Boer, D., & Voelpel, S. C. (2017). From listening to leading: Toward an understanding of supervisor listening within the framework of leader-member exchange theory. *International Journal of Business Communication*, 54(4), 431–451.

6   MacLaren, N. G., Yammarino, F. J., Dionne, S. D., Sayama, H., Mumford, M. D., Connelly, S., Martin, R. W., Mulhearn, T. J., Todd, E. M., Kulkarni, A., Cao, Y., & Ruark, G. A. (2020). Testing the babble hypothesis: Speaking time predicts leader emergence in small groups. *Leadership Quarterly*, 31(5), 101409.

7   Zenger, J., & Folkman, J. (2013). I'm the boss! Why should I care if you like me? *Harvard Business Review*.

8   Vianello, M., Galliani, E. M., & Haidt, J. (2010). Elevation at work: The effects of leaders' moral excellence. *Journal of Positive Psychology*, 5(5), 390–411.

9   Chartered Management Institute (2023). Taking responsibility: Why UK PLC needs better managers.

10  Lavigne-Robichaud, M., Trudel, X., Talbot, D., Milot, A., Gilbert-Ouimet, M., Vézina, M., Laurin, D., Dionne, C. E., Pearce, N., Dagenais, G. R., & Brisson, C. (2023). Psychosocial stressors at work and coronary heart disease risk in men and women: 18-year prospective cohort study of combined exposures. *Circulation: Cardiovascular Quality and Outcomes*, 16(10), e009700.

11  Seppälä, E., & Cameron, K. (2015). Organizational culture: Proof that positive work cultures are more productive. *Harvard Business Review*.

12  Maio, G. R., Pakizeh, A., Cheung, W.-Y., & Rees, K. J. (2009). Changing, priming, and acting on values: Effects via motivational

relations in a circular model. *Journal of Personality and Social Psychology, 97*(4), 699–715.

13  Brummelman, E., Nevicka, B., & O'Brien, J. M. (2021). Narcissism and leadership in children. *Psychological Science, 32*(3), 354–363.

14  Vater, A., Moritz, S., & Roepke, S. (2018). Does a narcissism epidemic exist in modern western societies? Comparing narcissism and self-esteem in East and West Germany. *PLoS One, 13*(1), e0188287.

15  Scholl, A., de Wit, F., Ellemers, N., Fetterman, A. K., Sassenberg, K., & Scheepers, D. (2018). The burden of power: Construing power as responsibility (rather than as opportunity) alters threat-challenge responses. *Personality and Social Psychology Bulletin, 44*(7), 1024–1038.

16  Daniel, W. (2023). Middle managers are so burned out that nearly half want to quit within the next year. *Fortune.*

17  Galinsky, A. (2023). Bad bosses forget one simple thing. *Business & Society.*

18  Sheridan, S., & Ambrose, M. L. (2022). My cup runneth over: A daily study of the energy benefits for supervisors who feel appreciated by their subordinates. *Journal of Management, 48*(2), 440–471.

19  Piff, P. K., Stancato, D. M., Côté, S., & Keltner, D. (2012). Higher social class predicts increased unethical behavior. *Proceedings of the National Academy of Sciences, 109*(11), 4086–4091.

20  Owen, D., & Davidson, J. (2009). Hubris syndrome: An acquired personality disorder? A study of US Presidents and UK Prime Ministers over the last 100 years. *Brain, 132*(5), 1396–1406.

21  Reit, E. S., & Gruenfeld, D. H. (2022). Considering the role of second-order respect in individuals' deference to dominant actors. *Journal of Experimental Social Psychology, 101*, 104326.

## 11: Breathe, Relax, Empower

1  Rushing, C., & Powell, L. (2015). Family dynamics of the stay-at-home father and working mother relationship. *American Journal of Men's Health, 9*(5), 410–420.

2  Schaeffer, K. (2023). Key facts about dads in the U.S. Pew Research Center.

3  Engstrom, H. R., & Laurin, K. (2024). Lower social class, better social skills? A registered report testing diverging predictions from the rank and cultural approaches to social class. *Journal of Experimental Social Psychology, 111*, 104577.

4  Williams, M. J., Lopiano, G., & Heller, D. (2022). When the boss

steps up: Workplace power, task responsibility, and engagement with unpleasant tasks. *Organizational Behavior and Human Decision Processes*, 170, 104140.

5    De Hoogh, A. H. B., & Den Hartog, D. N. (2008). Ethical and despotic leadership, relationships with leader's social responsibility, top management team effectiveness and subordinates' optimism: A multi-method study. *Leadership Quarterly*, 19(3), 297–331.

6    Anderson, C., & Galinsky, A. D. (2006). Power, optimism, and risk-taking. *European Journal of Social Psychology*, 36(4), 511–536.

7    Schaeffer, K. (2023). Key facts about dads in the U.S. Pew Research Center.

8    Cohn, D., Livingston, G., & Wang, W. (2014). After decades of decline, a rise in stay-at-home mothers: Chapter 4: Public views on staying at home vs. working. Pew Research Center.

9    Johnson, S. K., Podratz, K. E., Dipboye, R. L., & Gibbons, E. (2010). Physical attractiveness biases in ratings of employment suitability: Tracking down the 'beauty is beastly' effect. *Journal of Social Psychology*, 150(3), 301–318.

10   Zebrowitz, L. A., & Montepare, J. M. (2008). Social psychological face perception: Why appearance matters. *Social and Personality Psychology Compass*, 2(3), 1497–1517.

11   Braun, S., Peus, C., & Frey, D. (2012). Is beauty beastly? Gender-specific effects of leader attractiveness and leadership style on followers' trust and loyalty. *Zeitschrift für Psychologie*, 220(2), 98–108.

12   Graham, J. R., Harvey, C. R., & Puri, M. (2017). A corporate beauty contest. *Management Science*, 63(9), 3044–3056.

13   BBC (2018). What the average American CEO looks like. BBC Worklife.

14   Slaughter, A.-M. (2015). *Unfinished Business: Women, Men, Work, Family.* Random House.

15   Davidovitz, R., Mikulincer, M., Shaver, P. R., Izsak, R., & Popper, M. (2007). Leaders as attachment figures: Leaders' attachment orientations predict leadership-related mental representations and followers' performance and mental health. *Journal of Personality and Social Psychology*, 93(4), 632–650.

16   Easton, M. (2023, September 21). Women still do more housework, survey suggests. BBC News.

17   McMunn, A., Bird, L., Webb, E., & Sacker, A. (2020). Gender divisions of paid and unpaid work in contemporary UK couples. *Work, Employment and Society*, 34(2), 155–173.

18   Rovnick, N. (2015, July 17). Women and money: The struggle to juggle. *Financial Times.*

19 Guinote, A. (2007). Power and goal pursuit. *Personality and Social Psychology Bulletin*, 33(8), 1076–1087.

20 Hartog, D. N., & Belschak, F. D. (2012). When does transformational leadership enhance employee proactive behavior? The role of autonomy and role breadth self-efficacy. *Journal of Applied Psychology*, 97(1), 194–202.

21 Galinsky, A. D., Gruenfeld, D. H., & Magee, J. C. (2003). From power to action. *Journal of Personality and Social Psychology*, 85(3), 453–466.

22 Lammers, J., Stoker, J. I., Rink, F., & Galinsky, A. D. (2016). To have control over or to be free from others? The desire for power reflects a need for autonomy. *Personality and Social Psychology Bulletin*, 42(4), 498–512.

23 Lammers, J., & Imhoff, R. (2021). A chronic lack of perceived personal control increases women and men's self-reported preference for high-status characteristics when selecting romantic partners in simulated dating situations. *Social Psychological and Personality Science*, 12(7), 1345–1357.

24 Williams, M. J. (2014). Serving the self from the seat of power: Goals and threats predict leaders' self-interested behavior. *Journal of Management*, 40(5), 1365–1395.

# INDEX